FEATURES AN EIGHT-PAGE PHOTO INSERT
OF THE DIVINE MOTHER, AMMACHI

"A feast for the soul . . . Throughout this fascinating spiritual adventure and personal pilgrimage, Savitri Bess introduces us to Ammachi, the great Holy woman from India. Bess lovingly offers us lessons, insights, and prayers that might very well break open your heart and change your life! Partake and enjoy!"

—Patrice Karst, author of *God Made Easy*

"Fathers and their muscles have murdered religion. Mothers and their milk can revive it. . . . [A] fascinating physical and spiritual journey on the modernized, yet ancient path of Ammachi. This work provides the best education on this path— the path of using creative power, Shakti, to do good."

—Dr. Anoop Chandola, Professor of East Asian Studies, University of Arizona

"A spiritual page-turner . . . A wonderful primer for those who are curious about what having a guru would be like. Bess takes the reader behind the scenes to show us that a declared spiritual path intensifies all the struggles and failures. . . . She takes us to the deep end of the pool. . . . The combination of personal stories of seekers further along the path, direct quotes from Mother, and a historical framework that explores the Mother energy in all her forms, makes this a seeker's classic."

—Maureen Walsh, CEO, Life Works, Inc.

Also by Savitri Bess:

Offer Me a Flower: A Spiritual Quest

The
Path of the
Mother

Savitri L. Bess

Ballantine Wellspring™

THE BALLANTINE PUBLISHING GROUP

NEW YORK

A Ballantine Wellspring™ Book
Published by The Ballantine Publishing Group
Copyright © 2000 by Savitri L. Bess

Grateful acknowledgment is made to the following for permission to reprint previously published material:

Mata Amritanandamayi Center, San Ramon, California: *Excerpts from* Awaken, Children! *Vols. I–VIII by Swami Amritaswarupananda.* © *1991, 1992, 1993, 1994, 1995, 1996. Excerpt from* Man and Nature *by Sri Sri Mata Amritanandamayi, translated by Swami Amritaswarupananda.* © *1994. Excerpt from* Eternal Wisdom: Upadesham Part I *compiled by Swami Jnanamritananda, translated by Dr. Nambudiri.* © *1997.*

Mata Amritanandamayi Mission Trust, Kerala, India: *Excerpt from* Ammachi: A Biography of Mata Amritanandamayi *by Swami Amritaswarupananda.* © *1994.*

The photographs of The Holy Mother Ammachi are reprinted courtesy of Mata Amritanandamayi Center. Copyright © Mata Amritanandamayi Center 1999.

Cover design by Kristine V. Mills-Noble
Text design by Ann Gold

www.randomhouse.com/BB/

A Library of Congress card number is available from the publisher upon request.
ISBN 0-345-42347-X

Manufactured in the United States of America

First Edition: May 2000

10   9   8   7   6   5   4   3   2   1

TO MY MOTHER, RUTH L. BESS,
WHO GAVE ME THE BIRTH THAT LED ME TO AMMACHI

*Whoever comes into the river of Love
will be bathed in it, whether the person
is healthy or diseased, a man or a
woman, wealthy or poor. Anyone can
take any number of dips in the river of
Love. Whether someone bathes in it or
not, the river of Love does not care. If
somebody criticizes or abuses the river of
Love, it takes no notice. It simply flows.*

—Ammachi

Contents

Part V: Surrender

Part VI: Contentment and Yearning

Acknowledgments

Acknowledgment of the highest order goes to Sri Sri Mata Amritanandamayi Devi, also known as Ammachi or Revered Mother. When I asked her what I should do for my *sadhana*, my spiritual practice, she said to write a book. Little did I know what was in store for me. The process has been one of my most challenging and effective learning experiences. I went to Ammachi with the manuscript at every step along the way. She encouraged me to continue when I wasn't sure if I should, and she assured me that she was overseeing the editing and rewriting process.

With Mother as the guide, I was led to all the right people to bring the book to completion. I am grateful to them all. My friends Priscilla Logan and Michael Mandell listened with tender ears to a few of the beginning chapters and then introduced me to my agent, Adrien Gordon. Adrien worked relentlessly after introducing me to one of my editors, Parvati Markus. Parvati edited the initial proposal, polished up the finished book, and was a solid source of support all the way through. My friend Rita Sutcliffe read the entire manuscript and offered valuable suggestions. Marsha Skinner appeared on the scene in the beginning stages to do some rearranging and cutting—I refer to her affectionately as my Kali editor.

I am grateful to my first writing teacher, Nancy Wall, and to the people in my Taos writing groups: Linda Sonna, Jerry Delaney, Katherine Naylor, Laura Golden, Paula Brooke, Rosalie Deer Heart, and others whose names I'm sorry I don't remember. Many dear friends supported me at various times, including Helen Luce, Ahmayo Bohm, Beth Morris, Vaishistha (Robert Orr), and my sister, Wendy Smyth. My aunt, Gretchen Figge, gave me the means to buy my earthship home in Taos—the perfect environment for writing this book. I am grateful to M.A. Center in San Ramon, California, for giving permission to quote Ammachi. Many thanks to my fellow devotees at the Amma Center of New Mexico and the Amma Center of Maui for providing an encouraging setting for the final stages of writing and editing.

A big, warm thank-you to Ballantine Books, whose efforts made it possible to introduce at least some aspects of the Mother to readers and spiritual aspirants. My Ballantine editor, Cheryl Woodruff, has been another kind of mother, leading me gently and wisely into the extensive additions and rewrites that brought the book into its final form.

Introduction

For there to be life, there must be breath. The Mother is that breath to me, and for this reason I have dedicated my life to the Path of the Mother.

My spiritual search was not a wandering quest; I tumbled into it by accident, or, to put it in Eastern terms, through destiny, twenty-seven years ago. I had stormed in and out of a marriage within a year's time, which caused me to have serious doubts about myself. The unsettling inner sense was as if the strong fibers that once held me together had diminished into the morning mist, into the fragile strands of a spider's web. However, I didn't see the sparkle of the rising sun on the dew or notice the diamond-like jewels of water that lined the intricate design. I was aware only of a disturbing unfamiliarity. While I pondered my condition, I didn't dwell on it for long.

I decided to further my studies in weaving, entered the University of Washington, earned a master of fine arts degree, taught at the university for a year, poured my soul into my fiber-art work, and began to enjoy success in various exhibitions.

In my university extension class I had a student, Connie,

whose yoga and meditation studies attracted my attention; she seemed unusually luminescent and serene. One evening I asked about her practices and what it all meant. During a brief conversation, she told me that *yoga* is the study of the self. I didn't know that self meant supreme soul; I had thought the term referred to my own self. However, she didn't have to say any more. The word *self* alone rang a tone of familiarity inside the fabric of my being. In that instant, during the coffee break in my fiber-art class, I knew that if I ever needed inner guidance, yoga was the route I would take, not psychology. It made sense to me that if I were to know my self, I would know everything.

Soon after, I went to Denmark on a Fulbright grant to study prehistoric Danish textiles and to weave my own creations. I don't know what the catalyst was, but it snapped something inside me during the early spring of my yearlong study. Perhaps it was the dreary Danish winters, or the basement room I lived in, or the dark, makeshift kitchen in the hall where I couldn't escape gazing at a large photograph of the face of a perfectly preserved Bronze Age man. His skin had been tanned in the Danish bogs where he apparently had been thrown as a fertility sacrifice. What I do know is that one day I found myself no longer able to cope with even the simplest of tasks and I cried incessantly for no obvious or understandable reason. I knew that if I went to a hospital, my state of emotional fragility would have been diagnosed as a nervous breakdown or some other psychological disorder. In retrospect, I can say that what I experienced then was a spiritual emergency, a crack into cosmic consciousness, an opening into a realm for which I had no context.

My sensitive condition was my cue that it was time to find a yoga teacher. After hunting in the Copenhagen Yellow

Pages under the many yoga listings, I called the instructor nearest my apartment. She told me that a *swami*, a Hindu monk, was visiting from India and that there would be no yoga classes while the Indian holy man taught and lectured every night for the next ten days. Naturally I planned to attend. My boyfriend had expressed concern over my emotional state and wanted to come with me. We pored over Copenhagen street maps, took a series of buses to a distant corner of the city, climbed a dark stairwell into a large flat where about twenty or thirty Danes had gathered. We all sat on the rough wooden floor while a wiry, ascetic-looking young man with long black hair translated into Danish for the English-speaking Swami Satyananda Saraswati.

The Hindu monk's words filtered into me in the form of vague images. While slipping into and out of the world of fragmented words and filmy visions, I clung to the inner picture, which had the greatest calming effect. It assured me that if ever I were to become lost in a vast and stormy ocean, with practice I would know that a thin thread forever attached me to a great mother whale. At the end of the talk we were asked to sit quietly for a five-minute meditation. Ordinarily, staying still for even one or two minutes would have been impossible for me. However, I found myself floating with ease into an unaccustomed silence.

After a bout with high fevers and a cold, I began taking yoga classes from the Indian monk's disciple, the Danish translator, Swami Janakananda. My emotional symptoms cleared up as I absorbed myself in the depths of meditation, in the world within the world of my inner self.

While I was reluctant to return to America and would rather have stayed in Copenhagen studying yoga, I went on to my new teaching job at an art college in Philadelphia. In the spring, indescribably strange feelings began to surface once more. Since my Easter break was a few weeks away, I decided to find a place to go for a spiritual retreat. Once again I searched the Yellow Pages and found a yoga *ashram*, a spiritual retreat, in the Pocono Mountains; it was there I was to meet the American Jewish woman Swami Lakshmi Devi, who would become my first *guru*, or spiritual teacher. I had no idea that through choosing a motherly spiritual teacher I was about to begin my worship of the divine feminine.

At home in Philadelphia, in between teaching and weekend visits to the ashram, I began to create unfinished woven images out of a crunchy, transparent plastic twine and hardware-store jute. The coarse yarns seemed to emerge out of my fingers to form symbolic tapestry images, like Morse code from an unknown sender telling me that my self, as I knew it, was dissolving. My thrust toward success in my career was powerful, but there was a pull toward spiritual life that was beyond my comprehension or control.

Even if I was destined to give up my life as I knew it, I wasn't ready to stop cold. My solution to fording the transition between worlds was to seek a six-month National Endowment for the Arts grant to explore Tantric art. This would provide me with a good professional excuse to live at the ashram and find out if it was a road I would be able to follow. When I was awarded the grant, I intuitively knew I must burn all bridges to the past and leave behind the security of my accumulated laurels. I concluded that I must be completely unencumbered before I would be free to plunge wholeheartedly into the unknown. I gave up my profession as a college art instructor and fiber artist to live with my guru as a Hindu renunciate, a person whose only goal in life is the spiritual quest.

I did not comprehend fully that I had been on the Path of

the Mother until ten years after my first spiritual teacher's death, when I met the Mother of Immortal Nectar, Mata Amritanandamayi, also known as "Ammachi," an Indian saint who considers all as her children. During one of her yearly visits to America, I watched thousands of people come to her one by one. For hours I sat spellbound, witnessing as she held them in her arms, listened to their tales of woe, and wiped tears from their eyes with her delicate brown hands.

After minutes in her lap, signs of transformation shone on all their faces as this small, round woman's boundless love caused children, the elderly, the infirm, and the able, to walk away smiling or weeping. That time I wasn't searching for a spiritual master and was taken entirely by surprise when something slipped into my heart and told me that my meeting with Ammachi had marked the end of my search. Not that I had reached spiritual enlightenment or the final liberation from birth and death—far from it. I had found the mother whale. I had found the sure way across the ocean. After twenty-two years, without even looking for it, the image I had received during Swami Satyananda's lecture in Denmark had become a reality. There was no doubt in my mind that my spiritual thread was attached firmly to this woman and, through her, to the Mother of the Universe.

OVERVIEW: ON THE PATH OF THE MOTHER

Let them [Mother's children] study their own nature first. Then they will see the essence behind everything in this world.

—Ammachi

The story of my own journey is part of this book, as are the stories of gods and goddesses, saints and seekers, and the paths and practices I want to share with you. But mostly, I want you to meet the Mother, whom I will present to you in both a very personal way and an abstract, universal way. The purpose is for you to find your own unique relationship with her.

The Divine Guide

To experience the warmth and wisdom of great souls or *mahatmas* is a blessing; they are the embodiment of divine love. Following the custom of many cultural traditions in ancient and modern times, I have chosen as a source for sage counsel throughout this book Ammachi, whose story is told in Part I. Many believe that mahatmas such as Ammachi are born into human bodies as a result of humanity's cries for help. (Amma means "Mother"; Ammachi means "Revered Mother.") *The Path of the Mother* would not be complete without including the age-old custom of seeking advice from a great soul.

The Shadow (from a Spiritual Perspective)

She who creates us, nurtures us, and protects us, she out of whose womb the whole universe is born, has been hidden in the unconscious shadow of our Western culture for thousands of years. Her warmth, her smile, her whisper in our ears, her gaze of a million lifetimes, awaits our remembrance. She beckons us to uncover her multifaceted identity, summons us on a journey through the labyrinth of our own darkness, our own mystery, with the Mother herself as our guide.

Since she has been neglected for so many thousands of years in the West, many of us now long to know about her. Because of her incomprehensible nature, it is necessary to contemplate who she *might* be. Why is the feminine considered mysterious? Why is Goddess Kali black? Why is there so much secrecy around the Black Madonna? Why do we consider *black* scary? Why is dark associated with intrigue? You are likely to find many answers to these questions within the pages of this book.

The shadow refers to both the good and the bad aspects of ourselves, others, and the world of which we are unaware. The shadow is the unconscious mind, or that which is not seen, understood, or remembered. On many levels, both the divine and the demoniacal can reside there, until every detail about the entire universe is revealed. Because of its concealed nature, it is a complex subject and is dealt with at length in Part IV, The Shadow from a Spiritual Perspective.

The Stages

I have noticed six cyclical and nonlinear stages on the journey with the Mother. These will be addressed relative to each of the six parts. Stage one is getting to know the Mother; stage two, love and rapture; stage three, the Mother's discipline; stage four, the shadow; stage five, surrender; and stage six, contentment and yearning. The final liberation, a notion that will be discussed all the way through the book, is not included as a stage because, once attained, it is permanent.

The stages are cyclical; they happen over and over again in many different ways. Myths and personal accounts are used for illustrating each stage. Most of the stories contain elements of all of the stages, demonstrating a kind of microcosm of our entire spiritual journey.

The stages are nonlinear in the sense that one does not necessarily follow another. For instance, stage four can be followed by stage one, stage three by stage two, and on and on in innumerable patterns. Sometimes more than one stage will take place at the same time. Usually their motion resembles an ascending spiral. It can appear as though you have returned to the same spot. In reality, the same location could be a little higher up on the spiral. If you have been doing your practices regularly, you will notice a subtle, sometimes dramatic shift each time you return to the same stage. Sometimes your progress can appear to be unnoticeable, and you might think you are not getting anywhere. Ammachi likens this sensation to riding on a Boeing 707 to the other side of the world, to India or Australia: you don't notice that you are going anywhere until you land at your destination.

Evolution . . . is a slow process. It requires a lot of cutting,
polishing, and remolding. It needs a lot of work and requires
immense patience. It cannot be done in a hurry.   —Ammachi

The Practices
Woven in and among the stories and commentaries are suggestions for spiritual practices, including meditation, creating an altar, communicating with the Mother, work as worship, selfless service, singing, accessing the shadow, prayer, cultivating contentment and yearning, and more. The practices form the foundation of the Path of the Mother. They lead us to the Mother within.

The best way to approach inner work is with an attitude of knowing nothing. To illustrate, Ammachi tells a story about a great scholar who went into the forest to seek the advice and wise teachings of a mahatma. The educated man was in a big hurry to learn meditation. The mahatma insisted on offering him a cup of tea before discussing meditation. The scholar, too restless and impatient to wait, said, "Forget about the tea. I want to learn meditation right now."

The mahatma said, "Why are you in such a hurry? There is plenty of time to relax and have a cup of tea. Then we can discuss the matter." With that, the mahatma ambled slowly into his hut to prepare the drink. Returning to the scholar with the pot of hot tea, the mahatma sat down, handed a cup to the scholar, and began to pour. He poured until the cup was full and then continued pouring, causing the tea to spill into the saucer.

The scholar waved his hand in the air and said, "Stop pouring! The cup is full." But the mahatma kept pouring, with the tea now overflowing onto the ground. The scholar shouted, "Are you blind? Can't you see the cup is full and spilling over!"

"Yes," the mahatma responded. "The cup is full and can't contain another drop. Now you know that when a cup is full, it cannot contain any more. How then can you, who are brimful with information, listen to me about meditation? It's impossible. First empty your mind; then I will talk to you. Meditation is an experience; it cannot be explained verbally. Meditation happens only when you get rid of your mind and your thoughts."[1]

Ammachi further explains that when we think we are knowledgeable, we are really ignorant because we are closed down. Once we think that we know, we tend not to listen— we only speak. However, when we are beginners we listen intently with openness and receptivity. In order to know, we need to be open. "The process of opening is painful, but once it opens up, the beauty and charm of the divine flower of the heart is indescribable and eternal. . . . If you can remain an innocent beginner, that is the best way for this opening up to happen."[2]

> *The deepest knowledge is available only when you learn how to participate with your whole being, only when you learn the art of bowing down before all creation in utter humility.*[3]   —Ammachi

Part I

Getting to Know the Mother

Once concentration is attained, you are in contact with the inner Mother, that means your own self. Even when you meditate on the name or the form of a god or goddess or Mother, you are, in fact, meditating on your own self, not on some external object.

—Ammachi

Ammachi

What are the greatest qualities of a Mother?
Love, forgiveness, and patience.

—Ammachi

At an ashram in southern India on the Arabian Sea, in a forest of coconut palms on a thin peninsula between the ocean and the quiet backwaters, I lived with Ammachi, believed by many to be the Great Mother Kali incarnate. I had felt compelled to go to India after meeting her. When Ammachi's four-day stay in New Mexico had ended, my longing to be with her was so intense that I lay on the ground prostrate, praying and begging for the means to go to India and study with her. Three days later my storage shed was broken into and two oriental rugs were stolen; I received insurance worth the exact value of a roundtrip ticket to India.

In the middle of India's rainy season, I was sick off and on with high fevers, asthma, and bronchitis. Even though I felt weak, I went to sit with the Mother while she met individually with thousands of Indians and a few hundred Western devotees. My heart leapt with joy when I saw an empty place just behind Ammachi. I rushed to the spot before someone else could take it and found myself sitting within arm's reach of her.

She sat cross-legged on a tiger skin, on a platform that was just high enough for devotees to kneel in front of her. They could rest their heads on her shoulder or lap while she stroked them and offered her unique form of *darshan*— vision of a holy one. From time to time she also offered words of comfort and advice. A life-size image of the Goddess Kali, black with red tongue hanging out, stood in an enclosure just behind Mother. A veil of smoke from burning sandalwood drifted in the air. I was happily squeezed between the enclosure and Ammachi's platform, only slightly aware of my sticky body, wet from the hot temperature and high humidity.

To my dismay, my sense of delight quickly diminished into a dense fog of negative thoughts. There's Jennie, standing in everyone's way right in front of Mother; she has no consideration. She talks with Carol late into the night, disturbing our sleep; if they would get up at four A.M. as they're supposed to, they wouldn't do that.

I was appalled at myself. What was I doing? I had Mother right in front of me and all I could think about were other people's faults. I must not think that just because I'm behind her and she's busy hugging thousands of people, she won't know I'm feeling so negative.

My critical, analytical mind continued. Look at Judy coming for a hug when she's just been yelling at Susan for not cleaning the kitchen well enough. How can she smile like that, knowing she's such a bitch? Doesn't Ammachi know? Mother must not know, because—look—Amma touches her so gently under the chin, smiles at her so sweetly.

No strength of will or self-admonishment would stop my negative thoughts, which drifted into shadowy crevices in my mind and provoked unpleasant memories to surface like a film of dark images from my past. I thought of the time I had yelled at a young swami at an ashram in Pennsylvania until he had lifted a bronze Buddha and tried to hit me with it. I had been so enraged I wanted to take a knife and penetrate his flesh a thousand times.

Oh, dear Mother, can you accept me this way? wondered my horrified logical mind. There was no way to stop the train of thought. In Denmark, angry for no good reason at my boyfriend, I'd thrown glasses, shouted sarcastic criticisms; he'd become so furious he tried to choke me.

Mother, they tell me you like to take all our sins, but isn't this too much? You don't really want me to sit next to you with such thoughts, do you?

Helplessly I watched the inner film of my shadow side: I saw myself verbally abusing my mother, my sister, my lovers, my friends. For what seemed to be lifetimes of disharmony and despair, I raged on and on, watching myself in gnarled and ugly visions.

With my mask of piety now fully dropped, I began weeping like a small child. Ammachi, I prayed, if you're really my Mother, then you'll love me through all of this, won't you? If you're really a Mother at all, won't you still love me?

At that moment, a woman who was leaving the ashram wanted my place so she could spend some final moments near Ammachi. Distracted from the litany of my sins by this interruption, I wiped my eyes and got up to give her my seat. Ammachi turned all the way around; her black eyes penetrated me with a dark stare that silently said, Where do you think you are going? You're not finished yet.

My heart thumped against the inside of my chest. Obediently, I sat back down. She does know, I thought. Relief flooded through me. There had been a space deep inside where I had struggled for years with self-hate, negativity, and anger. Ammachi's obvious acknowledgment of my silent prayer suddenly filled that chasm with self-acceptance and unconditional love.

For perhaps another hour, with total abandon now, my mind replayed tapes of my life's errors, my blackest hours. Gradually, as the dark visions faded, tears fell out of gratitude and awe. Slowly I felt a blissful energy emanating from Mother's body, filling me with light and love just as a river fills a lake. Words cannot begin to describe my sense of joy and inner contentment.

The above story is one of my countless introductions to the Mother. At the time I had no idea of the extent of the Mother's love, and I certainly did not realize her love was so unconditional as to include the shadow. Stage one of getting to know the Mother includes learning about her on all levels, and can include glimpses of all six stages. Consciously or unconsciously we all have an image or an idealistic view of the Divine Mother. We know at least some aspect of who she is from our experience with our own mothers. We've been in her dark womb, experienced oceanic bliss in her amniotic fluid, struggled out through her birth canal, smelled her body, tasted her milk, listened to her cooing, and rested at her breast in her arms. Bonding with our own mothers can give us at least part of the information we need in order to know the Divine Mother.

Even people who grew up motherless or did not bond with their mother at the time of birth understand the concept of the perfect mother. They know what the perfect mother would have done for them, and how her presence would have comforted them.

There are many ways to know the Great Mother—

through a stormy day at the ocean, the whistling of the wind through pines, a grandmother teaching you how to sew, an uncle taking you fishing on a secluded lake, a father strolling with you through the woods, a teacher showing you the secrets of the animal and mineral kingdoms.

For me the ocean has always been a source of inner peace. Even before I knew the meaning of contemplation and meditation, I sought inspiration and comfort from the sea— gazing at sunsets, walking on the beach, swimming in ocean swells, watching waves crash against the rocks, exploring tidal pools. Without realizing it, I had experienced the Mother in the sea. She was constant; she was fierce; she was gentle; she was moody; and she was vast.

While I was in India, Ammachi often would take us to the beach to meditate after dinner, after the dishes were done. All at once she would emerge, seemingly from nowhere, usually around ten P.M., beckoning for us to follow her to the shore, a five-minute walk past thatched huts, banana trees, and coconut palms. Word would get around that Mother was going to the beach.

The first night I learned about it, I had noticed the ashram was conspicuously empty. Guessing what had happened, I dashed barefoot down the path, picked my way through the sand and over the rocks. The quarter moon, mottled and pale, hovered above the dark waters, its dim light playing with shadows on the waves. Like apparitions rising from the rocks and sand, the crowd of some one hundred devotees were silhouettes clumped together, silent and immersed in meditation. Perching on a rock a few feet from the edge of the group, I closed my eyes and sank into the calm.

All at once, through the sound of waves lapping onto the

shore, I heard singing, muffled in the humid salt air. At first I wasn't certain I'd heard anything at all, and wondered if it was a voice out of my imagination. When I opened my eyes, Mother was standing in her white robes, not more than fifteen feet away, her arms reaching to the sea, supplicating, chanting a melodious Sanskrit hymn—one verse, then an echo, a choral response from the crowd: "You are creation; You are creator; You are the breath of life in all nature."

Suspended in a stillness that was beyond time, I barely noticed when she'd stopped chanting and slipped away, the crowd padding behind her to the ashram.

There will be times when we think we know Mother, and other times when we haven't the slightest notion who she is. Watching Ammachi chanting to the ocean gave me still another view, one of the Mother worshiping the Mother in nature. As she continuously emerges from behind her myriad veils, we will find ourselves spiraling in and out of stage one over and over again, as illustrated in the following story.

At a retreat in La Fonda Hotel in Santa Fe, Ammachi's first disciple, Swami Amritaswarupananda, affectionately referred to as Swamiji, gave a lecture in the ballroom. He talked about how none of us really knows the Mother, that all we know are the multitude of masks that she presents to each of us for our own unique guidance. We don't really know her, he repeated over and over again. Disturbed by this notion, I thought to myself, Her tenderness with each person who comes into her lap causes me to weep. Her presence fills me with an inner peace I've never known. Don't I qualify to know her even a little bit? Beneath my logical musing was the urgent question, How can a child not know its mother?

In the afternoon everyone meditated on the roof with Ammachi. I sat in the back where I could stay under cover, protected from the rain, as I felt a fever coming on. Afterward, I rushed through the drizzle to be one of the first people in the line inside the tent, which was set up at the other end of the roof. Ammachi had begun to pass out the first of 730 dinner plates. After five or six people, my turn came. She held my plate back, and said, "Children." Knowing that she likes to serve the children first, I searched immediately behind me, finding one mother with a baby. Then, not wanting to go into the rain to locate more children, I sheepishly squished myself back into another line.

This incident and the question about truly knowing the Mother plagued my mind. That night my fever broke several times, and, after sleeping fitfully in clammy moisture, I woke up in the morning with a hacking cough. I contemplated quitting the retreat and driving home to nurse my physical misery in the comfort of my own bed. I struggled through the thickness of my mind, remembering that each of the times I've been ill around Mother, love had been the underlying message. Shocked with myself for thinking of leaving for the sake of a feverish cold, I thought, A child doesn't leave its mother when it's sick; it *goes to* its mother.

The next morning, Swamiji continued the previous day's topic, giving me some clues to clarify my original question. He told us we must be innocent like small children in order to truly know the Mother. Behind all her myriad faces—her concerned face, her scolding face, her terrifying face, even behind her smiling, compassionate face—lies a particular kind of smile that never changes. It is a smile in her eyes that dances in eternity. I wondered about the smile and was struck by a new level of understanding about innocence. When Mother didn't want to "feed" me on the roof, I received a subtle message beyond the obvious communication—it wasn't just because she wanted me to round up the children. I realized that my fear of meditating with her in the rain showed a lack of trust, a lack of the childlike quality that would have allowed me to know that as a mother she would not have permitted me to come to any harm.

Filled with remorse, my heart swelled in surging waves as we waited after the lecture for Ammachi to arrive. The minutes passed slowly. I sat down, stood up, sat again, and then left the hall to go to the bottom of the ballroom stairs, where I could catch one of the first glimpses of her when she entered. Also waiting were several mothers with their very young children. Not knowing from which direction Ammachi would appear, I constantly glanced back and forth, wondering if she would come down the hall from the elevator or if she would come the other way up the stairs from the lobby. With my heart nearly breaking with longing, I envisioned myself as one of the toddlers in Ammachi's arms, and wondered if being that small was the only way to be in her love. Even while tears filled my eyes, I couldn't stop smiling when the little ones would squeal with delight while they played, or when they would cry and carry on if they lost sight of their mothers. I shifted my weight from left to right. Mother was late. Then, seemingly out of nowhere, Ammachi swished by, scooped one of the infants out of its mother's arms into hers, motioned for the others to follow her, glided up the stairs, and disappeared into the hall.

I dashed to the other door in time to see Ammachi sweep down the aisle to the front where she would lead meditation and give *darshan*. Before handing the smiling toddler back to its mother, Ammachi sat the baby next to her, put its legs in cross-legged position, and placed its hands on its knees in a meditative pose. Everyone laughed, and then we proceeded with the guided meditation. After sitting for twenty minutes with my eyes closed, my entire being was consumed with a love that knew no words. I was powerless to comprehend my burning hunger to be in Mother's arms. Hoping that my intense yearning might be an opportunity to merge into her, I closed my eyes, trying to sit without fidgeting.

After meditation, unable to contain myself, I pleaded with a hostess to let me into the short line where the elderly, the disabled, and mothers with very young children were given first preference. She asked me to wait about fifteen agonizing minutes and then let me in. As I moved forward on my knees toward Mother's lap, tears streaming down my face, my eyes were focused on Ammachi's soft, round torso. I was seized with the sense that her white, sari-clad body was swarming with cells of love and that, for fractions of seconds, I experienced myself sliding through a crack in her cosmic womb, falling into her infinite ocean of compassion.

One of her attendants alerted me that my turn had come. Still immersed in the vision of her as a great white sea, I dove into her arms. The shock of bumping into a solid body was disorienting. I struggled to understand the change in my perception. Remembering that I had yearned to be small like a baby, I awkwardly cried out "Ma, Ma, Ma" as she pressed my face onto her breast. As I grappled with the fact that she was not a watery ocean, she pushed me not more than five inches away from her to put sandal paste on my forehead. Simultaneously I looked into the black liquid of her dark eyes, which had expanded into infinity; time ceased to exist, and the lights of the universe with a joy beyond wonder danced into mine.

When she had finished applying sandal paste, traces of my initial disturbance surfaced. I remembered my desire to merge with her. As I walked away, twinges of regret mingled with bliss. For flashes of seconds I had been dissolved in starlight in the black of her eyes, and then my mind slipped into prefabricated walls of thought. I wondered if I had closed the door to the very experience I had been seeking. Mixed emotions tumbled around inside of me as I wound my way around the hundreds of people waiting to come to her. By the time I reached the back of the ballroom, I had settled into joy. With Mother's grace, my pestering mind couldn't take away the all-pervading feeling that flooded my being—somewhere inside of me I am a child who knows its Mother. For several weeks I felt radiant and peaceful from the afterglow of Mother's love.

The incident showed me that my love and affection for a physical representation of the Mother can evolve beyond yearning for her beautiful, loving self into an experience of her more subtle, eternal, all-pervasive essence. It was a confusing mixture of realities. My disorientation helped me become aware of my constantly shifting perceptions, leading me to wonder what was real. For moments I perceived Ammachi as an ocean of bliss. When I bumped into her physical body, I was plunged into an even more intense yearning to experience her universal, all-pervasive quality. I paused long enough, while tumbling through multiple realities, to see the smile Swamiji had spoken of. There I stopped in an eternal moment only to have my mind enter, drawing me out of the experience. The Mother's smile was unveiled for seconds, and I, carrying too much shadow baggage, probably could not have tolerated any more grace than that.

Swamiji Amritatmananda, another one of Ammachi's first disciples, tells a story that draws us further into stage one, further into the mystery of who the Mother is and how she meets our most compelling needs. Twenty years ago, Swamiji Amritatmananda, a tall, statuesque man, known at that time by the name of Ramesh Rao, came to live in Ammachi's ashram in Kerala. He was twenty years old, an Indian from a well-to-do family. Ramesh's parents, who were against his entering the spiritual life, were trying to have him arrested and hospitalized for mental instability. To protect her young disciple, Ammachi sent Ramesh to the Himalayas to hide. There he wandered, begging for his one meal a day from pilgrim rest houses where spiritual aspirants can receive alms.

One day, in Gangotri, someone was sponsoring a festival, a feast for hundreds of holy men and ascetics. As Ramesh meandered though the throng, he was very moved by one of the seekers he spotted in the crowd. He couldn't explain it, but there was something about him Ramesh found attractive. The two sat together for the meal and, after chatting for some time, the stranger invited Ramesh to visit his home, a cave on the banks of the holy Ganges River. It is the custom in the Himalayas for ardent spiritual aspirants to live in caves and do meditation practices there.

The grotto, not more than ten or fifteen yards from the roaring river, was small, with hardly enough room to seat two people. Swamiji Amritatmananda, noting that he had not told his fellow seeker about Ammachi, recalled the conversation in the cave: "I asked him, 'Who is your spiritual teacher, your guru?' Surprisingly, my friend said, 'I don't know who my guru is.' I found his answer to be strange because he was doing very good spiritual practices. I wondered how it was possible that he didn't have a guru. Then he told me, 'Of course I have a guru, but I don't know who that guru is.' Again I found his answer to be very unusual, so I asked, 'Could you please explain what you mean? How is it you have a guru, but you don't know who that guru is?' "

Swamiji Amritatmananda's eyes glowed like lakes on a full moon night as he continued the story. "My friend told me that he had left his home in southern India at an early age, wandering in the Himalayas searching for a guru but never finding one. After coming upon an empty cave, he settled there. Daily he practiced meditating on light, something he had learned from books. One early morning while he was meditating he saw an enormous light, like a thousand or ten thousand suns. Slowly, slowly the light reduced in size, finally taking the shape of a human being. He stared at the light, as slowly, slowly it came toward him. Gradually, the light turned into a form covered with a white sari. After some time a figure emerged—a black lady draped in the white sari. With a beaming smile, she walked toward him. Then, opening her arms in greeting, she said, 'Son, I am your guru. I am your guru. I came here to initiate you.' "

Recalling the incident, Swamiji was silent for a few minutes, gazing into space, eyes welling with tears. "My friend was crying. After a while he said, 'In that moment she gave me a mantra. But I don't know who that lady was.'

"I got excited, certain the lady must be Ammachi. I pulled a small photograph of Ammachi out of my bag; I cupped the picture in my palm and held it in front of my friend. 'Do you know this lady? This is my guru.'

"As soon as he saw the picture, he snatched it from me, went into a state of ecstasy, and began dancing. I also was in a blissful mood. I don't know what happened, but I felt Ammachi's presence. After about an hour and a half, we returned to a normal state of consciousness. My friend was staring and staring at the photo. Then he nodded and said, 'This is the same woman who came to me in meditation.'

"For a long time we sat silently, with the sound of the Ganges River flowing.

"After I left his cave, I continued wandering for about eight or nine months until I received a message from Ammachi that my parents had stopped their search. So I returned to the ashram in Kerala. The incident in the Himalayas impressed me so much that I wanted to know if Ammachi had really come to this man whom I now felt was like my spiritual brother. One day I asked her, 'Are you his guru?'

"But Ammachi was very tricky. She just walked away without answering. Several times I asked her, and, like a small child, she would skip away, saying, 'Oh, I don't know anything about that.'

"Finally, I couldn't stand the suspense. I had to know the truth. I caught hold of Mother's feet, saying, 'Mother, I won't let go until you tell me the answer.'

"With that, Mother became very serious. She closed her eyes. Her body became like fire. I got a little scared, felt as though I was in the presence of something very powerful, some cosmic energy, like the fire of the universe.

"Then Ammachi spoke: 'Do you think you five or six boys are my only disciples? No. A lot of seekers and holy men wandering in the Himalayas are meditating upon me, doing their practices for the good of the world. Some in other parts of the globe as well. They are all my disciples. I initiated them.' "

Swamiji laughed. "I was still a little frightened, but I felt the whole area—the trees, the sand beneath me, the air, the sky—was saturated in a blissful mood."

With a warm smile, eyes twinkling, Swamiji said, "So, that's the story."

Who is the white-robed woman whose voice is the primary guide throughout this book?[1]

Ammachi's mother, Damayanti, tells us that she had a dream of giving birth to the Indian god Krishna the night before Ammachi was born. Ammachi's father, Sughunanandan, a devotee of Krishna, had a dream about Devi, the Universal Mother. Neither parent gave much credence to their visions. Today, both of them throw their hands in the air and laugh about the times they went through with Ammachi as their child. It was not possible for them then to conceive that their strong-willed daughter would someday draw crowds from all over the world, and that they would be among those who approach her to receive her blessings of infinite love.

On September 27, 1953, in the Idamannel family, in the rather backward fishing village of Parayakadavu, where Ammachi's ashram sits today, Ammachi was born. Undoubtedly one could hear the sound of waves lapping on the shore during the event, and perhaps men were chanting boat songs while hauling fishing nets onto the beach. Her mother had crept across the sand into a thatched hut and crouched in labor for the rather unexpected birth; she still remembers the ease with which Sudhamani, as Ammachi was called, came into this world. None of the usual pains or signs that had preceded the births of her first three children accompanied this one. Above all, Damayanti says she will never forget the brilliant smile on her newborn's face.

Sudhamani, Ambrosial Jewel, was born with dark blue, almost black skin, much like the color of Krishna or the Goddess Kali. However, neither Damayanti nor Sughunanandan saw the skin color as a sign of divinity. They thought something was wrong and went to doctors to try to cure it. While Sudhamani's skin grew somewhat more pale in color as she grew older, she was always darker than her brothers and sisters. Even today Ammachi's skin will take on a blue-black tone when she is in a particular devotional mood. However, because of the dark color, she was the subject of potential social stigma, not to mention a possible difficulty in finding a suitable husband.

The prejudices prevalent at the time of Ammachi's birth revealed some aspects of India's own shadow—the shadow of a culture that preferred light brown skin over dark, and a society whose family members fretted over dowry and marriage of the sometimes unwanted female babies. In addition, India was generally seen as a society whose families practiced religion with devotion but often without the wisdom and deeper understanding necessary to go beyond the external trappings to reveal the essential truth. Ammachi's parents were no exception.

At a very early age Sudhamani saw that her family's desire for status and respect determined their attitude and subsequent behavior toward her. Their social desires blinded them from being able to love her unconditionally. Instead she was often abused and beaten. In a sense we can say that this little fishing village where Ammachi was born represented conditions that are prevalent all over the world. Many of us come from families in which there were serious problems about loving well. Many of us have experienced some form of abuse.

Often our social and religious consciousness develops in response to our life experience. This may have been true of Ammachi, who today often speaks about the need for unconditional love and patience during child rearing:

They [children] grow up seeing the conflicts, arguments, disputes, hatred, fighting and finally the separation of their parents. They never experience what love is, which is what they are supposed to learn from the mutual love between their father and mother. The parents are the two Gurus which the children see from birth until they come into contact with the world. If the seed of love is not sown at home, it cannot sprout or blossom.[2]

Ammachi's parents did not separate, as is so common in the West. But her father often was out to sea fishing in order to support his family, leaving an ailing and often irritable Damayanti alone to take care of the children.

Ammachi was the fourth of nine children. She was precocious from the first smile at birth. She walked and talked at six months, recited prayers at two, and composed devotional songs from the time she was three. Villagers would delight in listening to little Sudhamani's love songs to the Indian god Krishna, the flute-playing lord. Eventually neighbors learned the songs and joined with her while she sang. Everyone was attracted to her charming ways and her natural concern for others.

As Ammachi grew older the spiritual qualities that made her so delightful as a toddler caused disturbance in the household. The shadow side of her family's self-restricting social mores rose to the surface, with Ammachi as the scapegoat. She performed exceptionally well in school, and even memorized poems she overheard while walking past upper-grade classes. However, she was forced to stop her studies after the fourth grade to help her sick mother. Sudhamani took over most of the household duties instead of her older sister because it was thought the older sister would have a better chance of finding a good husband if she finished school. Ammachi sought solace in her love for Krishna. She carried around a pocket-size picture of the black-skinned deity and imagined that he accompanied her everywhere, especially while she did the household chores.

Krishna, beloved in all of India, is well known for his amorous nature. His beauty and magnetic charm attracted the devotion of all the cowherding *gopis* and *gopas* in the village of Brindavan where he lived thousands of years ago. He was known to steal the gopi women's garments while they bathed in the river, and other such amusing pranks. Sometimes, late on moonlit nights, he would play haunting, enchanting music on his flute, and in that way lure the women from their homes, down to the river to dance with him in love. When he would leave the village, as he was known to do from time to time, they would pine away from despair and loneliness, until one time when he left they discovered that he was not really outside of themselves, but rather his love existed within their own hearts. Through their intense and sometimes painful love for him, they merged with him—they became Krishna's love.

What was it about Krishna that stole Sudhamani's heart? We might imagine that she loved his indomitable nature, his dark blue skin, his love of everyone no matter what they said or did, his playfulness, and his apparent contradictions. Krishna's behavior was determined not by any standard code of living, but was driven by divine love alone.

There are many tales of Krishna's childhood, of his fantastic powers and the pranks he and his boyhood friends played. One day they went with paints in hand to a house where two of their teachers, both rather strange characters, were sleeping. Krishna and his friends painted clown faces on their teachers, who, when they awoke, pointed and laughed at each other. But when they saw themselves in a mirror, they stopped laughing and quickly went to wash their faces.

Like the gopis of Brindavan, we can imagine that as a girl Ammachi longed to catch glimpses of Krishna with his gold silk garments, his peacock feather stuck in his black, flowing locks, and his flute. Like them, Sudhamani thought only of him while she cooked, washed clothes, fed cows, and fetched water from the well.

Today Ammachi tells us that she preferred to work hard because the more household tasks she was given, the more opportunity she had to think of her beloved. Dressing her younger brothers and sisters for school gave her the chance to imagine she clothed Krishna and his consort Radha. In line at the water pump, her lips moved incessantly with Krishna's name.

From Damayanti Amma, Ammachi says she learned perfectionism. In fact, Ammachi claims that her mother was her guru:

> Damayanti Amma was, in a way, my Guru. She inculcated diligence, devotion and discipline in me. She observed all of my actions meticulously. If there was even a little rubbish left over in the courtyard after sweeping she would beat me. When all the vessels were washed, she would scrutinize them and if there was even a slight trace of dirt, she would scold me. . . . If even a speck of dust or ash happened to fall into the cooking pot, punishment would follow.[3]

Often while Sudhamani walked on the beach to a relative's house to help with their chores, she would swoon upon seeing a dark cloud that reminded her of her beloved.

She would fall unconscious on the beach, reveling in a glittering world beyond our normal range of consciousness, where Krishna danced and played his flute for her.

At a very young age Sudhamani was acutely aware of the poverty and suffering in her village. She was disturbed by the plight of the poor and would steal food and bangles from her own family to give away to those who suffered and were hungry. Ammachi, who always refers to herself in the third person, explains how her concern for the poor affected her spiritual quest:

> She [Ammachi] started an intensive spiritual search for the root and reason of sorrow. Because she saw so much misery with her own eyes, she wanted to discover the roots of such untold pain. Very soon she had the realization of the fundamental importance of helping suffering mankind to understand the meaning behind sorrow and how to prevent it. She felt an inner urge instructing her to help poor and suffering people through a life of service.[4]

Sudhamani's spiritual quest included long hours of meditating and devotional singing after she had finished with her chores. Sometimes she refused to come inside, and her father would feel obliged to sit with her in the sand to protect her from the bad reputation the family could get from letting her stay out alone at night. Often her father or her brother would reprimand her when she danced, sang, and cried out for Krishna while others tried to sleep.

Her parents were in despair as to what to do with their young Sudhamani, whom they began to suspect was mentally ill. Beating and scolding did nothing to alter her strange behaviors. While Sudhamani usually was silent when her mother and father reprimanded her, sometimes she would

argue back. Her mother would say, "Don't speak!" Sudhamani would reply, "I will speak!" In these moments Ammachi longed for her real mother. One time when she
overheard Damayanti complaining to Sughunanandan about
her, Sudhamani yelled from the other room, "You are not my
mother. You are my mother-in-law!"

Ammachi considered the ocean to be her real mother, and
sometimes slipped away from her work to pour out her
heart's miseries to the vast, expansive waters. Ammachi describes one period in her life in which she suffered great
despair:

> Later, when she [Sudhamani] was feeling unbearable grief
> because she hadn't yet seen God, she turned against the
> whole world. She felt angry at Nature. She would say, "I
> don't like you at all, Mother Nature, because you make us do
> things that are wrong!" She would spit at Mother Nature and
> shout at her using whatever words came to her mouth. It be-
> came a form of madness.
>
> When food was placed in front of her, she would spit into
> it. It was a very difficult condition. She was angry at every-
> thing. She felt like throwing mud at anyone who came near
> her. When she saw someone suffering, she would think that it
> was because of their selfishness, and that they were just expe-
> riencing the fruits of their karmas. But this attitude soon
> changed. She started thinking, People are making mistakes
> out of ignorance; if we forgive them and love them, they will
> stop making mistakes. If we get angry at them, won't they
> just repeat their bad actions? When these thoughts came, her
> heart was filled with compassion. Her anger disappeared
> completely.[5]

In her late teens and early twenties, Sudhamani developed an intimacy with nature. She would call out to

the breeze, ask if it had seen her lord. She would plead with the stars and the moon to tell Krishna that she waited for him. She would lie down on the road, lean against a cow, talk to it as if it was Krishna's. She began to imagine that everything was Krishna, until gradually she noticed that he no longer was outside of her but dwelled inside of her.

No one suspected her merged state of consciousness until one day she passed by a neighbor's yard during a Krishna holiday. Many villagers were gathered together listening to a recitation of the ancient tales of Krishna. Sudhamani was drawn into the yard in a blissful mood. She lay down on the branch of a small tree in the exact body posture Krishna was known to assume. The villagers saw in her face, in her smile, the perfect attitude of their beloved Krishna. They were convinced she was possessed by him. She never tried to explain the truth of her experience.

The villagers longed to see her in this mood again, wanting her to perform a miracle. Ammachi tells us that it was their belief that created the miracle. She asked them to bring a pot of water. It turned into buttermilk and was distributed to all. Then, from the remaining drops of buttermilk, she told one man to touch it with his finger. It turned into gallons of sweet pudding that everyone ate. They loved Sudhamani's attitude of Krishna (Krishna Bhava) so much that she agreed to assume it three times a week. During these times she often would become playful, just like Krishna was known to be. She would peel a banana to offer to an elderly Krishna devotee, and, without fail, when the devotee closed her eyes and opened her mouth, Sudhamani would withdraw the banana, teasing in this way over and over until finally she would pop the banana into the devotee's mouth.

At one point her family attempted to have her betrothed,

but Sudhamani vehemently refused. A frustrated Sughunanandan went far away to a city where he was not known
by anyone to consult a famous astrologer. Sughunanandan
asked when would be a good time for his daughter to marry,
to which the astrologer replied that such an act would only
bring catastrophe to the family. The astrologer told Sughunanandan that Sudhamani was a mahatma (great soul) and
not to attempt to have her given away in marriage.

However, Sudhamani's spiritual quest was not over. Now
that she lived with Krishna inside of her, she missed the bliss
of yearning for him. One day a globe of brilliant light appeared before her. Out of it came a vision of the Mother of
the Universe, so extraordinary, so beautiful, that Ammachi
now longed to see her again. Before, Ammachi had thought
Krishna was everything. Now, with the appearance of the
Mother, an even greater longing arose within her. She pleaded
with Krishna to take her to the Mother, but even with his
help they could not find her anywhere.

Sudhamani became like a small child calling out, "I want
to see my Mother! Where is my Mother!"[6] At this point
in her spiritual practices it became difficult for her to perform daily chores. She would gaze at the sky or the trees
and be overcome with uncontrollable tears or laughter until
she would fall unconscious. Often she would wade into the
backwaters at dusk, and slip into a trance upon hearing the
sound of evening devotional chanting coming from nearby
homes. She would go to take a bath and forget her towel; she
would fetch the towel and forget her soap; then she would
lose herself in the bathroom for hours until someone, usually
a neighbor or family member, would find her there. One
neighbor in particular loved Sudhamani deeply, took pity on
her, and often helped her get dressed and eat.

Sudhamani's eldest brother supported the family's disapproval of her strange behaviors. One day he became so enraged that he forbade her to live in their house. So she made her home on the beach under the stars. Since she no longer tolerated normal food, animals provided her with sustenance. Dogs would bring packets of rice, a cow would lie down and offer its udder. She had nursed two baby sea eagles who had fallen from their nest and now they would drop fish for her to eat. Sudhamani's mother sometimes tried to grab the fish and cook it for her, but usually Sudhamani ate it raw. A black-and-white dog became her friend. She would lay her head on her canine friend as a pillow, speaking to it affectionately as "Mother."

In the months before her enlightenment, the spiritual practices Sudhamani had done fervently for her whole life reached their final stage. On the beach in the small fishing village where she was born, the twenty-two-year-old Sudhamani's tormented craving for the Divine Mother became extreme and her prayers incessant. She describes her experience:

O Mother, my heart is being torn by this pain of separation! Why does Your heart not melt seeing this endless stream of tears? O Mother, many Great Souls have adored You and thereby attained Your Vision and become eternally one with You. O Darling Mother! Please open the doors of Your compassionate heart to this humble servant of Yours! I am suffocating like one who is drowning. If you are not willing to come to me, then please put an end to my life. Let that sword with which You behead the cruel and unrighteous fall on my head as well. At least, let me be blessed by the touch of Your sword! What sense is there in keeping this useless body which is a heavy burden for me?

Her anguished pleas culminated with the Divine Mother appearing to her, dazzling like a thousand suns. In her own words:

> Each and every pore of my body was wide open with yearning, each atom of my body was vibrating with the sacred mantra, my entire being was rushing toward the Divine Mother in a torrential stream. . . .

[Sudhamani cried out]:

> O Mother . . . here is Your child about to die, drowning in unfathomable distress . . . this heart is breaking . . . these limbs are faltering . . . I am convulsing like a fish thrown on the shore. . . . O Mother . . . You have no kindness toward me . . . I have nothing left to offer You except the last breath of my life. . . .

Sudhamani then lost all contact with the external world and entered a sublime realm:

> The Divine Mother, with bright, gentle hands, caressed my head. With bowed head, I told Mother that my life is dedicated to her.
>   Smiling, She became a Divine Effulgence and merged in me. My mind blossomed, bathed in the many-hued Light of Divinity and the events of millions of years gone by rose up within me. Thenceforth, seeing nothing as separate from my own Self, a single Unity, and merging in the Divine Mother, I renounced all sense of enjoyment. . . .
>   Today I tremble with bliss recollecting Mother's words: "Oh my darling, come to Me, leaving all other works. You are always Mine." . . . From that day onward I could see nothing

as different from my own Formless Self wherein the entire universe exists as a tiny bubble. . . .[7]

Now Sudhamani avoided all human contact; she dug deep holes in the sand where she lived in the bliss of complete union with the Divine Mother. Relatives and villagers who had thought her mad before now were convinced of her mental derangement. She says these were the happiest days of her life.

However, Sudhamani was not destined to remain forever in rapture on the shores of the Arabian Sea. After some time she heard a voice from within her say:

My child, I dwell in the heart of all beings and have no fixed abode. Your birth is not for merely enjoying the unalloyed Bliss of the Self [Supreme Consciousness] but for comforting suffering humanity. Henceforth, worship Me in the hearts of all beings and relieve them of the sufferings of worldly existence. . . .[8]

After she received this message in late 1975, Sudhamani began to manifest the attitude of the Divine Mother (Devi Bhava). She became known as Mata Amritanandamayi, Mother of Immortal Nectar. She is affectionately and respectfully referred to as Ammachi, Revered Mother.

The two sea eagles would sit like sentinels on the roof of the small temple while Ammachi ministered to hundreds of devotees. Even though many recognized her divinity and came from many parts of the world, it took several years for her family and most villagers to adjust. Even today some villagers doubt her. Many, including her father, continued to harbor the belief that she was possessed. One day her father became very angry with Devi, the Mother of the Universe, and told her to leave his daughter's body. She warned him that his daughter's body would perish, but he insisted she go away. Sudhamani fell over dead, remaining with no heart-beat or breath for eight hours. Ammachi tells us that she had left her body and hovered over the scene. She watched them mourn and prepare for her cremation, watched her father lament his mistake, and heard them chant mantras to appease the goddess. Their prayers gradually drew her into her body, and her father from then on understood not to interfere. Ammachi came back to life in the mood of Krishna, smiled, saying to her father, who was a staunch devotee of Krishna, "Without *Shakti* [the divine feminine] there can be no Krishna."[9]

Today she takes hundreds of thousands into her arms and ceaselessly offers them overflowing love and compassion. To extend her love, she travels all over the world. She has built ashrams in several cities in India and in the United States. In India there are elementary schools at all the Indian ashrams, computer schools for the poor, a major technical school, a major hospital for the poor,[10] a hospice, orphanages, and twenty-five thousand homes to be built for the homeless.

In a land where only men have performed temple worship services for thousands of years, she has been overseeing the training of women renunciates to do the rituals in the several temples consecrated by Ammachi throughout India. Ammachi says that long ago women used to perform religious rites. In addition to personally guiding more than four hundred resident disciples and running the many charitable organizations, she is very accessible to everyone who comes to meet her. She sits for many hours a day, sometimes as many as eighteen hours, to receive devotees and answer personal questions.

Hinduism and the Mother

You are creation; you are creator; you are
the breath of life in all nature. . . . Devi,
Devi, Devi.   —Ammachi

Once upon a time, a long time ago, while the gods were resting in the heavens, evil influences infested the world. The demonic forces, led by a powerful and unrighteous king, had become widespread and uncontrollable. A messenger was sent to alert the gods who were lost in deep sleep, but it took centuries to awaken them. By the time they opened their eyes, darkness had pervaded the land. Wickedness prevailed. Once roused from their heavenly slumber, the gods with their mighty weapons were unable to vanquish the evildoers. The gods' weakness in the midst of the abominable and fierce turmoil allowed these vile powers to rage on. There was only one way to bring the world back into balance: Ask the Mother of the Universe to intervene.

The gods, fuming with anger, raced through the sky in their chariots to Devi's home on top of the mountain in the Himalayas. They summoned the goddess through her power, which lay within them. Great lights, like glittering rainbows, came forth out of their bodies, infusing the entire

29

world with a brilliant luster. Like a luminescent vessel of fragrant gold at the end of the colorful rays, the different lights concentrated, combined into one as the body of the Great Mother. Wonderstruck upon beholding her as she sat in blinding radiance on her jewel-studded throne, they bowed down before her and sang hymns of praise. As a symbol of their urgent request, they entrusted their ornaments and weapons to her and prayed for her to wield them for the benefit of all mankind.

The all-compassionate goddess, who is the author of both the good and the demoniacal, had been watching and waiting. She gladly agreed to assist in eliminating the evildoers from their wanton devastation. In order to bring balance back into the world, she consented to intervene. But first, because of an agreement she had made a long time ago, the bad king would have to come to her.

The great and wicked monarch who now ruled heaven and earth was told by his messengers that there was a goddess whose beauty and charm were beyond compare. The king's subjects wondered why their all-powerful king had not seized her as his own. The king listened intently as his advisers described her swanlike elegance and grace. He quickly realized that the love of this one woman was the only important possession he lacked. Filled with ravenous desire, he sent his most loyal subject to offer her the king's hand in marriage. In haste the royal messenger made his way to Devi's snow-capped mountain abode. With sweet, persuasive words he promised her gems and precious metals, all the luxuries of the world.

She graciously thanked him, but reminded him of a vow she had made many years ago: "Only a man who conquers me in battle, removes my pride, and equals me in power shall be my husband."

The messenger said, "My dear lady, even the gods are unable to face my lord and his brother in battle. How can a single woman expect to defeat them?"

Devi said, "It is true, your king and his brother are mighty and strong. However, I am bound by my promise even if it was ill-considered. Do not lose your dignity by being dragged by the hair to your king. Go back and tell him what I have said. Let him do whatever he considers proper."

The messenger returned to the wicked monarch with Devi's proclamation. The king strutted back and forth, puffed up with pride, and did not remember that the woman he desired was the Mother of the Universe, the creator of all that is. He thought her foolish and haughty. In a rage, he commanded his forces to enter into battle with her.

A great war ensued. Devi rode into battle on her lion. The magnificent beast's mane shook, its muscles rippled, and it roared while biting off warriors' heads. With the utterance of the sacred sound, *hum,* Devi burned one of the army generals to ashes. She frightened thousands of soldiers with the *twang* of her bow while her goddess warrior attendants brandished their weapons. This angered the monarch's brother, who came at her with his club. She dismounted her lion and marched toward him. Each of her steps caused the entire world to quake. The sound of her ankle bells penetrated into the stratosphere with their ringing. Undaunted and unable to recognize her identity, he rushed at her with his army. Devi called upon the terrible form of the Goddess Kali—black, with tongue hanging out, a garland of skulls strung around her neck, blood dripping from her teeth. The heavenly beings cheered as Kali raised her sword and trident, advancing triumphantly toward the enemy. She bellowed like a thousand lions, pierced the enemy lines, flung elephants aside, and devoured their riders. The wicked brother showered Kali with arrows that she crushed like matchsticks in her gaping white teeth. With wild fury Kali slaughtered his armies, and with her sword she severed his head.

The king, who cherished his brother's life as he did his own, flew into a rage. He raised his fist, told Devi she was arrogant, and challenged her to fight him alone without the help of her goddess warriors. Obligingly she withdrew the feminine beings into her body. Her loud, untamed laughter echoed off the distant mountains as she said, "These goddesses are but my own powers; I stand alone."

He lunged at her with his sword and mace; he pulled her up into the sky where they fought with missiles that flew across the expansive space like comets. With one dart, Devi pierced the king in his chest and threw him down lifeless onto the ground. The entire earth shook upon receiving his fall.

Those who had been trembling in fear as they watched now became tranquil. Sacred fires blazed peacefully, the blue sky cleared, and the sun shone brilliantly as the throngs of onlookers sang these hymns of praise:

> Salutations again and again and again to the Devi who is at once most gentle and most terrible, and who is blue-black in complexion.
> Salutations again and again and again to the Devi who abides in all beings in the form of power.
> Salutations again and again and again to the Devi who abides in all beings in the form of peace.
> Salutations again and again and again to the Devi who abides in all beings in the form of sleep, of thirst, and of hunger.

Salutations again and again and again to the Devi who abides in all beings in the form of reflection, of meditation, and of happiness.

Salutations again and again and again to the Devi who abides in all beings in the form of forgiveness, of modesty, and of faith.

Salutations again and again and again to the Devi who abides in all beings in the form of loveliness, of good fortune, and of activity.

Salutations again and again and again to the Devi who abides in all beings in the form of memory, of contentment, and of intelligence.

Salutations again and again and again to the Devi who abides in all beings in the form of error and of confusion.

Salutations again and again and again to her who, pervading this entire world, abides in all beings in the form of consciousness.

Salutations again and again and again to her who is the author of everything.[1]

—*Devi Mahatmayam* (Glory of the Divine Mother)

Perhaps one of the reasons we in the West are drawn to Hinduism, once past the initial exoticism, is that it reveals spiritual paths often obscured by cultural and religious shadows. Seeing the perfection inherent in the core of another culture's belief system frees us from the preconceptions and misconceptions of our own culture. Expanding our minds—by transporting them into concepts foreign to our normal way of being—can break the spell of old patterns. After sloughing off the surface trappings of our own heritage, we might be led down into the beauty and love inherent within them; we might discover that the Great Mother was always there.

That is the other gift a Hindu view gives us: the enduring presence of the divine feminine.

Even though at our American ashram on the East Coast we worshiped the Mother twice daily, adorned her image with flowers, offered her sweet rice, and chanted her names, it was not until my first journey to India that I began to get a tiny glimpse of the broad spectrum of her power and grace. In Hindu India, great rivers are named for goddesses; the ocean and the earth are considered the Mother, the trees her arms, the mountains her breasts, the plants her nourishment, the sky her lover.

Usas, Kali, Lakshmi, Kamala, Parvati, Aditi, Saraswati, Devi, Gayatri, Shakti—all names of Mother as God. There is a goddess of the sun, a goddess of dawn, and another of starlit nights. There is a goddess of wealth and beauty, a goddess of wisdom and aging, a goddess of learning and of speech. There is a goddess of destruction, and a goddess of all-devouring time. They are all the Mother.

In contrast I realized the extent to which we lack her influence in our Western society. In the West we have a powerful force in the Catholic tradition in the form of the Virgin Mary. Yet the message of Mary's position as *only* the mother of God, not worthy to be considered Mother *as* God, pervades most Western belief systems.[2] By the year 200 c.e. "virtually all the feminine imagery for God had disappeared from orthodox Christian tradition."[3]

Mary Magdalena adds another dimension complementary to that of Mother Mary. However, Magdalena's commanding influence during the formation of early Christianity was all but erased from the scriptures. Instead she is commonly remembered as an unfortunate prostitute who simply underwent a conversion, not recognized as the great feminine force to which Jesus himself alludes.[4]

My own unconscious response to the absence of Mother as God in our Western religions led me to seek a more complete approach to my inner truth through the religion of Hinduism.

In Hindu India, the Mother, who has been obscured in the shadow of Western religions for thousands of years, is considered to be the sum total of the energy in the universe. While present-day India is primarily patriarchal, throughout contemporary, historical, and prehistorical times, Hindus have never ceased worshiping Mother as well as Father. To have an example of living Mother worship in a major world religion can help us piece together vestiges of the power of the feminine force exiled from Western spiritual traditions and illumine the Path of the Mother.

Initially the Mother's multifaceted appearances, from fierce to benevolent, seductive to repulsive, might feel very strange to some. Others of us might welcome the wide range of feminine expression immediately. For all of us, the staggering unfamiliarity can help shake us out of the realm of heady logic into the realm of our hearts, into the soul of the Mother.

Sanatana Dharma, the real name of Hinduism, means Way of Eternal Truth, and carries the belief that truth existed before human beings did. *Sanatana Dharma* assumes that it is the purpose of all human beings, on whatever path, to seek enlightenment. The unadulterated absolute that the religion of Hinduism brings to life says everything and everyone comes from, lives in, and goes to the same source: the

river of love, the supreme soul, the eternal truth, the Great
Mother.

In fact, Hindu is a name given by the British to the people
who lived in the Indus Valley. For all the inhabitants of this
great valley, religion was a way of life, an integral part of
each day, from sunrise to sunset, in work, in prayer, in family
life, in everything they did—it was *Sanatana Dharma.* When
the British arrived they wanted to name the many forms
of worship that were practiced there. So they named the
Moslems, the Parsees, the Sikhs, the Jains. To the others, too
numerous to designate, they gave the name of Hinduism,
and these people became known as Hindus. In those days
everyone saw all of the many ways of life as equal in value,
as paths to enlightenment.

All these different religious groups worshiped side by
side and in harmony with one another. Even today, the true
Hindu embraces all religions and all spiritual practices as
well founded. I have met many Hindu families who came
to America to settle. Some wanted to give their children a
spiritual education, so they sent their little ones to Catholic
schools or Baptist schools, not understanding that the spiritual approach in these institutions was exclusive, not inclu-
sive. These families became disillusioned when their children
came home with tales of religious prejudice. One example
was of a child in the third grade who had won an academic
contest that promised him dinner at the teacher's home, but
the award was withdrawn because he was Hindu.

Because Hinduism recognizes that the entire creation ema-
nates from the Mother, it embraces all spiritual traditions,
sees all ways as valid paths to the supreme. The volumes
upon volumes of Hindu scriptures include monumental
epics, philosophical treatises, endless laws of how people

should conduct their lives, and rituals for every imaginable event and condition. Within the vast philosophical and devotional works, Hinduism acknowledges that there is only one absolute truth, which is eternal and beyond logic.

Even though there are thousands of gods and goddesses in Hinduism, the religion is not polytheistic at its core. These multitudes of divine beings serve the purpose of elucidating the fact that the one God or Mother is *everything* and that there are layers and various dimensions of existence beyond our normal perceptions. *Paramatma,* or supreme soul, is the name often given to that one genderless, formless, nameless being who pervades all and is all. Customs that include the feminine have not been removed from Hindu scriptures as they have been from our Western Bible. Instead, Indian sacred writings that describe the Mother as the source of all are numerous.

Mother India's traditions have not forgotten out of whose bodies we are born. Many temples have engraved in stone such graphic feminine images as the *yoni*, or vagina, with the symbolic red blood of the menses smeared on it, or the spread legs of female figures with infants emerging out of the yonic passage. A few temples in India are encrusted with carved figures depicting sexual acts, representative of the divine union of masculine and feminine that causes the universe to remain balanced within its cosmic dance.

Hindu India is the only country in the world today where the Mother remains widely worshiped in an unbroken lineage that goes back in time thousands of years. In central India there is a prehistoric megalith that is still used in rituals in much the same manner, one supposes, as it was during the time of the mother goddess cultures of 3000 B.C.E. "All over the Indian subcontinent, monuments dating from as early as 8000 to 2000 B.C. symbolize the great active power in the universe, the feminine principle, Shakti."[5] Many of these ancient Devi shrines are still held in reverence today.

The Sanskrit word for sanctuary means womb-chamber. In prehistoric times domes were built and caves used as temples with their entrances resembling the Great Mother's yonic passage. Mother-Goddess figurines with exaggerated buttocks and breasts are prolific in many parts of India. Often the Mother statuettes show signs of having been touched on their yonic parts, evidenced by the wearing and discoloration that has occurred over centuries of repeated tactile acknowledgment. The genital area is regarded as the source of all life, the focus of the Mother's cosmic energy; her menses time is known as the flower; her breasts, belly, and yonic entrance are revered as sacred.[6]

Hindu scriptures elaborate upon countless goddess legends and prescribe rituals and guidelines for living a life steeped in dedication to the Great Mother, or Shakti. She is known to be the activity in all things, the great power that creates and destroys, the primordial essence, the womb from which all things proceed and into which all things return. Mother Shakti is associated with "independence or freedom because her existence does not depend on anything extraneous to herself. . . . She is even regarded as substance, because all possible objects are latent and manifest in her womb."[7] At the time of dissolution when she returns into the void, she is neither male nor female, nor neuter, nor does she have form or attributes of any kind; at this point she is the ultimate aspect of reality; she is both Shakti and Shiva.

Shiva is the masculine energy, the supreme lord, the great ascetic and meditator. In Hinduism, the male aspect represents pure consciousness, which is inactive; the female aspect symbolizes the primal force, which is active. The Shiva *lingam*, a stylized phallic symbol, stands for an eternal column of light, the purest form of Shiva. Interestingly, one of the largest laser beams in the world is named Shiva. The lingam commonly sits in the yoni. The two images as one represent the cosmic masculine and feminine, the great absolute. The lingam comes *out of*, not *into* the yoni, illustrating the nature of the universal male and female, suggesting the feminine principle, which is the active force in *both* males and females—she is the primordial power. Whatever exists is dependent upon her. She is THAT which is energy in all forms and all beings. The masculine is inert without the feminine. There cannot be one without the other.

Today the relationship between Shiva and Shakti is honored amid the most patriarchal traditionalism of Hindu India. An example lies within one of the most elite and highly respected of Indian philosophical systems. The Shankaracharya Jagadguru,[8] considered to be equal in stature to the Catholic Pope, inherits the position of serving his followers by representing Shakti, the Mother of the Universe, in the form of the Goddess Sarada.[9] Her divine presence in the temple of the south Indian village of Sringeri, in Karnataka province, has inspired and guided the actions of an uninterrupted heritage of Jagadgurus or universal spiritual figureheads since c. 800 C.E. "Through the person of the Jagadguru, she dispenses her grace."[10]

The Indian saint Shankara, an incarnation of Lord Shiva, the first in the line of these Jagadguru religious authorities, settled in Sringeri after he saw an auspicious and unnatural occurrence: a cobra, with its open hood, shaded a frog in labor pains from the scorching midday sun. Twelve hundred years later I could feel the love that must have existed between these two natural enemies as I walked barefoot over the four hundred acres of holy land, met the smiling eyes of men and women mothered by the presiding Goddess Sarada, crossed the Tunga River in a pole-driven boat, watched monkeys at play in the tropical forest, and passed by enclosed tombs of the thirty-five Shankara Jagadgurus where Shiva lingams are worshiped daily to acknowledge the passing of these great souls into the cosmic ocean of bliss, the ultimate union of Shiva and Shakti.

The average Indian is inundated daily with feminine religious symbology in the nearby temple, in the worship room in every home, in the scriptures, in the customs, and in religious celebrations. One such religious event is observed for ten days in October or November, according to the changes in the lunar calendar. In Sringeri, His Holiness, the Jagadguru, dons the jewels, the dress, and the crown of the supreme goddess or Devi. This Indian spiritual figurehead embodies the Great Mother of the Universe in a ritual attended by thousands of India's most humble and most elite.

> *Except [from] our own mistaken habits of thought, there is really*
> *no justification for the popular conception of God as He. God may,*
> *with equal justice and propriety, be considered She.*[11]
>
> —The Greatness of Sringeri

≈

Repetition of Name

> *There are quite a lot of sootlike stains in our mind. All of that will*
> *get washed away when we chant the Divine Name.*[12]
>
> —Ammachi

How does all the above information about the Mother and Hinduism relate to any of us who were born and raised in the Western world with Western customs and traditions, a blend of cultural mixtures from all over the world? How can we possibly retrieve Mother worship practices that were lost from our Western religious heritage long, long ago?

It may require a stretch of the imagination to convert the stories of love and wisdom from another culture into our own. While most of us in Western societies have not acknowledged God as Mother, it can give us courage to do so when we see that within the vast range of Hindu practices, the Mother has been worshiped without ceasing for thousands of years.

How can we start? One certain and easy way is by chanting a divine name of the Mother. It is a form of meditation, a practice described in more detail on page 44. In many religions the world over, repeating a divine name is used to quiet the mind.

Repetition of name can be done anywhere—while cooking, cleaning, showering, gardening, hiking, or resting. Chanting before important meetings or other potentially stressful situations can calm you and make your mind clear. It is most effective if you feel love or compassion or beauty or awe while you repeat the name. If these emotions are not available in the moment, the repetition of the name is itself a way into the divine within you. Ammachi explains: "Each one can choose a deity according to . . . [your] . . . taste and mental makeup, which will serve as a ladder to attain the Supreme."[13]

There are many names of Mother from all faiths. Feel free to choose one from the examples below or create your own name for the Great Mother. Some of you might prefer a name that is not identified with any particular faith:

Holy Mother of the Universe
Holy Mother

Divine Mother
Mother of the Great Light
My Beloved Mother
Mother of All Creation

If Mother's Christian name appeals to you, there are many ways to say the Virgin Mother Mary's name:

Hail Mary, full of grace
Mother Mary, full of light
My Dear Mother Mary
Oh Sweet Mary, Mother of Christ

Or perhaps a woman saint inspires you:

Mary Magdalena, my heart of passion
Oh, Therese of Lisieux, of the baby Jesus
Clare of Assisi, my holy inspiration

Maybe you are called to the mystery of the Black Madonna:

I bow down to the holy Black Mother
Prostrations to thee, Black Virgin

In Judaism, the bride of God is *Shekinah*, which means She Who Dwells Within. The Jewish *Shabbat*, or Sabbath service, is a celebration of the union between the inner God and his *Shekinah*. The possible uses are many:

Beloved Shekinah
Blessed be Shekinah
Shekinah, Mother of all creation

Hinduism has countless names for Mother:

Kali, Kali, Maha Mata (Great Mother of creation, preservation, and destruction)
Lakshmi Devi (goddess, Mother of wealth and beauty)
Saraswati Ma (goddess, Mother of learning, speech, and the arts)
Shaktimayi Amma (Mother, the primal feminine force)
Durga, Durga, Maha Maya (warrior, Mother of the great illusory power of the universe)
Para Shakti (all-pervading feminine force)

In Buddhism, the Mother comes in the form of these goddesses:

Tara (goddess, Mother of compassion)
Kuan Yin (goddess of compassion)

Sometimes repeating a whole phrase inspires our hearts to open to her love:

You are creation, you are creator,
you are the breath of life in all nature.

Oh Mother Divine, please give me refuge
in your nurturing arms of compassion.

Oh Mother of the Universe, lead me out of loneliness
and help me open my heart to you.

My dear Mother, you are the rhythm of life,
the ocean of bliss, the light of the sun and the moon;
you are the mystery of this universe.

Oh gracious and compassionate Mother,
please bless me with your vision in every minute of my day.

Holy Mother, Divine Mother, help me to be free.

To begin, sit in a comfortable position in a chair or on a pillow. One way to start is to first say out loud the sound "Ma, Ma, Ma, Ma, Ma" for a few minutes. Take deep breaths in between each series of "Ma, Ma, Ma." Uttering sound is calming and uses the breath. "Ma" means Mother in languages all over the world. Notice the silence between names. As time goes by, the silent space gets bigger and bigger.

Once you've chosen your sacred name, say it quietly to yourself. You may notice that your mind wanders away. This is normal. When you become aware that you've strayed from repeating the name, simply bring your mind back to the task. One way to prevent your mind from getting distracted is to use beads as a reminder. Get a bracelet or necklace with same-sized beads on it, like prayer beads. Hold them in your hand and, using your thumb and middle finger, go from bead to bead each time you say a name. This technique is the same as the rosary in Catholicism or *japa* in Hinduism.

In the beginning, Ammachi suggests it is easier to move the lips while saying the name; then, after a while, let it become a mental repetition. Let the name rise and fall with each inhalation and exhalation until it becomes a continuous repetition. Sometimes the mind becomes still, then the chanting of the name will stop on its own. At this point you can simply sit and enjoy the peace and inner silence.

At first I was resistant to repeating a divine name, a *mantra*. We hadn't used a divine name in my ashram in Pennsylvania. In India, everyone at Ammachi's ashram was silently chanting the divine name given to them by Ammachi or by another spiritual master. I saw their lips moving or noticed them fingering their *japa* beads. After two years, I wondered if I should stop being so stubborn and ask for a mantra from Ammachi herself. During one of her swami's lectures on meditation, someone asked if it was okay to use the mantra in place of meditation. The swami laughed and said, "The mantra is your meditation."

Now I was interested. Secretly I began saying the common response to Ammachi's 108 names, *Om Amriteshwaryai Namah*, salutations to the Mother of Immortal Bliss, just to see if it would really work for me, and if it would help my meditation. I found it to be a useful way to banish unwanted thoughts and it aided in calming my mind even when I wasn't sitting in meditation. During the summer of my third year after meeting Ammachi, I asked Amma to initiate me with the divine name of my choice. She always asks what name we would like to be identified with and adds a seed mantra, a *bija*, such as *aim*, *hrim*, or *srim*, to make the name stronger, to infuse Mother's energy into the name. After hearing her repeat the secret name and *bija* in my ear, I felt the thread between Mother and me had been established in a very personal way.

While it is auspicious to receive a divine name from a master such as Ammachi, it is a vital spiritual practice to chant a name of your own choosing in the meantime. Once you've selected a name, it is recommended not to let anyone know it or hear it.

Ammachi explains further the advantages of chanting:

Not knowing that you are the power behind the entire universe, not realizing that you are its very life force, the totality of all existing energy, you identify with your mind, with its different thoughts and feelings, and you say, "I am so and so—I am angry, thirsty, hungry, etc." You identify with the outside, not with the inside. Once you are identified with the inside, then there is no longer any inside or outside, because you have transcended both.[14]

≈

Creating an Altar

Amma [Mother] is not a guest. She is your Mother. There is no need of any elaborate preparations to receive her. Your love for her is more than enough, there is nothing to worry about. Whatever you offer with your own hands is like ambrosia to Amma.

—Ammachi

The exteriorizing of Mother helps awaken the mystical realization that she is inside us. Most of us more easily become transported to feelings of Mother's love when we see or hear something or someone that reminds us of her. For each of us that something or someone will be different. Creating an altar helps establish the visual stimulation to remind us of her and awaken our hearts to her.

Amma [Mother] always remembers you, but your remembrance of Amma is equally important.[15]   —Ammachi

As with the names, there are many possibilities. It is best to choose a picture that matches the name you use for name repetition. Many bookstores, churches, Indian import shops, oriental art galleries, and spiritual centers of all faiths sell religious pictures. Take your time and let the entire process of making an altar be filled with a sense of the sacred.

Some of you may want the inspiration of a past or present

living Mother whom you can imagine holding you in her arms or looking into your eyes. I've introduced you to Ammachi. There are many other Hindu and Catholic saints—Jillellamudi Mother (introduced at the end of Part I), Anandamayi Ma, St. Clare of Assisi, St. Theresa of Avila, St. Catherine, St. Joan of Arc, St. Mary Magdalena, and St. Therese of Lisieux, whose story is told in Part VI. You can research the image you choose to learn more details that will inspire you.

One of the most powerful examples of Mother comes to us in the form of the Virgin Mary. She is known for her infinite patience as well as her incomparable suffering and humility. She accepted without complaint the modest stable surroundings as the only place available for the coming birth of the Christ child. With the support of Joseph, she nursed, fed, cared for, and raised the one who was to become known as the King of the Jews. When Jesus was crucified on the cross, Mother Mary and two other Marys were the only ones willing to remain with Jesus. They weren't afraid to expose themselves to the dangers of possible criminal conviction and death. Mother Mary's qualities of unending dedication and love gave her the instinct to stay by her son as he hung pierced and bleeding. The many artistic depictions of Mary holding her departed son in her lap show us the quality of unimaginable sorrow of the Holy Mother who had lost her only child. After enduring sadness beyond compare, Mother Mary shows still another quality inherent in the Universal Mother—that of forgiveness.

The Black Madonna is Christianity's expression of divine mystery, a symbol of the elemental and indomitable wellspring of life. She was shrouded in secrecy for hundreds of years, even though there are countless Black Virgin images in churches throughout Europe. Some religious authorities claimed she was dark because of the smoke from the candles and incense. But why, then, were her garments unstained? Possibly associated with esoteric teachings and initiations, her image was undoubtedly influenced by goddess depictions from the Near East and India. Like the Hindu Goddess Kali, the Black Virgin is a tribute to the darkness out of which we are all born and to which we all go, the source of creation.

Kuan Yin is Buddhism's goddess of compassion. "She is the child-bearer, creator . . . friend and intercessor. She is the goddess of life itself."[16] Originally Kuan Yin was male, known as Kuan Shih Yin, the Chinese name of the *bodhisattva*, the divine incarnation known as Avalokitesvara, "the lord who regards the cries of the world." Kuan Yin was transformed into a feminine figure in a time when such a revolutionary act was necessary for Buddhism's survival. She is testimony to humanity's cry for the divine feminine in a tradition that had been dominated by the patriarchy. The gentle, graceful depiction of Kuan Yin was believed to have been inspired by statues and paintings of Mary encountered along the Silk Road, the trade route. The connection was drawn because, in China, no image so personally appealing, so delicately elegant, had ever been seen before. Now there are countless myths and legends about Kuan Yin. Poems such as the following were inspired by her and spoken in her voice, as if directly from her:

Thirsty and footsore, as you walk in the heat of the day
Sudden disasters come out of the sky, out of nowhere—
Like a bird whose nest has plummeted out of a tree
To find yourself in peace, go deep into the wilderness.[17]

Hinduism offers thousands of forms of the goddess to appeal to myriad emotional predispositions. Saraswati, consort of Brahma, is the goddess of learning, speech, and the arts; she is depicted as slender and graceful, holding a stringed instrument. There is also Sita, wife of Rama; Radha, beloved of Krishna; Soma, the goddess of divine intoxication; Durga, the warrior goddess portrayed earlier, who rides a fierce lion, combats demons, and destroys illusions; Mahadevi, the ultimate reality, the creative, transcendent female. Kali and Parvati are presented in later chapters.

The Mother in her most seductive form comes as Kamala, or Lakshmi, consort of Vishnu, the preserver. She is the goddess of wealth and beauty. She and her sister the moon goddess were born out of the churning of the ocean of milk at the time of creation. Lakshmi is of luminous golden complexion, sits on a pink lotus, and is attended by two white elephants who continuously pour water over her. Adorned with precious metals and gems, wearing a white silk sari, she is also known as the one clad in water, symbolic of her abundance and fertility. As the goddess of prosperity and purity, she is magnetic and full of grace. Where beauty and wealth can tend to be a breeding ground for pride, to meditate on Lakshmi means it is essential to cultivate humility and charity.[18]

There is a quality from which none of us can escape while on the Path of the Mother, or on any path—growing old. An image honoring old age might appeal to some of us. In addition to Mother's beauty, love, wealth, nurturing, and care, there exist aspects of her that often challenge our ability to acknowledge and dispassionately accept even the most distasteful of her characteristics. One such aspect that commonly is frightening to many believers is known as the beholder of smoke, or Dhumavati. She is the opposite of the goddess of youth and seductive beauty. She is a Shakti without her Shiva, the old, eternal widow, also recognized as the d one or the quarrelsome one. Dressed in dirty rags, g, broad teeth, her hair dry and tangled, she rides a chariot carrying a banner with a crow inscribed on it. She is Mother at the time of the deluge; she is unorganized, destructive energy. Poverty-stricken and lacking radiance, her face is wrinkled and distorted, her eyes are harsh and lifeless. Dhumavati's right hand is raised in blessing, an invitation to perceive the love of Mother in all aspects of life, beyond attraction and repulsion.[19]

The altar scene should make your heart swell with love and your mind expand beyond daily concerns. Several pictures can surround your main altar. Other pictures to support your main choice could include animals and landscapes. Ammachi is my main focus. I also have pictures of Kali, Shiva, and Krishna on my altar. Jesus, Mary, and St. Therese and a few others adorn smaller shrines around my house.

> *Your altar is not just a place to keep pictures. . . . Try to make it serene like a temple. . . . The remembrance that "my Lord" or "my Amma" [Mother] can step in at any moment will certainly help you keep the room clean and tidy, for you will want to make it suitable for Him or Her to come in and be seated.[20]*   —Ammachi

The next step is to decide on the location of the altar. While it can be situated anywhere in your house or apartment, it is critical that it be in an inviting spot, one that lures you to sit in front of it regularly. The ideal is to set aside a small room for this purpose alone. Most homes in India are built with a little meditation and worship room.

Additional altar objects include a candle and something fragrant to burn such as incense, sage, or cedar. Your incense holder could be traditional or it could be a rock with a hole in it.

Tend to your altar daily by offering flowers, leaves, or food. After you've offered some delicacy and done your meditation or prayer, then you can eat the blessed food, which is called *prasad*.

In reality, one's own heart is the temple, but we have not yet realized that. Therefore, we need an external temple as a reminder of the internal one.[21]   —Ammachi

≈

Kundalini Shakti[1]

> There is a Ganges [holy river] within us
> which has the power to purify our mind.
> That is why it is said that Ganges flows from
> the head of Lord Shiva. When we reach
> perfection through meditation, we come to
> him, the possessor of ambrosia. The pure
> Ganges rises up from within. . . . The
> Goddess Ganga hiding in the matted hair of
> Lord Shiva . . . represents the Kundalini
> Shakti. . . . Its endless flow is the flow of the
> Ganges.   —Ammachi

On my first trip to India I stayed for ten days in the small village of Sringeri in the mountains of Karnataka, the home of the Shankaracharya Jagadguru mentioned earlier. Before dawn every morning I went to worship in Sri Sarada temple. I watched Hindus bathe in the cold, crystal waters of the Tunga River before entering the gray stone sanctuary. In the spacious, dimly lit building, some thirty Indians clustered around the life-size, ornately decorated, black granite image of the goddess. A priest chanted in the ancient Sanskrit language while most of us sat cross-legged on the smooth-as-glass polished rock floor. After about half an hour, another priest came out of the small enclosure that housed the goddess and rang a bell nonstop for several minutes.

We all stood up and, with joined palms, gave our obeisance to the feminine deity while another priest waved a flaming camphor lamp from head to toe, up and down, around and around the Mother Goddess. Her black stone shimmered, rippled in the play of light; her primeval eyes seemed to move as if in an ancient dance. The hair on my body literally stood on end when musicians blared forth with piercing, primal sounds on larger-than-clarinet-sized double-reed instruments, accompanied by a big drum, the *mridungam.* To my Western ears there was no obvious hallowed tune, yet my belly and my heart vibrated with their own knowledge. We penetrated into a core of sacred that went beyond sweet and lovely, which until then had been my primary association with holy music. These bellowing, syncopated rhythms fractured all preconceptions and awakened in me the vast, great silence of the Mother herself.

Every day filled my senses beyond their normal capacity. I was inundated with sights and sounds to which I was totally unaccustomed: the temple echoed with the chanting of fifty boys reciting *Vedas,* sacred texts, for several hours every morning as part of their priestly training; women spread colorful saris on the ground to dry near the sacred river; a mother elephant and her baby stood outside the temple, occasionally kneeling and trumpeting upon the commands of their keeper; priests smeared honey, milk, water, and coconut oil onto Shiva lingams, the huge black granite phallic images protruding out of stone yonis.

My brief visit culminated during an overnight stay on the coast of India's Arabian Sea, a stopover in a small but busy city before my flight home. As I lay on my hotel bed reading, I heard the sound of boys chanting, a faint reminder of the same voices I had heard in the temple in the village a few days earlier. Now I experienced the chanting as a miracle and, in my reverie, didn't fully understand its source. Unable to move from a deep meditative state induced by the dronelike choir, I mentally searched the room for a possible origin of the voices: perhaps the humming of the fan vibrated like chanting. My book fell from my hand as I entered more deeply into a trancelike state. Gradually I became aware of an agreeable sensation pulsing below the base of my spine. In the small part of my rational mind with which I still had contact, I was aware that Kundalini Shakti, the coiled snake goddess, had been stimulated.

The tingling feeling gathered strength, gently undulated with a pleasant sensuality, a gentle orgasm, up the front side of my body, in the form of a double helix or interspiraling of two energy forces. I had never heard of Kundalini rising up the front of the body, but that was my experience, and it lasted for at least forty-five minutes. After the sensation faded, I lay immobilized, my body lightly throbbing, vibrant, and with a sense of being suspended in space.

When I was able to move, I got up to look out the window; there I saw that my hotel room was located at the corner of the building, one of four rooms that had a view onto the garden of an adjacent priest school. The sound of real boys practicing Vedic chants had tipped my senses just far enough to awaken within me one small part of Mother Kundalini's force.

It was an extraordinary experience. Unsought. Neither deserved nor undeserved, and totally unexpected, as a Kundalini experience often is. Since Mother Kundalini had only tickled me, had not risen up in a permanent joining with Lord Shiva, I was aware that I was susceptible to one of the greatest hindrances to spiritual growth: Letting the mind slip away from the Divine Mother and into arrogance. It is an easy attitude to fall into when she has gifted us with one or a series of experiences that change our lives forever. It is tempting to lapse into disregard as to who is the source of our ecstasy. We might even think that we are special, or worse, that we are powerful in and of ourselves, forgetting that the Mother is the cause of all and is the only source of true power.

So, before going on to explore Kundalini Shakti—the Mother in our bodies—and the inner universe of *chakras*, wheels of energy, here's a little Hindu story about how pride can impair vision.

There once was a great king who became puzzled as to the underlying cause of the universe. After observing the behaviors of countless learned men who seemed to lack faith in the divine, the king, in order to clarify his own doubts, sought the wisdom of a sage. The revered wise one responded by telling the monarch about an ancient conflict between the demons and the gods, or *devas*. The world had been in danger of being destroyed. By the mercy of the Devi, the deities won the battle. Not remembering the cause of their victory, the gods became proud and haughty, vainly repeating stories of their great conquests. Upon seeing that the gods had become deluded, Devi took pity on them. She appeared before them as a great and holy light, resplendent like ten million suns, yet cool like ten million moons, and dazzling like ten million lightning flashes.

They all wondered what this bright and incomparable

light might be. Indra, lord of the heavens, in order to resolve their quandary, sent the mighty fire god to question the light. As the fearless fire god approached the light, a heavenly voice called out and asked him who he was. He announced to that great light that he was the strongest being in the universe, and that through his strength alone he was capable of burning everything. The brilliant light showed the fire god a piece of straw and challenged him to burn it up. When he was unable to burn this dried fragment of grass he quickly returned to the *devas*, and told them to give up their pride, that their sense of supremacy was false.

Still not satisfied, not understanding the source of the light, Indra asked the stupendous wind god to go to the light and discover what it was. Once again, as the wind god came close to the magnificent light, a celestial voice spoke and asked him to identify himself. The wind god told the blinding light that by his indomitable power he could move anything and that it was because of him that the universe is alive and brisk with movement. The light challenged him to move the piece of straw that was lying at his feet. When he could not budge that weightless strand of straw, he gave up his pride and retreated. He told the hosts of *devas* to renounce their vanity, that it was not possible to know the nature of that holy light.

The gods gathered together, still curious, and pleaded with Indra himself to go to the light. The king of the heavens accepted the challenge and marched boldly toward the light. Much to his dismay, as he approached the phenomenal light it began to fade. Unlike the others who were humbled quickly, Indra was unable to give up his sense of superiority; he was afraid to go back to the assembly of gods and admit failure. Instead he took refuge in the great light. Out of the darkness a voice spoke to him, telling Indra to chant certain sacred goddess syllables. Since he was too ashamed to return home, the great and powerful Indra succumbed to her request and did as the voice had commanded.

After nine months of repeating the names of Devi, the light appeared to him in its original brilliance. Within the mass of light Indra saw a youthful virgin whose beauty was beyond any he had ever seen. When Indra saw this radiant goddess, the hairs on his body stood on end, he swooned with ecstasy, and his eyes filled with tears of love and deep devotion. Full of humility and awe, he fell prostrate at the feet of that exquisite and magnificent Devi.

After singing hymns of praise, Indra asked, "O Fair One! Are you that great mass of light? If this be so, kindly state the cause of your appearance."[2]

She answered, "After creating this universe, I enter into it as the internal controller of all; it is I that impel all individual souls to perform their actions; because of me the wind blows and the sun moves in the sky; from my power alone the fire god, the death god, and, you, Indra, do your respective duties. It is through my grace that you have obtained victory in the battle. All of you gods are merely parts of me. Therefore banish from your heart all your vain boasting and idle prating. With all your head, heart, and soul, take refuge in me; come unto my blissful and absolute form and be safe."[3]

And so it was that Indra, the lord of the heavens, experienced both from within and without the power of Kundalini Shakti, the vision of Devi, which caused him to swoon in ecstasy and bow down in humility.

*   *

The goddess of the great light sleeps within us all, waits to awaken in her own time and in her own way, sometimes for no apparent reason or with no obvious spiritual effort. Indra had no idea what he sought when he searched for the meaning behind the great light.

When only slightly aroused, Mother Kundalini can cause our physical body to respond like Indra's, with tingling and hairs standing on end. Any number of sources or experiences, such as hearing boys chanting or seeing a splendid sunset, can stimulate the initial sensations of Devi's energy throbbing within us. Even while she lies dormant in her coiled-up position in the first chakra, Kundalini Shakti pulses with life in everything we do—play, work, rest, even sleep. Each of her energy centers embodies various fundamental human needs or qualities. We might feel her currents generating within us in the form of urges, even longings or obsessions, not dissimilar to those we experienced as an infant when we wanted milk, touch, comfort, security, or the sound of our mother's voice.

In the first center, located at the base of the spine at the perineum, which is between the anus and the posterior part of the genitals, lies the essence of the root cause of our existence—Shakti's original desire to create. This chakra is at once our primal urge to be, and our primal urge to unite with the absolute. In order to be well grounded in life, it is essential to have a healthy relationship with our first energy center. Like a tree spreading roots into the ground, the first chakra can give us the vibrant sense that we are intimately connected to the earth and all of life. Since it is associated with sexual instincts and creative impulses, this chakra's arousal from any source can cause powerful, sometimes disturbing, erotic feelings. Yet, Kundalini's more gentle awakenings can cause a highly pleasurable, mysterious tickling sensation at the base of the spine, such as my experience in the hotel room on the coast of the Arabian Sea.

Like Indra in the above tale, the snake goddess's journey up the spine can create a flooding of great light throughout our being, causing us to lose consciousness of everything but her. Our burning desire to follow a spiritual path receives its initial motivation from the root chakra. This sacred energy center supplies us with the drive that propels us out of our mother's womb and the longing that takes us to Great Mother at the end of our cycle of lives.

The second center, located at the lower abdominal region below the navel, is the womb, our first home, the source of our sense of security. Its nature reveals itself in our wishes for physical comfort, family, and home. If we are out in the wilderness, the first activity we undertake is to create shelter. We can live for many days without food, but without proper cover the elements of nature can destroy us quickly. The condition of homelessness can produce deep feelings of instability and lack of a sense of belonging. In our society, many of us take home for granted, but when we don't have a living space or are in the process of buying or building a house, it can cause almost insurmountable stress.

A large part of our life is spent gathering physical and emotional security. For the spiritual seeker, this chakra has to do with finding comfort and security by relaxing into the arms of the Mother. It represents trust in the most basic and most elevated sense of the word.

The third center, seated at the navel, is the umbilical cord, the origin of our nourishment, our vital connectedness to everything that is. It mobilizes our incentive to hunt, gather, grow food, and to acquire wealth, fame, name, power. To understand this chakra's meaning, we might imagine ourselves suspended in space, floating in the amniotic fluid of the Great Mother's womb, attached to her by our cord and receiving all the nourishment we could ever need. When we lose the awareness of our eternal connection to Mother's cosmic belly, we tend to seek nurturing in stressful ways, such as pursuing hurtful relationships or seeking approval from nasty bosses. This chakra strengthens itself when we stop being drawn toward unnecessary acquisitions, destructive relationships, and endless or unrealistic attainments. Relaxing into the inevitable ups and downs of life's daily rhythm helps us realize that the Mother of the Universe provides for us even in the worst of circumstances. A sense of personal empowerment based in our faith in the all-nurturing Mother leads to a well-developed third energy center.

In many cultures, particularly those of the Western world, the healthy expression of the first three chakras has been neglected and distorted. In an attempt to fill the gaps created by not honoring these energy centers, many individuals tend to thrash around, grasping at anything that remotely resembles their unmet needs. Blind yearnings and feelings of unworthiness often are at the root of these chakras' misplaced expressions. Many people in our culture cherish the qualities inherent in the fourth through the seventh chakras. However, like attempting to play music without a beat, or growing a tree without roots, expressions of the upper energy centers can falter if the first three are not strong.

The fourth chakra is the heart center, the eternally bubbling spring of both personal and universal love. Herein lies our longing for sharing, devotion, charity, selfless service, and compassion. The heart is the middle, the center, the connection between the lower three and the upper three chakras. The heart draws us to the Great Beloved. Its beat pumps the moisture of life through our being. Its yearning stimulates Kundalini Shakti to rise and join with Shiva at the top of the head.

The fifth, residing at the throat, is the source of the original sound, the primal roar, our first cry, the Mother's lullaby, our unique song. It is the center of expression and communication. The sixth, located at the point between the two eyebrows, is the site of the universal light—our inner vision, inspiration, and intuition. Indra's vision of Devi is an example. From the third eye come our impulses toward knowledge, self-realization, and enlightenment. The seventh chakra, at the crown of the head, represents the state of being beyond desires, longings, cravings, and needs. It is here that the awakened Kundalini Shakti meets with the pure consciousness of Shiva and unites into one the polarities of masculine and feminine.

As we explore the potentials of these energy centers, we find that each one can manifest in opposing extremes. The root chakra can take us from obsessive, unmet sexual desires to soaring exalted heights of union with the beloved. The heart chakra can carry us from states of loneliness and suffering to exhilarating feelings of brotherly and sisterly love. Each of the chakras is affected by the others. There is no true separation between them. Awareness of the different energy centers can help us know our true nature and the great Kundalini Shakti who lies both within and without.

Ammachi reminds us not to focus unnecessarily on Kundalini Shakti's awakening:

The concept about kundalini rising is a *bhavana* (creative imagination). We can have the concept about God as well. It is the same idea. Whether you follow the path of devotion or the path of *karma* or the path of *jnana*, this awakening of the kundalini must happen. The difference is that a devotee calls the same kundalini shakti as Krishna, Rama, Devi, Jesus, or Buddha. Children, do your *sadhana* [spiritual practices] properly and sincerely. Do not waste your energy and time thinking, When is the kundalini going to awaken? Will it rise up if I follow this path or is the other path better?[4]

≈

Meditation

Meditation is not simply sitting with eyes closed. It is a state of unbroken concentration like an endless stream. . . . —Ammachi

How do we find the Mother within? One way is through meditation, a practice that lays one of the foundations for spiritual growth. Two techniques are presented: Focusing on the breath and fixing the mind on a point inside the body.

Like the stages on the journey with the Mother, meditation practice is cyclical and can follow much the same pattern as the stages. The experiences will come in any order, over and over again. In the beginning you are getting to know the techniques. Next you might fall in love with the experiences and have dreamlike visions of great beauty. At some point you will find discipline is necessary, especially if you tend to falter in your regularity. Shadow material can come up in the form of difficult emotions or unpleasant inner pictures. Surrender happens when you let go into the process and feel accepting of all experiences. Yearning and contentment are the fruits of your practice. As you encounter different experiences you may benefit by referring to the relevant sections in this book. For now, try not to worry about what is to come. Just begin the meditation techniques without any particular expectation about them.

You should give up this idea about becoming more spiritual. . . .
That very thought can sometimes be a hindrance.[5]   —Ammachi

Meditating will affect your day in a positive way no matter how simple the practice or how long you do it, or no matter what stage you are experiencing. Not only does the mind become more clear in meditation, but you become more relaxed and filled with inner peace. It brings brightness into your soul. You will become more alert and more open.

Ammachi advises in the beginning to develop love for your daily routine. If you are unable to meditate or concentrate, try repeating the names. That process will help your mind quiet down if neither of the techniques that follow are working for you on a particular day.[6]

First, prepare the area where you will meditate. The dimly lit room where you have the candle on your altar helps provide the right mood. It is best to sit on the floor with the buttocks raised just enough so that the knees touch the floor, creating a tripod of support (knees and base of the spine). Keep the spine straight. If for any reason you have difficulty sitting on the floor, feel free to sit on a chair. Use the same chair or pillow every day so that this chair or pillow carries the vibration of meditation in it.

Make certain you will not be disturbed during meditation practice—no phone calls, no visitors. This can be facilitated by having a particular time for meditation, either early in the morning and before bed, or whenever you would be least likely to be disturbed. If you must pull the phone plug just for this time, do so. This is your sacred time.

You might wonder how long you should meditate every day. Start out sitting for ten minutes in the morning and the same in the evening. Later, build up to longer time periods. Eventually, if possible, sit for twenty or thirty minutes. Perhaps on designated days, like Saturday mornings, allow yourself forty-five minutes to an hour to meditate. The important part is to be regular. There are subtle beings both inside and outside, similar to plant and animal *devas*, who get used to your connection with them, and they like to know you will always be there.

> *To get rid of the old habits and replace them with new ones, a regular timetable will be very helpful.*[7]   —Ammachi

1. Focusing on the breath. Sit quietly for a couple of minutes and let your breathing be normal. Close your eyes. Notice your breath as you breathe normally. Remain aware of your breath. When your mind wanders away, gently bring your concentration back to your breath. It is important not to judge the wandering mind—you will only become frustrated if you do. It is the mind's nature to slip away from your control. Your task is simply to be aware that it has wandered and to bring it back to focusing on the breath. As you breathe, try to watch the thoughts.

> *Can you see a thought rising in your mind? Can you see how the thought works and how it dies? Once you are able to see a thought clearly, that very thought becomes impotent.*[8]   —Ammachi

You might wonder what to do when emotions come up. Let them come. Let the emotions, even if they are distressful, be the focus of your meditation—they will subside naturally. Then come back to focusing on the breath. In Hinduism, emotion is the same as the mind. The thoughts produced by the mind are the cause of emotions. Surprisingly, you will find that if you concentrate only on the sad or anxious feeling, without a thought attached to it, the emotion will disappear.

> We will get spiritual strength only if we still the mind. . . . The mind will run around when we sit idle. "Where is my child? How is my wife? Has she gone to the office?" It will wander like this. Meditation is to stop such wandering. In the beginning stages of our spiritual practice, the mind may continue to roam about. This can be stopped only through constant and determined practice.[9]
>
> —Ammachi

Sometimes aches and pains in your body will become pronounced. Focus on these until they quiet down, then, again, come back to the breath. Be aware of the quiet between breaths.

Continue watching your breath and watching your thoughts. Let the whole process have its own rhythm, with the rising and falling of the breath being the central core of the meditation.

> If you can see with a subtle eye, you find that there is a gap between thoughts. This gap is thin—thinner than a hair's breadth—but it is there. If you can keep the thoughts from flowing without control, as they do now, this gap will increase. But this is possible only in a mind which is concentrated on a single thought. It must dwell, not on many thoughts, but on one single thought.[10]
>
> —Ammachi

2. Fixing the mind on a point inside the body. Follow the same pointers given under breathing. Using the candle to help your one-pointed concentration, focus on the flame for a few minutes. Now close your eyes and let the afterimage of the flame rest in your heart or at the point between the eyebrows.

> *Meditation can be done while fixing the mind either between the eyebrows or in the heart. . . . One should continue doing meditation with the conviction that one's Beloved Deity is in one's own heart.[11]*
>
> *One may get a headache and pain in the eyes if one meditates on the spot between the eyebrows. Insomnia also may occur. If so, meditation should be stopped temporarily. If restlessness occurs, then it is best to meditate in the heart. In the beginning it is better to meditate in the heart. After having the feeling that the heart is full, it is not so dangerous if meditation is shifted to the spot between the eyebrows. In any case, it is best for householders [those who live in the world] to meditate in the heart. One will feel a cooling effect by meditating in the heart, whereas heat is experienced if one meditates between the eyebrows.[12]*
>
> —Ammachi

On some days meditation will be easy for you, and on other days it will not. Whatever you do, don't let obstacles or disappointments stop you. Just as with any undertaking, meditation can have ups and downs. Perseverance always brings success.

≈

In the beginning the mind will not be inclined toward meditation. It should be subjugated very tactfully. You will not be able to catch a chicken if you run behind it, but it will come if you call it after putting its food nearby. In the same manner, do not run after the mind to control it. By slowly questioning and tactfully instructing it, you can get it in your hands. Ask the mind, "O mind, why are you running after these objects [of the world]? Are you getting any benefit from them? Don't you know that these things are ever-changing?" Thus, the mind should be tamed and eventually directed away from the world of matter to the world of Spirit.[13]

—Ammachi

Jillellamudi Mother

Mother exists forever and includes
everything within Herself. She who is
everything and everywhere is Mother. It is
not correct to say "Mother of the Universe."
The Universe is itself the Mother.

—Jillellamudi Mother

The twentieth century has brought a number of incar-
nations of God as Mother into the world. Anasuya Devi,
otherwise referred to as Jillellamudi Mother, Amma, or the
Mother of All, was one of them. She lived a life exemplifying
the path of wisdom and knowledge, teaching that spirit and
matter are from the same source. Her method of awakening
those who came in contact with her often took the form of
blunt, poignant, sometimes playful questioning. The course
of her life demonstrates a way of supreme knowledge that
utilizes the mind as the primary method of removing veils of
ignorance. Through poignant inquiry, she taught that everything is divine. She is also well known for exhibiting the
Universal Mother's celestial game of hide-and-seek, which
she played masterfully from the time of her birth in 1923
until her death in 1983.

Before she was born, her father, Sri Sitapati, had two visions that portended a divine birth. Once while he was con-

templating the death of five of his six children, he saw a luminous form of a five-year-old girl that dissolved into the
form of the Hindu god, Vishnu, and his consort, Lakshmi.
While he experienced peaceful bliss from this first vision, he
did not give it another thought until his next vision, which
came in the form of a dream, in which he saw an adult
woman with an enormous vermilion *kum-kum* mark on her
forehead, typical of the mark worn by most Indian women,
only uncommonly large. Richard Schiffman, in his warm,
vivid account *Mother of All*,[1] describes the following dialogue in the dream:

> Sri Sitapati asks the woman, "Who are you?"
> "I am the Mother," she answers.
> "Whose Mother?"
> "I am the Mother of All," she replies.[2]

Sri Sitapati's curiosity as to the significance of the dream
led him to seek an interpretation from a scholar who predicted the birth of a divine child into his family line. Even after this obvious message, Sri Sitapati thought it all sounded
too far-fetched and superstitious for his practical mind. Several decades later, when the first devotees were beginning to
gather around his daughter in the town of Jillellamudi, he
recognized that her distinctive features, including the unusually large *kum-kum* mark she wore, were those of the
woman in his dream. He also began to realize that the child
in his first vision looked just like his daughter had when she
was young.

Soon after the dreams, Anasuya Devi, or Amma, as she is
often called, was conceived. During the pregnancy, Amma's
mother, Rangamma, often felt waves of bliss and joy that

were so intense she would experience spells of uncontrollable laughter alternating with tears, unusual for a woman
who was known for her quiet and retiring disposition.

Amma was born just before sunrise; as if to announce the
event, trumpets, bells, and drums blared forth from a nearby
temple where a special holy day was being celebrated. As
the midwife raised the knife to cut the umbilical cord, she
became transfixed by a visionary experience. In Schiffman's
words,

> The knife [for cutting the umbilical cord] . . . became transfig-
> ured before her startled gaze into a trident (a Hindu emblem
> of divinity) and the rope, which was to be used to tie up the
> umbilical cord, seemed to elongate to the point where she
> could no longer make out either end of it. When the confused
> midwife glanced down, she observed, to her growing won-
> der, a sacred conch (the symbol of Aum, the original vibra-
> tion of creation) on the infant's abdomen. As she gazed at the
> conch it became transformed into a lotus flower, in the heart
> of which a divine figure moved fluidly in ecstatic dance.[3]

In later years, Anasuya Devi explained that she was fully
aware at birth; she amazed her midwife and others who had
been present at the birth by relating explicit details, even
precise conversations.

When Anasuya was only nineteen months old, her mother
found her seated in a classical yogic cross-legged posture
under a pomegranate tree. The mother became distraught
upon seeing the child's eyes turned upward. She ran to pour
buckets of water on her, hoping to bring her out of what she
thought was an epileptic fit. When that didn't work, her
mother ran for the doctor, who administered several pungent

liquids into the child's nostrils. None of these harsh proce-
dures changed the meditative mood of Anasuya. Later
she slowly returned to "normal" consciousness of her own
accord.

A similar episode occurred several days later in the presence of an aunt. Several days after that second episode, an
old wise man dressed in the orange robes of a swami saw the
child and told the mother, "Your child is a manifestation of
God. This is your last birth." Even after such obvious signs
and messages of divinity, her mother reflected on the experiences briefly and soon returned to treating Anasuya as an ordinary child.

From an early age Anasuya, whom everyone even then
called Amma because of her compassionate nature, took pity
on the poor and downtrodden. Much to her family's distress
she would give away gold bangles, rings, whatever she had
to help the needy. When she was challenged as to whether
the recipients were worthy of her gifts, she would claim
there is no such thing as worthiness, only neediness.

Her precocious nature was especially dramatic at the time
of her mother's passing when Amma was just five years old.
As death approached, her failing mother asked where Anasuya would stay when she died. Amma responded that she
would stay "everywhere with anybody." Her mother, frustrated by her vague response, asked how she would find elders to love and care for her, to which Amma replied, "I
should take care of them, shouldn't I? Those who are best
able to look after others are the true elders."[4]

Soon after, when her mother had breathed her last breath
and everyone was grieving and lamenting, Amma asked
what was wrong with her mother and why was everyone so
unhappy. Thinking she didn't understand, her father said,

"She is dead, your mother is dead!" Someone else, fearing the concept of death would be too disturbing for a child, said, "Your mother is only sleeping."

"If she is only sleeping, why does everybody weep? Mother slept every day. Why didn't people weep every day?" Amma wondered pointedly.[5]

There was a disturbed silence in the room, as none knew how to answer this question. Her grandfather, a well-known lawyer, took Amma and Sri Sitapati upstairs and out on the veranda to rest and be away from the weeping relatives. Here the conversation continued. Schiffman details the following dialogue, which began when the grandfather struggled to answer Amma's question as to the nature of death:

> Amma followed up quickly with another question: "Where do people come from in the first place?"
>
> "From the mother's womb," he replied.
>
> "Is the child always in the mother's womb?" she pressed.
>
> "No they aren't."
>
> "Then how do they get there? Where do they come from in the beginning, Grandpa?"
>
> "God sends them."
>
> "Then where do people go? You said [of my mother], 'She has gone.' Where does she go?"
>
> "To the cremation ground."
>
> "If the body is not sent to the cremation ground, does it mean that the person is still alive? In that case let's keep Mother right here."
>
> "What kind of questions are these!" [her grandfather] exclaimed with a bemused smile.
>
> "Tell me, Grandpa, where do people go?" the child demanded sternly.
>
> "To God," he replied.
>
> "Why?"

"It is His will."

"The one sent by God, returns to Him at His will. What is there in this to weep over?" she reasoned with a gentle persuasiveness.

Even in this most sorrowful time, [the grandfather] could not suppress his pure joy at the child's wonderful analysis. Laughing out loud and hugging and kissing Amma, he exclaimed in amazement, "Where did you learn all of this [spiritual philosophy]?"[6]

Amma was forbidden from attending the cremation because she was too young. However, she further astonished her grandfather, who had returned from the ceremony early, by describing in detail the entire rite, which she had observed in the flame of a kerosene lamp.

After her mother's death Amma was passed around to several different relatives to care for her. Because she was so independent, mature for her age, and free-spirited, the relatives rarely concerned themselves with her whereabouts and let her roam the city freely by herself. One day she went into one of the goddess temples, where she spent the day asking pithy questions to devotees, some of whom regarded her as impertinent. Later she brought some flowers and *tulasi* leaves to the goddess and laid them on the floor before offering them. The priest was enraged and scolded her for the sacrilege of putting them on the floor before offering them to the goddess. Amma retorted that the flowers had grown out of the ground, and asked him if that was sacrilege, to which the priest had no answer.

While Amma was taking a closer look at the statue, the priest accidentally locked her into the compound when he left for the day. During the night she removed the decorations on the statue and began to wonder if the stone image

was God, or if the precious ornaments on the Mother Goddess's image were God, or if in fact the worshipers were
God. Her train of thought led her to the fact that the statue,
the ornaments, and the devotees all have as their source
the earth. She concluded that the earth was God and therefore only the earth was worthy of our worship. As described
in Schiffman's account, Amma picked up a handful of soil
and spoke out loud to Mother Earth, to the soil she held in
her hand:

> You tolerate patiently when plowed or trampled underfoot.
> You calmly bear the good and the bad without making any
> distinction between the two. . . . Though they slaughter Your
> own dear children and make Your tender body spill with
> blood; though they break Your heart with axes, still You do
> not condemn them. You do not abuse them. You will never
> punish them. On the contrary, even the most wicked You take
> upon Your lap to comfort and refresh. . . .
>
> [Amma then] fell prostrate on the ground as if to embrace
> the all-embracing Earth. . . .
>
> Again she said: "Mother! How sacred is Your life of unpar-
> alleled selflessness. How divine a life so full of sacrifice and
> universal love. Therefore I address you as the Supreme God-
> dess of forbearance and patience. I wish for all people to wor-
> ship You alone. I desire that all should adore You day in and
> day out."[7]

The next morning when the priest returned, Amma was
standing facing him as he entered the compound. Her form
appeared so luminescent that he was certain she was the
goddess herself standing before him. He fell prostrate at her
feet and went into a state of trance. When he opened his
eyes, she had disappeared, at which time he became confused, wondering if he had indeed experienced the vision of

the Mother. He ran to the stone image of the goddess, which he had been worshiping for many years by rote, fell down before her, grabbed her feet, and asked her if she had come alive and if his vision were true.

Meanwhile, the trustee of the temple arrived, did not recognize the priest's blissful state, and demanded to know why the goddess had been stripped of her jewelry and sari. Amma had removed all the clothing and jewels during the night, which the priest, in his reverie, had not noticed. Now even more bewildered, the priest searched in a likely place and found the lost jewels. But by this time the patron was angry, accused the priest of stealing the jewels, and fired him, telling him never to return.

The priest left the compound, sad and dejected; as he made his way slowly through the streets to return home, he ran into Amma. His heart was so heavy he didn't immediately recognize her as the child of his morning vision in the temple. Absentmindedly, he asked whose little girl she was. She told him she belonged to whomever she was with at the moment. Closing his eyes, the priest drifted into a dreamy mood, remembering his experience earlier in the day. He confided in Amma that today he had seen his Mother in the form of a divine child. When he opened his eyes, he saw Amma disappearing down the road. He ran after her, frantic to find out if she, indeed, was the child of his vision.

His chase ended at the railway station, where he found her seated under a tree. Panting from running down narrow streets, he asked her if she was the one who had given him the vision of the Mother. She teased him, telling him she was afraid he was coming to steal her jewels again. Astonished that she knew the circumstances of his dismissal, he fell at her feet and cried out, "Mother, do not cover me up again with your *maya* [illusion]. . . . Take me quickly into yourself."

She continued to tease him by responding that she was not a Mother, but only a small child. Now totally mystified, the priest wandered away.

Later in the afternoon, Amma was sitting at the temple trustee's doorstep when he arrived home. He asked who she was, to which she responded that she was a relative of the temple priest, that she was his mother's sister. Amma, in describing herself in this way, alluded to her relationship to the Mother Goddess of the temple. Amma proceeded to tell the trustee that the priest was a good man who didn't deserve to be deprived of his job. The trustee became uncharacteristically contrite, and was inspired to go to the priest's house, apologize, and reinstate him. The priest, surprised by the behavior of his employer, looked out the window and saw Amma wandering through the crowds of people in the street.

"Mother!" he called, and ran down the stairs to find her, but to no avail. With a heavy heart, he returned home and prayed: "Mother, why do you play hide-and-seek with this child of yours? Be kind enough to grant him your [vision] completely and permanently. I cannot stand being tossed about in this cradle of the world any longer. Amma, unveil this curtain of [illusion] and take me into your blessed lap once and for all!"[8]

Little Amma went to stay with still another relative in 1929. While she was wandering the street through the bazaars alone, she overheard a lecture being presented by a local swami, a highly regarded scholar. Daily, for one month, Amma sat down quietly in the back of the room and listened to the swami's teachings, and daily she would leave before everyone went filing up to prostrate themselves at his feet, an Indian custom. The swami became intrigued with Amma's beautiful, luminescent eyes. Since she never approached him, he could no longer contain his curiosity and beckoned for her to come to him. When asked who she was, she responded that that was exactly what she was there to find out. When he asked her to which caste she belonged, she responded, "To the caste of the sperm and ovum."[9]

The swami, thrilled by her answer, wanted to give her a mantra; but Amma was willing only to come and listen to his teachings, not to be taught. One day she referred to him as her child; when he asked her why, she responded that it was her destiny. Now he was even more enchanted with her and especially eager to initiate her with a mantra. She insisted that she did not want a mantra because his explanation as to its meaning was not good enough.

"In that case, you please do it yourself," the swami offered.

"Are you asking me to give you a mantra or to explain what mantra means?"

"According to your pleasure. I leave that to you. Both are needed in my case," he admitted with a broad grin.

"Then in what capacity should I act?" Amma questioned playfully.

The swami was overjoyed. Happily abandoning the reserved dignity and pious demeanor of his profession, he drew Amma into his large arms and kissed her paternally. "Though you are outwardly a child, in reality you are Mother! What class do you attend?"

"I don't go to any school, I have only come to this school. But this seems to be a school without a teacher."

"Yes indeed, Mother," the swami agreed, his portly form quivering with laughter at this latest blow to his [ego].[10]

During the next days the tables completely turned, with Amma now the teacher and the swami the student. She spent a few more days with him teaching him about mantra, about what is real and what is not, and about the nature of Mother and Father. When he asked her how others viewed her, she responded that everyone viewed her according to their own capability, according to each person's ability to expand. After he conclusively identified her as the Mother of the Universe in child form, she left, never to return. Before going, however, she cautioned him about the impossibility of ever grasping her true nature with the limited use of the rational mind.

Throughout her childhood she unveiled herself to those who were ready to see, she ministered to the ill and dying, and she continued to shock her traditional relatives of the high Brahmin caste by helping the outcasts who were in need. When she entered her teen years, it became time to choose a husband for her. She did not object, as many of her relatives did, when a cousin from a poor Brahmin family was chosen to be her betrothed. She experienced the symbol of the yoke in the Hindu wedding ceremony as indicating the equality of the male and female within the marriage, a perfectly balanced relationship in which the two walk unerringly together. Amma identified marriage as a state in which each partner revered the other as god or goddess, and therefore the union itself represented a means through which one could attain higher levels of consciousness.

Her husband was a simple man who didn't seem to have much interest in philosophical matters. She intended to set an example that through marriage one could attain perfection by shedding selfishness and egoism and maintaining devotion to one's spouse no matter what the conditions. Amma, as the exemplary wife in the Hindu tradition, served him, obeyed him, and revered him throughout her married life. In the beginning her husband did not understand her and was often cruel and physically abusive to her. Through her marriage she taught that everything comes from one source, even negativity and pain, and that no life circumstance can bar us from the goal of self-realization.

Amma stepped down considerably from the comforts and freedom to which she was accustomed. She joined her husband, who had taken a new job as village officer, in the small town of Jillellamudi. There she worked in the fields, carried water from long distances, bore three children, and lived a harsh life. When the countryside wasn't dry and wind-parched, it was flooded from the monsoons. The villagers were backward and ignorant; they were afraid of her, and several attempts were made on her life by the use of poison. Most of these ill-wishers became devotees in the end. Amma preferred not to discuss the circumstances of these difficult times.

After ten years of enduring severe conditions, circumstances changed as people from near and far began to hear about the holy woman from Jillellamudi. With permission from her husband, Amma cooked and ministered to the needs of many pilgrims who came to visit. Even when he objected to some of her wishes with regard to the growing numbers of devotees, he usually relented and gave his permission. In the end her husband was transformed and became one of her devotees. Ultimately he was a willing partner in the formation of the ashram that grew around their home.

During one of her *darshans* with a small group of devotees, one curious man asked her what she thought about. She replied that her mind was constantly occupied with what to feed her children. Over and over again she would say that her main concern in life was to nourish the hungry, rich or poor. To that purpose she cooked for everyone who came to visit and eventually had a staffed kitchen that was open twenty-four hours a day. Before she met with anyone, she would make certain they had been fed.

Her visitors included scholars, whom she baffled with her almost heretical interpretations of *Advaita Vedanta* (philosophy of nondualism). There is a famous "rope/snake" metaphor that has been used for hundreds of years to explain how the supreme reality, or Shakti, is not that which we see: A rope lies coiled on the road; someone walks nearby and mistakes it for a snake. The proponents of this ancient and highly revered philosophy explain that in order to realize the true reality, one must cease superimposing what we perceive daily (the imagined snake) on the true reality (the actual rope), and in that way one would come to understand the illusory quality of the world.

Amma, however, insisted that the world and what we see *is* the true reality. She said the problem lies in thinking that there is something beyond that which is right in front of us— whether it be a rope or a snake. The mistake, she said, is seeing two.

Amma said, "In my view, God does not exist separately somewhere. You are all God. There is nothing existing apart from what we see before us."[11] Imagining something to be something else is what is unreal. She said that the illusory quality of the universe refers to its changing nature, not the unreality of that which changes.

In further response to those philosophers and teachers who taught that all we see is illusion, Amma said, "How could it be so? If my foot hurts, how can I believe that the pain does not exist? If I am very hungry and you are eating, what meaning is there in your telling me to think that my hunger does not exist?"[12]

Over and over again scholars would challenge her view, citing scripture as their authority, and over and over again

Amma would explain that the scripture represents a description of someone's experience and, as such, is not to be mistaken as the experience itself. Since the experience of the absolute cannot be put into words, scriptures have become subject to interpretations which cannot impart the original personal experience that inspired the scriptural writing. In other words, the resultant scriptural interpretations do not necessarily reflect an experience of the true reality.

Amma's view is clearly illustrated in the following encounter she had with an arrogant swami who came with his disciples to meet her:

Swami: How does this Universe appear to you?

Amma: Trees appear as trees, houses as houses—each one as it is, different from another.

Swami: If so, where do they come from?

Amma: From the Universe, surely.

Swami: What? You know the tree must have a seed—who ordained that the seed come?

Amma: "What is" has come as seeds.

Swami: If "What is" has come as seeds, where did all things come from?

Amma: It is not like something coming to one place from another. "What is" is everywhere, and THAT has itself become all that we see.

Swami: (anger in his voice) So what is Advaita (nonduality)? . . . Have you at least heard the words?

Amma: (Picked up a banana.) I think this is Advaita. (Peeled off the skin and held both parts.) This is *dvaita* (duality).

Swami: You said that the Universe is the *Adhara* (basis) for all that we see. What is the Adhara for the Universe?

Amma: The Universe is its own Adhara.

Swami: You say the Universe is its own Adhara, but on what do you base your statement?

Amma: I.

Swami: You have perception, but no scholarship. Do study the scriptures thoroughly!

Amma: Scriptures do not yield experience; experience yields scriptures.

Swami: (Enraged) The scriptures were not written just for you; they are for everybody, and they are the authority! (He left abruptly.)[13]

At a later time Amma explained that all scriptures, doctrines, and religions are the same. "All appear the same to one who practices; they appear separate only to one who pounds tables. Don't all religions have the saying, 'Love all'? . . . Although the way I express it may differ from the way others have said it before, the *bhava* (mental state) is the same. . . . Yes, duality is seen—division is there. To feel the ONEness in the duality is Divinity. Duality is always seen; it is mind that feels the ONEness."[14]

Another common belief among scholars and teachers along the spiritual path is that we must conquer our mind, our senses, and the elements of nature. According to Amma, " 'Conquering' simply means understanding. 'What is' is Mind. . . . To say that the five elements [of nature] are conquered does not mean that they cease to exist—indeed a living being is itself a combination of the five elements. Understanding is conquering. We begin by wanting to conquer Nature *(prakriti)*, only to realize at last that Nature is itself God."[15]

In the midst of the scholarly debates, the joy, and the feeling of celebration that pervaded the "House of All," as the ashram was called, a tragedy occurred. Amma's daughter Hyma, who suffered illnesses and chronic headaches throughout her short life, died at the age of twenty-five. Amma showed visible signs of grief that seemed to personify the archetypal sadness of motherhood in the face of a child's death. At the burial, one devotee spoke aloud what most probably was on the minds of everyone present, "Why has it happened like this even to you?" To which Amma responded, "I wanted it this way and then got it done. In this, nobody else is responsible. I made the dagger, and then with that dagger I stabbed myself."[16] Amma presided over the ceremony, and placed her daughter's body in a shrine so that the devoted Hyma, beloved by all, would serve those who came to pray.

Amma often insisted that she was not a guru and had no disciples; "Mother does nothing. All things come at their proper time," she would often say. Many people who came to her ashram were confused that she did not assign austere spiritual practices or tell students to meditate so many hours in a day, as is the custom of most male-dominated spiritual institutions. Some people could not believe that any spiritual progress could be made with such lack of discipline. But Mother herself clarified by saying, "What is to be attained by seeing Mother? Seeing Mother is itself attaining."[17]

Amma was a classical, compassionate Mother in every sense of the word. At the House of All, one devotee was suffering with a high fever and unable to sleep. He thought he could no longer bear the pain and prayed to Amma to come in a white sari, sit on his bed, and massage his aching body. No sooner "had this desire arisen, than he felt the cool touch of a hand on his forehead. Opening his eyes, he was amazed to see Amma in a white sari sitting at the edge of the cot, her face wreathed in smiles. 'Have you called me?' she inquired as she started massaging his body."[18]

Even to devotees who lived at great distances from Jillellamudi, Amma would appear if needed. One devotee in Portland, Oregon, had such an intense devotion for her that she was impelled to come to him in a vision. He subsequently wrote to Amma about his extraordinary experience, gave the date, described the color and design of her sari, and was later told that the day had been her birthday and the description of her sari was precisely that of the one she wore. When another devotee commented that it was unfortunate that this American would never have a chance to meet her, Amma replied, "Though he is there and you are here by my cot, the truth is that this child of mine is closer than you are."[19]

While Amma claimed not to be the cause of the countless miracles that happened around her, her devotees believe she was, and still is. Her insistence on disclaiming responsibility for anything was because she wanted her disciples to understand that Shakti alone is the cause of all things, miracles and otherwise.

One can go to Jillellamudi today, participate in an active program, and pray at the temple where her sacred relics are enshrined. Accommodations are available at the House of All. Her original home still stands, with the addition of an adjacent meditation center where one can sit, meditate, and feel Amma's presence. There is a college and high school where students learn the Sanskrit language and study scriptures, and a medical center with care available to the rich and poor, free of charge. At the dining hall, her heart continues to express itself through her unending concern that her children be nourished—food is served twenty-four hours a day to all who are hungry.

*   *

A few more words from Jillellamudi Mother:

"Mother" means the One without a beginning and without an end, the One who is the Beginning and the End—that which has become everything and which cannot be comprehended—the limitless, resistless basis of all.[20]

When love becomes primary, it isn't possible for there to be a single person who isn't loved. You will love death, you will love life—love alone will be important.[21]

To make one who hops like a frog (in pride) move like an earthworm (in humility) is my way.[22]

I need one veil to disguise myself; I need another to exhibit my disguise to you. There is always a veil within a veil. Mere words cannot remove them. These veils will not allow you to pass through with your baggage.[23]

Mother's love? Love itself is Mother.[24]

I am not God and you are not the devotees; I am not the guru and you are not the disciples; I am not the guide and you are not the pilgrims. I am the Mother and you are the children.[25]

Mother is like the Earth, which assimilates filth as well as good things. Whether a thing is good or bad is your concern; the Earth and the Mother make no such distinction.[26]

How can we call that emotion which changes its hue every moment "love," my child? True love never changes. What stays only for a moment and then disappears is not love at all.[27]

Today people are throwing flowers at me; tomorrow they may throw stones. I welcome anything. That kind of impartiality must become natural. That alone is liberation.[28]

≈

Witnessing Meditation

*[Witnessing] is a state in which you remain constantly detached
and untouched, simply watching everything that happens, without
the interference of the mind and its thoughts.*   —Ammachi

So how can we attain this state of detached love and acceptance of all things, all events, all people? The practice of witnessing is one step in that direction. One striking observation we could make about the Jillellamudi Mother is the detached love she held for all people and things. Even as a child, she viewed the death of her mother with complete dispassion. The inspiration she offered the temple priest and the scholarly swami came out of her detached witnessing state of consciousness. She knew God permeated everything and that all emotions, negative and positive, came from one source alone.

Why is a witnessing state desirable? Most of us feel better when we are not identified with emotions or events, especially negative ones. It is not pleasant to *be* anger when we are angry. Yet anger when we are not identified with it can be a useful emotion, such as in the occasional need for a show of anger when disciplining children. Another example might be with a friend who was unhappy about an episode in her life. You may have helped her by expressing sadness, even though you weren't really sad, or even though your experience of sadness might have passed immediately after.

One time I went to Ammachi about my nephew, who had just been diagnosed with liver cancer. Amma let out a sound of suffering that seemed to come from the depths of the ocean. Her look of horror combined with her voice connected with my own feeling more deeply than even I had realized. Yet as soon as I left her presence she was smiling, radiant, paying attention to someone else. She had entered into my grief for my benefit, but had never left her connection to all that is.

Ammachi suggests that being in a witnessing state of consciousness, *sakshi bhava,* does not mean we can't carry on our daily activities or express emotions as Amma did with me regarding my nephew. Amma explains: "You may be concerned about your children's studies, the health of your parents and your wife, and so on, yet in the midst of all these external problems you remain a sakshi, a witness, to all that happens and to all that you do. Within, you are perfectly still and unperturbed."[29]

Ammachi reminds us that we experience witnessing states every day and we just don't notice it. For instance, we might walk in on our neighbors who are arguing. It is possible for us to watch the argument and not have an attachment to it, not get involved with all the negative feelings. In this situation we are more likely to see the problem more clearly than the couple who is fighting or if we were the ones squabbling. If we do get involved with our friends who are fighting, we are not likely to be of much help.

Another example of witnessing often happens while riding in a car, train, or plane. We observe the scenes we are passing, but we are not intimately involved. Looking out the window can be a peaceful experience because of this witnessing state.

*If this ability to witness can happen during certain moments of
our lives, we should be able to experience it constantly, in any
situation. This can be achieved because it is, in fact, our real
nature.*[30]   —Ammachi

The following practice can help to clear the mind after a day
at work or a day at home mothering. The technique is useful
for flushing out the day's thoughts and activities, leaving
our minds clear and quiet. Eventually the practice teaches
the mind to be more observant and detached while an activity is taking place.

Begin by closing your eyes and observing your breath, as
in the breathing meditation. Then mentally review the entire
day—from the time you woke up in the morning to the present moment. Watch the events of the day as if you were
watching them on a movie screen. While the aim is to remember everything, it is not necessary to see minute details,
nor should you anguish over things you don't recall. The
ability to see everything will come after practice.

Similar to the breathing meditation, the attitude you want
to hold in the witnessing meditation is one of detachment,
almost as if you were observing something that happened to
someone else, or viewing yourself from a distance. In the
event that your emotions become activated, let the feelings
be there in a detached way, not connected to the thought or
the exchange that caused the feelings. In other words, suspend your mental review of your day and let your emotions
move through you (even tears of sadness or hurt) without
thinking about the event associated with the feeling. The
feelings will go away when they are not connected to an activity. When the emotions pass, resume watching the movie
screen of your day until you reach the end of the day. Now,

carry on with the process of witnessing in the present as with the breathing meditation.

To become a witness is to really wake up and become conscious of everything that happens, both within and without. But in reality, there is no within or without. In that state of supreme witnessing, you become the center of everything, just watching all the changes occur. The changes never affect you because now you have become the center, the very life force of everything.[31]   —Ammachi

≈

Part II

Love and Rapture

*For the lover to wholeheartedly receive
and welcome the beloved, pure love
prepares the mind by chasing away all
the enemies of love. This results in a
constant flow of the lover's heart
toward the beloved. There is an
unquenchable thirst to drink in the
beloved, an unappeasable hunger to eat
him up and an immeasurable intensity
to become love.*

—Ammachi

The Lure of
Divine Love

Only in the state of love will the beautiful,
fragrant flower of freedom and supreme bliss
unfold its petals and bloom. —Ammachi

When I first went to India to be with Ammachi I had an intense inner resolve to merge with her, to be released from all suffering. On occasion I would stand on the roof of the seven-story concrete building, looking over the coconut palms to the Arabian Sea and crying out: "Mother, I don't want any more spiritual experiences, just liberation. Mother, please!" Then one night while in Ammachi's presence, I prayed silently, pleading for her to set me free.

Two evenings a week the large, wooden, sliding temple doors would rumble open, revealing the platform in front of the altar where Ammachi, with long black hair flying free and wearing a colorful silk sari, jewels, and a gem-studded crown, would sit on a throne assuming the attitude of the supreme goddess, Devi Bhava. While bells rang and conch shells sounded, a monk, clad only in an ankle-length orange cloth wrapped around his waist, would wave a flaming camphor lamp around and around in front of Ammachi. She would sit immobile with eyes closed. As if coming out of a trance, she then would toss a handful of flower petals toward the devotees and onto her own head in acknowledgment of her exalted state. Many believe that her appearance on these special nights helps us envision the Divine Mother in her heaven—it intensifies our experience of her.

My heart would swoon when I saw her in Devi Bhava. I would feel transported to a colorful paradise where only joy prevails. On these festive nights, some thirty or forty Westerners would be allowed to sit on the platform with her, and would line up at two rear entrances waiting to be let in, women on one side, men on the other. The air was electrified with anticipation. At the appointed moment the doors would fly open and those who had been waiting would run, pushing, shoving, and crowding onto the raised area to sit near Ammachi. Meanwhile, thousands of Indians would stand at two front doors that opened onto either side of the platform.

On one particular night I longed to sit next to Ammachi; a bitterness surfaced within me as I watched the Westerners bounding like a pack of monkeys to sit close. My usual response was to linger in the back until everyone had found their seats. Tonight I reluctantly stayed behind as was my custom. In a state of mental anguish, I prayed, "Mother, will you take me to the goal even if I stay back, don't run and push to be near you?" Just minutes later, someone gave me a seat a little closer. I felt a smile warming inside of me.

All at once one of Mother's female Indian renunciates approached me, beckoned for me to come quickly. She grabbed my pillow and bag, put them down right next to Mother and motioned for me to sit. Mingled with my state of shock and delight, my indefinable pleasure, was a feeling of embarrassment to be seated in such a prominent spot. I struggled to make myself very small, which I am not—while I am thin, I am too tall ever to hope to be inconspicuous.

Once settled, at first I couldn't take my eyes off Ammachi, her captivating smile, her glowing brown skin, her colorful sari. But soon my gaze shifted to watching the devotees coming to her. I was confused as to why I was unable to contemplate her exquisite form and was so magnetically drawn to stare only at the people. As much as I would remind myself over and over again to look at Mother, I was impelled as if by a will other than my own to watch the individuals moving forward in line.

Gradually my senses were pervaded by an unprecedented perception. Even though I saw distinct faces, smiling or crying, ugly or beautiful, sick or healthy, young or old, I unmistakably, without exception, saw them all as Mother. To make certain what I experienced was real, I would look away at the ceiling or at one of the several large fans. Without fail, each time I brought my gaze back to the devotees coming up to Amma, the vision of Mother in everyone had not altered. Even more amazing was the feeling of tender passion for each one, the same feeling I have for Ammachi.

There was another aspect to the phenomenon that amazed me. I sat so close to the throngs of people urgently crawling on their knees toward Amma that I was constantly bumped by them. This poking and pushing ordinarily would have upset and angered me, but on this night it was a different matter. I actually relished each minor infliction because each shove and knock felt like love pats from Mother herself. For five hours I sat in silent awe of this blessed experience. Even though I was filled with wonder, there was an effortlessness to my sense of self that made the event seem ordinary, as if the love of all beings was the natural order of life.

Even into the next day, my heart was filled with so much love for every person who crossed my path that I could have held each of them in my arms forever. Then my mind entered in: "I don't want this sweet rapture to leave me, ever." The thought of losing the feeling made me anxious, yet I still bathed in the grace of it all. I was so thrilled I wanted to share the experience with Mother. I wrote a note to tell her what had happened, asked her if I could please keep this new perception of life while I traveled the path toward final liberation. In her broken English she said in my ear, "Mother happy." For weeks I felt the inner glow of Mother's love in every human being. Then gradually it faded, to return only on occasion.

The story of love takes us to the second stage on the Path of the Mother. Here we are swept into bliss and rapture beyond any we have ever experienced before. While in stage one, the love we feel tends to be more abstract and distant; in stage two, our love for her becomes deeply personal and all-encompassing.

It would not be unusual to have an experience of this second stage early on in your relationship to the Mother, sometimes before stage one. Often she gives us samplings or previews of what is to come so that we have some sense of the goal, some indication that it is worthwhile to embark on the journey in the first place. Unwavering devotion and longing to be merged with the Mother are some of the characteristics of this stage. It can also be a stage in which we experience being bathed in light, merging with the absolute, having visions of divine beings, or having the sense that all is one. Consumed with love for her, our longing brings feelings of ecstasy.

To love someone greatly is one of the simplest and, at the

same time, most advanced of spiritual practices. Love alone will take us to the deeper spiritual truth within.

Often, before the actual event of divine love takes place, there will be some inkling of the longing. One of Ammachi's devotees, an American woman now living in Amma's ashram in India, is an example of love and rapture happening in the beginning. I will call her Rebecca, because she prefers to remain anonymous. Born Jewish, a tradition in which the Mother is not overtly included, Rebecca was never interested in the goddess image.

In India, Rebecca and I were sitting on the roof of the seven-story temple building at night, during Devi Bhava, the music wafting up from the loudspeakers. In telling her story, Rebecca felt it was important to step back in time, to when she was living in Berkeley, California, before she met Amma. She had a good job as a graphic artist and marketing agent for a printing company; she liked the people she worked for. There was no reason to leave her life as she knew it.

Before meeting Amma, Rebecca was involved with a different teaching, but without a living master. Many of the people in the group had known the master before he passed. Because Rebecca saw how deeply spiritual they all were, she began to feel a craving for a teacher. Somehow inwardly she knew she had reached a point when that would be necessary; these people could give her only so much, and she knew it.

One day I remember very clearly standing by a tree, doing tai chi, and praying somehow, really wishing for a teacher, and at the same time feeling this light come over me. I have a clear memory of it.

Shortly thereafter I moved to another part of town. Up the street from where I lived, I walked down some steps one day and accidentally discovered a little church. In the courtyard was a beautiful statue of Mary with her hands folded on top of one another. Sometimes I would go there and find somebody had put a flower in her hands. So there was a nice little atmosphere. I was never really attracted to Mary, but there was something special about this place, and, being Jewish, I would never hear about the Mother at all. It's Father, Father, Father. And so the concept of Mother didn't even enter into my mentality. But after a few times of going and standing in front of the statue, I felt something. I met Amma shortly after that.

Some of the people from the group I was involved with had gone to see Amma and were totally impressed. But I wasn't interested because they were the kind of people who would go to see every teacher, every guru, anyone and everyone, so here was just one more. However, one friend in particular told me, "You have to go, you have to go." I think because Amma was a woman, I thought, "Well, I want to see what this is about."

So I went to see her during the very last program she was giving in a church in Berkeley. I walked in. Even though I was early I had to sit way in the back; the church was packed full. It was in 1987, Amma's first year in America. Honestly, at that time I wasn't interested in Indian gurus at all. It was not the tradition I was involved in. I was very skeptical.

Mother walked in and sang some *bhajans* with her group, and somebody gave a talk. After that part was over, there was a big rush to line up to see Mother. I was thinking, Oh, brother, because I had to get up early for work the next day. My mentality came in, saying, I don't know if I want to wait; I have to get up for work . . . blah, blah, blah. Then my mind became very still and the thought went through, If this was Jesus Christ, wouldn't you wait? I always had a feeling for Jesus, even being Jewish. I thought, Well, yeah, I would wait if I knew it was Jesus.

So I waited and the line moved up and continued to move up for a long time. Then it was my turn. I can't really explain what happened because it's not something that is describable. The closest I can get is to say when Mother took me on her lap, she gave me an experience that she was everywhere and in everything.

I knew that this was the living truth; this was the real thing. I'd been reading books about saints and different masters. Before this moment I used to think, I'll go to India; I'll go to the Himalayas, but I'll probably never meet a teacher. Now I had no doubt that's what had happened—I'd met a master. It gave me hope that this sort of thing exists on the planet; it wasn't just in some book about masters who are no longer in their bodies.

I don't even remember how I got home that night. I just remember feeling very drunk. I do recall thinking, You're going to India. That's it. You're going to India. Then another part of me was rationalizing, Are you crazy? No way. But the insistent part was adamant, You're going; just forget it; you have to go.

The feeling of rapture lasted for quite some time. I remember being in my apartment and actually falling down in a kind of expansive state, swooning, feeling like pulling my hair out, thinking, My God, what is this? And who is she?

The thought of going to India was really pushing me. But Mother was leaving town and I didn't know when or how I would see her again. Here I'd met this woman saint and all of a sudden, Wham! and now I didn't know where she was. Soon after I heard from one of my friends that Ammachi was going to be in Mount Shasta in four days. Even though I continued to be in this rather inebriated state, I managed to get there.

On the mountain, at night, Mother was about to give Devi

Bhava in a small yurt. We were all sitting there on the grass with the yurt in the center. At a certain point the curtains opened and we saw Mother in her crown and colorful sari. When I looked, her skin was blue. I was staring at her, thinking, She's blue! The thought went through my mind, This is Krishna, even though I didn't actually know anything about Krishna.

Everyone spent the whole night imbibing Mother's presence. I remember going inside the yurt at one point; it was such a mystical feeling; I can't explain it; it was so divine. Then I fell into a deep meditation. Later, it was funny, because one of the hostesses asked the woman sitting next to me to move—after all, how many people can you fit into a yurt! The woman said, "I've been waiting for this for fifty years of my life and I'm not moving." And I wasn't moving either.

The next day during the regular *darshan* I had the urge to ask Mother if I could go to India. Only I was afraid because if she said yes, I'd be committed to going. Yet, somehow I managed to crawl over the people to hand the translator the message. She said, "Yes. You come. I'll pray for you."

When I left that yurt my whole body was literally shaking. I couldn't stop it, it was vibrating so powerfully. I had to drive the car down the mountain in that state. The interesting thing was the woman I was with was in a totally different frame of mind, blabbing away about all this worldly stuff. She had no idea what was going on with me.

Back in Berkeley, Rebecca, due to Amma's influence, continued having unusual spiritual experiences. However, because of her job and the major responsibility she had in the small company, she didn't feel she could go to India right away. She would have to give sufficient notice and get organized before leaving. In addition, she had always wanted to be in a relationship and she had met someone she was slightly interested in.

While Rebecca struggled with the notion of moving to India, Mother let her know in no uncertain terms that she was being guided and pulled by the divine. One experience happened while Rebecca was dining with the man she was interested in.

> I was sitting in a restaurant with him, just talking. All of a sudden, I can't really explain it, but I had a very palpable experience that God is love. It's like the whole presence, the whole atmosphere of the room changed and was filled with love. Somehow I knew it was Mother. I'd always heard that God is love, but the experience of it was something else. The tangible taste of it was very profound. I think Amma did that to show me how a relationship tends to pale in comparison to what I was striving for. I always thought I was looking for this love through a person. Everyone's different. For my path, Mother showed me very clearly that I would never find it that way.
>
> Another time, late at night, I was sitting in my bedroom; I had been holding a memory, a picture of Amma in my mind. All of a sudden the whole room became filled with light. It was bright like the sun. I knew it was Amma. So much energy came through my body, I could hardly contain it. Because of it I understood that in order to embrace this kind of energy, I would have to prepare myself for it. My mind and body were too dense to hold it.
>
> I was having all manner of similar experiences during the months after meeting Amma. And still I wasn't doing anything about getting to India. One day a friend of mine and I went to the bookstore to pick out some spiritual videos. I noticed one about the Mother, but I thought it was another Mother, not Ammachi. While we were watching, I saw

tropics, banana trees, and thatched huts, and I thought, What's going on? All of a sudden I saw Amma. I said to myself, Oh, my God. That's where I'm going? But it looked so primitive. I thought, I'm not going there! Yet I couldn't avoid the message: Mother had come onto the TV telling me I'd better come.

After that, I started to get to a low point. I really doubted whether I had the courage to go to India; I had heard so many negative things about it. I thought, Why are you giving up your life here and your job and all that? Are you crazy?

At the really lowest ebb, I went to my mailbox one day. There was a letter from India! When I saw it, my body started shaking. I thought, Oh, my God! I opened the envelope and the very first sentence was, "Darling Daughter, when are you coming?"

I thought, Okay, okay; I'm coming, I'm coming. So that was it. It was amazing; it really was. It still brings tears. But Mother knew. She had to do that for me. I was so dense.

Even after getting to India, Rebecca continued grappling with the notion of God as Mother:

It took some time for me to merge the notion of Mother and the physical as God. It confused me for quite some time because it was so deep in my psychology about God as Father. Changing my mental mind-set was something that couldn't be forced or intellectualized. The feeling of Amma's love was so great, the shift from God as Father to God as Mother happened naturally over time.

In Rebecca's story we saw love pulling her in, enticing her with its sweet nectar until she could no longer refuse the lure. While there were many attractive aspects to her life in

Berkeley, the Mother showed her a love far more powerful than she had ever experienced, a love that encompassed all, including the surroundings in a restaurant. Still Rebecca procrastinated. After Ammachi's original appearance in Berkeley, even after the spiritual experiences and subsequent feelings of ecstasy, the Mother had to continue persuading Rebecca in very concrete and physical ways. Though Rebecca had been praying for a teacher, even entertaining the idea of going on a spiritual quest to India, when the Mother appeared in physical form in the very town where Rebecca lived, she balked. Later Rebecca saw Mother on a videotape, then finally received something she couldn't refuse: a personal letter from the Mother, evidence of the Mother's never-ending love.

Chandra Pillai's experience of love and rapture challenged his beliefs about science and religion and his assumptions that maybe we don't need a God. Yet Chandra, a small man with a round face and a charming smile, is someone for whom the goddess was part of his tradition. As an Indian-born physicist employed at Los Alamos National Laboratory in Los Alamos, New Mexico, home of the atom bomb, Chandra's visionary encounter seemed almost paradoxical in the context of his job as a nuclear scientist.

Many aspects of Chandra's life didn't seem to make sense in light of his scientific and questioning mind. As a young man living in a small village in Kerala, India, he used to walk about a mile every Friday to worship Devi in one of India's thousands of goddess temples. Along the way villagers would heckle him, because in those days it was unusual for a teenager to be so religious. Chandra had always been attracted to temples and worship services.

In 1977, Chandra left India to attend graduate school in Oregon. His wife, Latha, and daughter, Lakshmi, joined him two years later. After doing research for his Ph.D. at the laboratory in Los Alamos, he and his family moved there. In their home they had a *puja* room, a place where most Indians keep an altar for personal worship. Even so, they were not active spiritual seekers.

In 1988, Cathi Schmidt of the Amma Center of New Mexico, just after she had first met Ammachi, wanted to learn Malayalam, the language of Kerala, and somehow found out about Chandra and Latha. Cathi telephoned the Indian couple to ask if Latha would be willing to teach Cathi their native tongue. On one of Cathi's visits to the Pillai home, Cathi told them about Ammachi and invited them to attend one of the programs. Chandra was only vaguely interested in meeting Ammachi. He decided to go to the gathering not because Ammachi was a saint, but because she was from Kerala. Chandra laughed, joking about the fact that not many holy people come to the United States from Kerala, only engineers and scientists.

Late in June, Chandra and Latha, with their daughter, Lakshmi, who was eleven, drove to Santa Fe to attend one of Ammachi's evening programs. Chandra remembers the first meeting well. While Mother was walking to the front of the tent, she looked at him; then they exchanged a few greetings and pleasantries in Malayalam. After the *bhajans* Chandra and Latha were impressed. The songs were more emotional than they had ever heard before, in India or anywhere else. Even so, as *darshan* began, the Pillais wanted to return to Los Alamos because it was late; Lakshmi had to go to school and Chandra had to go to work the next morning. Amma called them to her to give them *darshan*, individually, then together.

Chandra describes his experience:

When she put me in her lap suddenly I could feel the difference. I had never felt like that in anyone's presence. Even my own mother or father or anyone. Just being near Amma and touching her made a change in my surroundings. I didn't know what it was. She told us to sit near her, so we did. While I was watching her, I started crying quite a lot. I couldn't understand why. I wasn't sad. It was a sweet feeling while I was crying.

Chandra's wife Latha explained: "I felt we had been waiting our whole lives for her and didn't realize it. In India, for small things, we say, 'Amma.' And now here was the Amma we were always referring to."

Chandra continued:

After about an hour or two we left. I felt very good. I still remember the shirt I was wearing. When I was driving, I wasn't driving, I was floating. I didn't feel any weight. I was in the air. I had never felt like that. Nothing was in my mind. Usually I'm very careful, watching signs and noticing trees and houses. I don't remember any of those things on that night. It was a feeling that everything was very unimportant. I felt so detached, I could understand why everyone strives for that state. Because if you don't want anything, if you're not attached, you don't want to come back anymore. Now I knew there was a state of consciousness I could strive for.

The next day Chandra couldn't concentrate on his work because he was always thinking about Mother. "This had never happened to me. I've met many people, but now something was bugging me, a fire in my mind, something pulling me back to her. A craving. I called Latha and said, 'Let's go a little early today.'"

Latha, who had been listening with a look of admiration

and respect for her husband, laughed, saying, "I was so surprised. I had to drag him the day before, and now he wanted
to go early."

That evening Chandra and his family sat near Ammachi
again after the *bhajans* were over. Chandra noted that Mother
talked just like a regular person.

No lecture on spirituality. Nothing. She only asked me questions about my work, family, and such things. I wondered
why such a person who doesn't talk about religion could be
so appealing. We hear this same kind of talk from everyone,
but don't feel the same way. Amma doesn't look extraordinary, talk extraordinary; why is she so appealing?

We went to the airport to see her off. It felt like she
was taking a part of me, a part of my heart. In Malayalam
she said, "Son. Shall I go?" This is the way we say good-bye
in our language. It means "I'll be meeting you again." We
could feel she didn't want to leave us but had to go. It was
so sad.

Since that meeting with Amma I started thinking, Why? I
went through many doubts. I have a scientific mind. I always
have to have proof. We scientists don't believe anything that
cannot be proved. When I looked at life, I thought, I don't
need a God. Why do I need a God? I see a lot of people who
are very good people who don't believe in God. They give to
charity, live a nice life, don't hurt anybody. They are happy
and fine. So that means I don't need a God. Everything can be
explained and everything can be made the way you want it,
if you try and are smart.

In the beginning some people thought we were in a cult
and were afraid we would get brainwashed. I even wondered
about that myself. At the same time I thought maybe I'd have
enough intellectual strength to get out if I wanted to. But
would I be able to get out if I wanted to? It was an ongoing

process: I would analyze all along because I'd never had anything like this before. What was I turning into? Maybe I would become fanatical, give up my job and walk away.

So it was hard to accept someone like Mother. I had to admit there was another level that I hadn't experienced, hadn't seen. I had all the luxury and all the comfort in life, and now saw what I'd been missing all these years. When I saw Mother, I thought that the changes she was making me go through were all part of her game, that she wanted to show there is a level beyond what I see. Krishna says the same. The proof lies in the experience. Knowing the truth has to happen to everyone eventually.

I had gone to school and studied, but I never thought I would have a religious experience like they talk about in books; I thought these tales were only someone's imagination, that they weren't actually possible. I knew Krishna lived a long time ago, but I didn't think I'd ever know someone like him. Now, after meeting Mother, all I had read was making sense. I wished I had met her earlier in my life.

Then I began to think, Who is she? Why is she here? What is her mission? Then when I would see her, I saw only a regular person. I was very comfortable with her. Usually I am shy, sit in a corner to read books. I don't pay attention to people very much. In front of Mother I can say anything, including jokes, even jokes which I don't say in front of other people. She just smiles. She gave me the name Joker in the beginning. It's as if I am naked in front of her, with no secrets. I've never felt that in front of anyone. Not even in front of my family—I might make them mad if I tell a bad joke. But in front of Mother, nothing makes her angry. I forget everything else around me; I only see her, only the two of us.

I wondered, Is she going to tell me some day who she is? Maybe I'm not in a position to ask her this. Then I noticed another thing that attracted me—her knowledge of everything. When I found out she hadn't attended school past the fourth grade, I wondered how she could talk like she does, as if she'd studied all the books in the world and understood them in the most practical way. I'd never seen that. She is straightforward and clear. How can she know all these things? She sometimes narrates stories from Hindu scriptures using all the exact names. I don't think she ever read those books. Also her practical knowledge about science and her thinking about life in modern society—most swamis and holy people I've ever known don't like to talk about these materialistic things. When I heard about Amma and her schools and that she wants the best technical schools and hospitals, I was amazed.

One time I asked her, "Mother, you don't like scientists, right?"

She said, "I like science, son. But science has lost its heart." Mother told me that most scientists just want to be superior. They think they know the answers to everything and they are arrogant. It's not that she doesn't like science. Mother always sends someone with heart pain to a doctor.

Her interest in science and technology attracted me because she sees the good in it when used in the right way. We don't know what potential man can have. He can have anything he wants. Science can be a path. I'm a nuclear scientist. Mother says that when you reach a certain level, you don't need a lab. You can do it by thinking about it, by your willpower alone. I've found it interesting that when we do experiments we are always finding what we want to find. I realized that when a scientist wants to discover something, he can, because from his thought he's probably created it. But man has to know how to use this ability. What many scientists think about is how to hurt someone with their technology. Mother says that more advanced knowledge will be reached when man has evolved spiritually to want to use things for the good.

Over and over again Mother would clear my doubts every time I saw her—that's what science is supposed to do. All my experiences with her and the things she would say were leading my mind. Before I met Mother, science was one thing and religion was another; there was no connection between them. Science is against religion and religion is against science. Mother has shown me differently.

Slowly things became more clear. Most great scientists toward the end of their lives became very religious, such as Nobel physicist Albert Einstein, Nobel physicist Steven Weinberg, Cambridge professor John Polkinghome, Nobel laureate Charles Townes, and cancer biologist Carl Feit. They realized spirituality in the end of their lives. Although they didn't write it in books, they told about it in small conferences. Many of them became very devotional and pious, realizing, What have I invented? Just a speck in the cosmic knowledge. This realization made them understand there was a power behind their discoveries and inventions. With age, these kinds of religious thoughts can happen.

For many years I used to think, Why did Mother come as a mother, not a Krishna, or a soldier, or a politician who has power? Then I realized the motherly way is the only path left in the world which is pure and sweet. For a mother, her children are always precious, even if they are murderers or addicts. Mother always loves them. So maybe that's one reason why Mother came as a mother in this *Kali Yuga*[1] when everything is so corrupted. People don't trust anything anymore except maybe their own mother. You can always go to your mother when you are sad or you have a problem. She will never throw you out. Or if she does, she's doing it for your benefit. When I thought further and tried to compare Ammachi with Buddha, Krishna, and Rama, they all came for a certain purpose that is suited to that time.

Mother was changing me slowly, and I had the sense that

this had happened to me before. This is what I was looking for all my life.

To get on with the story of my experience: we always wanted Mother to come to our house. We nagged her and begged her. She always asked how far our house was from Santa Fe. "One hour's drive, then back one hour. Two hours; it's too long for you," we'd answer. We'd been coming to Friday *satsang*s [spiritual gatherings] in Santa Fe—every one since 1993. As my mind had become more clear, other things in our life became less important, so attending Ammachi's *bhajans* in Santa Fe was the only thing we wanted to do in addition to the *pujas* we'd hold in our home once a month.

After Friday nights we'd reach home around one A.M., but we were never tired. On the second Friday in August 1996, we left Santa Fe around eleven or so. I had given the *satsang* talk for the evening on the spot because no one was there to do it. I talked about fifteen or twenty minutes and told some Hindu story about Krishna. We went back home and I was feeling very uneasy because something was going on in my mind, but I didn't know what or how to explain it. Usually when we go back my mind is quiet. This time I was feeling an unknown turmoil.

I went to bed, but I was not sleepy. Latha fell asleep right away within two minutes. I was lying looking at the ceiling. I couldn't sleep. It was around two o'clock. Slowly I closed my eyes and started dreaming, a clear, awake dream; I was aware I was dreaming. The dream started in Santa Fe in June, at about three o'clock in the afternoon. Mother was giving *darshan* at a regular program. I was sitting with Mother when the program ended. She asked, "How far is your house from here?"

"About an hour," I said.

"I'll be there around six-thirty or seven in the evening."

I thought, Oh my God, she's coming! When we leave for Santa Fe, we just leave our house as it is, we don't clean it. I got excited and nervous. I went to Latha and said, "Mother is going to come to our house this evening. She wants to come before the evening program in Santa Fe. So what shall we do? I know, I'll go home and get everything ready. I'll pick up some *puja* stuff and get flowers. You stay here and come with Mother to show her the way."

Then, still in the dream, I went to the car and drove very fast. I parked the car on the street instead of opening the garage. When I got out of the car, I saw a white cloth in front of the house with flowers all over it. I thought, What is this? Then through our glass front door I saw light coming from inside, but not electric lights. In India we have a special lamp for the Shiva temple, a big fruit you can cut in half and make two lamps out of. It's like an avocado, but you can't eat the fruit because it's poisonous. You put oil in the halves, then insert cotton wicks. We put hundreds of them all around the Shiva temple during festivals; it gives a very good feeling. So I saw these lamps on either side of the steps to my house, and going all the way up to the third floor where our *puja* room is.

So, when I saw all these lamps and light coming from inside my house, my heart started pounding. I was alone and didn't know whether I should open the door. Finally, I opened it. Slowly, I stepped one step at a time. Then on the way up the stairs, I turned, bumped a lamp with my foot, and tipped it over. All of a sudden I woke up. My heart was fluttering so fast; I'd never seen these lamps except in temples, but now I was awake.

Then I felt a yearning to go upstairs to our altar. I didn't tell Latha. I slowly got up. My heart was pounding so much, and my yearning was so strong to go and meditate; I normally don't have such a powerful pull. After I got up I noticed there were no lamps, so I knew I'd had a dream and I was fine. I went upstairs; it was a little dark with only a night-light on. Usually I go and prostrate at our altar, then step back a few steps and sit there and meditate. Now I went very slowly. When I got to the *puja* room, I saw a form of a person sitting there in the dim light. I got a little scared. I didn't know what I was seeing. I put my hand on the floor and looked and asked in a soft voice, "Mother?"

As he described the phenomenon, Chandra touched his hand to his heart and made a sound, "Fffooff," to express his wonderment.

I had only said this one word, "Mother?" then I saw her little white dress, with the cloth over her head, sitting in lotus posture in a meditating mood with her eyes closed. I didn't know what to say. I was so surprised and a little nervous, but didn't feel like calling out. Now instead of going three steps back, I went ten steps back. My mind was thinking, How did she get here? Maybe it's not real. But there was nothing on the altar that had a form of a human being. We had only pictures.

Maybe half a minute passed, or more, then she opened her eyes, smiled at me, didn't say anything, then closed her eyes again. She didn't say anything. Slowly I started feeling that I didn't have a body. I was kind of floating in the air while sitting there; it felt like I wasn't touching the ground, like my body was gone; just air. But I could still see and feel everything around me. Then a light started coming from the back of her and the light became stronger and stronger and stronger. It became so bright it made me blind.

Chandra's voice quivered. "Then the Mother who had been in white clothes suddenly turned into the real Devi."

After becoming silent for a few minutes, head bowed, nearly whispering, Chandra narrated what happened next.

I could see the whole universe in her; everything was coming to her and everything was coming out of her: the sun, stars, the good and the bad, all of creation. It was hard to understand where it had come from and how the whole universe could be in such a small space.

The sight was just the way I used to observe things when we do experiments at the lab. There we try to look deep into atoms, try to understand the forces which hold the protons, neutrons and pions, maons, and quarks together. We see a wonderful and amazing world as grand and beautiful as the cosmos. Particles are being created and destroyed there, converting themselves into energy and energy converting to particles. Everything is in perpetual motion. Nothing is at rest even though all we see looks stationary from the outside. We can witness an exact mirror image of the universe in one tiny atom.

In my vision of Mother, nothing was separate from her. Whatever was happening in any part of the universe was happening through her, and not without her knowledge. What I saw before me was so bright and so beautiful, I don't know how to explain it. So beautiful. Now I could believe the things I'd read in the Hindu scriptures and the Bible. At one time I thought these were just good stories to make us feel good, but that the events were not possible in a real sense. Because of what I saw before me, I could accept as true the story about baby Krishna's mother prying open his mouth because he'd eaten some sand, then seeing the whole universe there. I could be certain of what the saint Meera Devi saw while she sang to Krishna. I could believe what Paramahamsa Ramakrishna experienced when he cried and prayed for Kali.

I don't know how long the vision lasted. Maybe ten minutes. I thought it was going to be permanent, that I was going to be in that state all the time. Then the light dimmed slowly and Mother went back to her more recognizable form and

disappeared. Slowly, I started getting all my normal senses
back: that I was sitting on the floor, that my body had feelings. I was crying very hard, and I was shivering.

Finally, I got up and shook my head. When I came down
to the bed, I was sobbing and shaking and feeling hot.

Latha said she woke up at that point, and when she
touched Chandra she thought, Oh my God he's burning.

Chandra continued: "For a while I didn't want to talk
about it. Later I was walking around outside and felt a
strong desire to go to India right away. I didn't know what to
do, if I should quit my job or what. But I wondered who
would take care of Lakshmi and Latha. I was very confused."

Latha called her family in India to seek guidance; she
asked her mother and sister to go to Ammachi's ashram to
ask about Chandra's experience and what should be done.
At first Mother didn't say anything. Finally Latha's sister insisted by asking Mother what Mother had done to Chandra.
Mother answered, "I haven't been to their house so I wanted
to go. Chandra is so innocent. When the mouth is open, the
sweets will come."

Chandra explained what it was like for him after the
experience:

Mother told my sister-in-law I should talk to one of the
swamis. So I called India. I told Swami all I wanted to do was
to meditate. But Swami told me not to. He said people like
me who don't have strength can fall into a bad state and become mad or something. I was so sad. And I got angry, too. It
was like being given a good thing, then having it taken away.
Why did she give it to me?

Then Latha described her dilemma.

I'd been with Chandra longer than I'd been with my parents, and now I was going to lose him. How was I going to take care of Lakshmi alone? I got so mad at Amma that she was taking away my husband. Why us? I wondered. The swamis are special and were born for these kinds of experiences. Why are we as householders getting this experience? Then when Swami said we had to keep Chandra on the worldly level, not to let him meditate, go to work, and slowly he will come back to his old state, I felt better.

Chandra continued:

Later Mother explained that I had that experience so many people can learn. God has appeared to many people in unexpected times; one doesn't have to be a renunciate or a monk.

However, after this happened to me, it was difficult for me to be around Mother. When she came to the United States in November, I stayed away from her; I'd go work in the kitchen or help with hosting.

With a sweet smile, her voice quivering slightly, her long, black hair draped over her shoulders, Latha described what happened when Chandra saw Mother again: "The swamis called him to come close to Mother. He came and sat a little near, then Mother called him to sit next to her. Slowly Amma talked to him and gently asked him to say a joke. He was crying so much, but once he started telling his jokes, he was okay."

Chandra said,

Still it's difficult for me to sit near her or look at her pictures; I start crying right away. My experience, though, changed my attitude about physics. I can see that science provides only a glimpse of the whole truth. When we look at the particles, at the atom, it is so mysterious, so beautiful, so wonderful. We've been splitting atoms for many years. Every time you split it, we find it is still smaller. Krishna said, "I reside in the smallest of the smallest." It means Krishna can keep on dividing the atom. When we see the experiments in physics we can see the amazing beauty of the whole creation. But we worry about fighting and making weapons. I think it is the destiny of man to go through the *Kali Yuga* and eventually we will learn from our mistakes; then we will realize how foolish we've been. We will realize there is a level way beyond what we now know. But we have to have the proof through experience. At least I had that vision of Devi and I can still contemplate what I saw. It was so beautiful.

In both Rebecca's and Chandra's stories, as in most of the personal accounts throughout this book, all six stages along the path figure in. The euphoria and bliss experienced in the two previous accounts stand out as representative of the love and rapture stage. As Chandra probed his doubts, he was exploring stage one, getting to know the Mother, in which more and more layers of the Mother's qualities were revealed. His skepticism, while demonstrating a healthy use of the intellect, was a manifestation of the shadow; his uncertainty indicated a lack of awareness of what lay underneath his conscious mind. Discipline is evidenced from Chandra's persistence to be close to anything that had to do with Ammachi and, over time, in his natural giving up of worldly diversions. Although not mentioned in the above tale, Chandra said Ammachi would scold him from time to time, and at the same time she would remind him that she could do this because he was part of her family—it's what mothers do with their children from time to time. Surrender happened when he became open and innocent enough to receive the full revelation of who Mother is. The stage of contentment and yearning became an aspect of his spiritual journey as he left aside other interests with only the strong desire to know, Who is she? After his vision, and after struggling for many months, he became content with his work in a new way. His more enlightened understanding of physics relative to the Universal Mother lent vigor to his pursuit of scientific experiments. At the same time, he continued to yearn to remain forever in the same state of consciousness he experienced during his vision of Devi.

In Chandra's story it is interesting to note Ammachi's very practical appeal amid the love and rapture before and after the vision. According to what Ammachi told Chandra long after his experience, he received the vision he had been longing for in previous lives. Just as Chandra observed there was no separation between science and religion, his story shows there was no separation between spirituality and worldly life. The Mother, through Chandra's experience, was showing him the connection between spirituality, work, and family life. We don't have to go to a cave in the Himalayas. Householders and physicists have spiritual experiences, too. In Hinduism, as in most religions, the family life is the spiritual responsibility for most people until later years. After the children are married and/or have a career, then ideally the parents retire to the forest or spiritual retreat where the full-time contentment and yearning can take place. Chandra has a beautiful and loving wife and a daughter who is enrolled in a premedical curriculum. The couple envision themselves retiring to a spiritual retreat in later years after Lakshmi is married and settled.

≈

Meditating on the Beloved Deity

The Inner Mother, whose true nature is infinitude and silence,
manifests visibly through this [external] body so that her children
can have a glimpse of the Mother who is deep within.[2]

—Ammachi

One way to cultivate or magnify your sense of love for the divine is to focus on your beloved deity as a meditation. Even though Rebecca and Chandra had natural tendencies toward devotion, their emotional feelings toward the divine had to be awakened. Regular practice of one or more of the following meditations can spark spiritual memories that have been lying dormant within you.

Just as with the breathing meditation, the following visualizations can cause negative and positive emotions to surface—sadness, awe, yearning, gratitude, lust, jealousy. Rather than trying to understand why, or wonder where these feelings come from, simply witness them without any judgment or interpretations of their origins. Feel free to direct all your feelings toward your beloved deity. As black absorbs all colors, the Mother ingests all negativity.

If you have a moody or passionate nature, you are a perfect candidate for the devotional path. Tears of emotion easily turn into tears of love and joy for the divine beloved. I've often found that I will get angry or jealous first, then fall into grieving for the Mother. More times than not, when I leave India, before I realize I'm sad, I am easily irritable and aroused to anger. Over the years I've come to recognize the symptoms. Saying the last good-bye to Ammachi or sitting quietly in meditation opens my inner pathway to love and yearning. Once my tears are released, the river of love can flow through me freely.

Two of the following visualizations focus on the feet. Worship of feet is a traditional practice in Hinduism for many reasons. The most obvious explanation is that touching a saint's feet causes us to feel a sense of humility and surrender to the divine. Sacred rituals to the feet cultivate qualities of devotion. Tenderly touching your beloved deity's feet can be likened to fondling the feet of your intimate loved one: boyfriend, girlfriend, husband, wife. In India it is common to see devotees kissing or patting a holy person's feet. In the New Testament, the highly emotional Mary Magdalena washes and anoints Jesus' feet. And Jesus bathes his disciple's feet at the Last Supper.

In a saint, feet are the most sanctified part of the body; it is a very favorable omen to touch a holy person's feet. Why? A saint's feet walk the earth, symbolizing their taking of a human body to teach us and help us to the goal of self-realization. The two feet represent the duality of creation: through worshiping or honoring the holy one whom we in the moment perceive as separate from us, we will ultimately attain the goal of oneness with the supreme.

Using your imagination, you might come up with any number of reasons why a holy person's feet are desirable objects of worship.

Fixing the mind on the beloved deity: You may choose any representation of the Mother of the Universe that appeals to you. Ammachi encourages the use of any form, male or female, for this process. Any male or female deity, in body or spirit, who has motherly qualities of patience, forgiveness, and love—Mary, Jesus, Kuan Yin, Krishna, Shiva, Saraswati, Durga, Lakshmi, Shekinah, Ammachi, Jillellamudi Mother.

The meditation can be done with your eyes closed, alternating with eyes open. Gaze at a picture of your beloved deity for a few minutes, then shut your eyes and focus inwardly on your memory of the image. Ammachi suggests we imagine that we are offering flowers at our beloved deity's feet. If the form fades away, we can imagine that we are mentally embracing the feet. Or, while chanting the divine name, we can pretend we are binding the deity from toe to head with the rope of repetition of name. Finally, visualize that you are undoing this rope, and continue imagining the deity. This binding and embracing can be repeated whenever the form fades away.

> *If you do like this the mind will not get a chance to think about other things.*[3]   —Ammachi

Mother Nature contemplation: Meditate on images in Mother Nature: a mountain, a river, a lake, a tree, an ocean. This can be done with the eyes open or closed and in combination with the breathing meditation. Loving nature can arouse an expanded sense of dispassion and awe.

An American woman, Marie Watts, attained self-realization after years of contemplating the night sky outside her home in Ely, Nevada. She believed that by looking at the perfection in nature we will eventually recognize that as our natural state of being. As a child, Marie used to gaze at the stars and imagine them to be the windows to heaven. Undoubtedly inspired by this childhood experience, she would lie outside on warm desert nights, and fix her mind on the absolute perfection of the star-studded desert sky. The culmination of her spiritual search occurred while she contemplated a sunrise in the Grand Canyon, Arizona. As she gazed at the rising sun in the grandeur of one of nature's most evocative formations, she was consumed by love and the absolute reality of all things.[4]

To cultivate this divine love through nature, Ammachi suggests the following visualization:

> *Imagine that the moon is the face of the Divine Mother. . . . As the wind blows, try to feel that it is the gentle caress of your beloved deity. . . . You can imagine that your beloved deity is calling you near, hugging you, kissing you, caressing you, blessing you, and then hiding in the clouds and coming out again a little later. By this kind of imagination you go deeper and deeper into your own consciousness.[5]* —Ammachi

Worshiping the beloved deity: Imagine your beloved deity, in this case the Mother, is standing in front of you. Try to see each and every part of her body, noticing the beautiful silk garments and the jewel-studded gold crown she is wearing. Invite the Mother to sit on a throne bedecked with rubies, emeralds, and diamonds. Then light an oil lamp and incense stick. Imagine yourself waving the lamp in a circle three times clockwise around the front of your beloved deity, from head to toe. Then do the same with the incense, slowly, and with loving concentration. Now picture yourself placing your beloved deity's feet on a footstool covered with a color-ful silk cloth.

First, lay a brass tray on the stool; then, carefully lifting the feet with one hand and pushing the stool under with the other, let the feet rest on the tray. Next, visualize yourself bathing your beloved deity's feet with different offerings: first with water, then coconut milk, now whole milk, and fi-nally yogurt mixed with honey. Enjoy the different ways these liquids feel on her feet. Afterward, imagine pouring rose water from a small pitcher to rinse her feet. With a soft white cloth, pat the feet dry, then gently lift them off the tray, removing the tray now filled with liquid, and place the feet back onto the stool. Now, put a garland of fragrant flowers around the Mother's neck. Then offer her sweet pudding, watching her relish the dish you have made for her. Envision her smiling at you and your heart opening to her. Finally bow down to her, thanking her for accepting your offering. Sit still for some time, feeling the afterglow of her presence.

≈

The Lover and the Beloved

Love just happens. Nobody thinks about how to love, or when and where to love. Nobody is rational about love. Rational thought hinders love. Love is a sudden uprising in the heart. Love is an unavoidable, unobstructable longing for oneness. —Ammachi

One of the ways divine love is portrayed in Hindu scriptures is through the relationship between the gods and goddesses. In addition to the abundant literature on this subject, artists often depict deities in acts of courtship, sitting in a flowery meadow gazing into each other's eyes, or resting with arms entwined under a tree. Representations of deities in postures of affection and lovemaking are common. The reason for these scriptural and artistic illustrations is that most of us are familiar with the palpitations of the heart when in the presence of our loved one. The sensual descriptions remind us in small part of what we might expect from union with the divine, the marriage of Shiva and Shakti.

Partnership is a path to enlightenment. When Indian couples get married in the thousands-of-years-old Vedic wedding ceremony, the woman is accepting her husband as her guru and god, and the man is accepting his wife as creatrix and goddess. Jillellamudi Mother's approach to her own marriage demonstrated the ideals of married life. In this *Kali*

Yuga, the age of the decline of righteousness, the idealistic notions of husband as god and wife as goddess have waned but are not forgotten. Every Hindu Indian is surrounded by frequent festivals and temples on every corner as reminders of the ultimate purpose of the relationship between husband and wife. Almost all Hindu Indians have in their homes an altar to remind them of the divine focus that is the goal of their relationship and the foundation of family life.

The following is a story adapted from the *Shiva Purana* to illustrate one example of a marriage between god and goddess:[1]

Without the connubial union of Shiva and Shakti, creation could not continue for long. But Shiva, the destroyer, was temporarily separated from his wife, Parvati. He was pre-occupied chanting scriptures and meditating in his home in the Himalayan Mountains. He was not engaged in his usual and necessary worldly occupation. Brahma, the creator, and Vishnu, the preserver, the two other gods in the Hindu trinity, were distressed. Without Shiva's active participation they were unable to create or preserve. So Brahma rode his swan to the abode of Parvati, sang hymns of praise to her, and supplicated her to incarnate, go before Shiva, and se-duce him back into wedlock. Parvati agreed, but first she mentally communed with Shiva to receive his consent.

Parvati took a birth in a royal family and was named Sati. From the time she was an infant, all she could think about was Shiva. She longed more than anything in the world to be with him. She drew pictures of him, prayed to him, and sang to him. When she was old enough to marry, with the per-mission of her mother, she performed spiritual disciplines aimed at fulfilling her desire to attain Shiva. She contem-plated his image, offered him cooked rice and puddings, and often went without sleep. On full moon nights she prayed to Shiva while meditating on the banks of the river.

Brahma now went to persuade Shiva to marry Sati. Shiva said he did not need a wife, but that for the benefit of the world, he agreed to ask Sati's father for his daughter's hand in marriage. Shiva went to the king to make nuptial agreements, and he met the beautiful Sati. When Shiva returned home to his mountain retreat to wait for the appointed wedding day, he no longer was able to meditate, but could think only of his betrothed. In order to pacify his restless mind, he decided he must marry her immediately. He summoned Brahma, and asked him to go to Sati's father to make hurried preparations. With this done, Shiva mounted his bull and flew through the sky with great haste to his wedding. His matted hair was tied in a knot on top of his head and he wore a tiger skin around his waist. The great festivity was attended by family and friends as well as Shiva's entourage of ghouls and ghosts. Everyone cheered and sang as Shiva and Sati, now united in wedlock, went off to their home in the Himalayas.

At last the heavenly beings were in harmony and the earth once again was restored to peace. Shiva and Sati lived in a mountain valley with flowers and lakes, with crystalline clouds and grassy plains, and with birds fluttering and chirping. Celestial damsels and semi-divine beings danced among the lotuses and blue lilies that were in full bloom. Shiva and Sati sported in this land of enchantment for ten thousand years. Shiva no longer was interested in meditating or chanting scriptures, for he found pleasure only in Sati, could think of nothing but his beloved wife. They teased and played and laughed. In union she entered into him and drank his juice. Day and night Sati stared at her husband's face, and Shiva, the great lord of destruction, gazed upon the comely countenance of Sati. And so it was that the god and goddess nurtured the tree of love, sprinkled it with waters of emotion, and caused the whole universe to rejoice.

> *Only a person who is completely detached can love others without any expectations. Attachment is not an aspect of real love. In real love . . . there will always be the knowledge of the changing or perishable nature of the body and the eternal nature of the Self.*[2]
>
> —Ammachi

Any one of us who has loved can identify with Shiva and Sati's longing to be in each other's arms for all eternity. This ancient tale is a reminder of the timelessness that pervades every love story. Love is universal. We all yearn for that inimitable feeling of loving and being loved. We all long for union. While many of us have experienced moments of feeling completely joined with our loved one, in reality most of us experience our beloved as a separate human being whom we love deeply. Perhaps the notion of "falling in love" came about because when we are in the presence of the beloved, we plunge into that place inside ourselves through which the great river of love runs.

When we fall in love, we want to do special things for the beloved. We want to treat our loved one as a god or goddess. Like Sati, who made special puddings and cakes for Shiva, we give chocolates and presents and flowers to the one we love. We make offerings.

Before and after they were married, Mark Wingard of Santa Fe, New Mexico, said he used to leave little presents for his wife, Dawn, at her front door, or in her car, or under her pillow—gifts such as flowers, earrings, imported perfume bottles, books. One time he wrote "I love you, I love you" in tiny letters all over a card from front to back. He said it was like writing a mantra, a repetition of a sacred name.

Mark, an attractive, kind-looking man with brown hair and mustache, described the nature of their relationship: "Even after nineteen years of being together, fifteen married, I see Dawn come into the room and my heart just gushes open. It's amazing to me after all this time. In some ways it's much better now than it was in the beginning. The spark of romance and the thrill is even stronger now."

Mark, a computer network analyst, told about meeting Dawn at a Buddhist function in Santa Fe. The 16th Karmapa, a holy man from a special lineage of Tibetan lamas, was about to perform the black crown ceremony. Just before the program began, from the opposite side of the room Mark spotted Dawn playing with her young daughter, Amber, a child from a broken marriage. With a broad grin and eyes sparkling, Mark recalled the incident. "I was intrigued, more interested in watching Dawn than I was in paying attention to the holy man. Even though we didn't actually meet on that occasion, I felt like we did psychically. Seeing Dawn for the first time in the presence of the Karmapa was about as auspicious as you could get."

Dawn, a slender, blond woman, responded: "I could feel someone watching me. I got really uncomfortable and sat down. Mark didn't tell me he'd seen me there until about a year into our relationship."

As the course of fate would have it, Mark's roommate was going to massage school with Dawn. The housemate introduced them. Mark commented that when they did finally meet, the introduction was quite unremarkable. Later Mark arranged for Dawn to be invited to a party he was having to celebrate Candelmas, the return of the light in midwinter.

When Dawn showed up, Mark felt a rush of excitement, saying to himself, "Ooooo. There she is!"

Dawn, an occupational therapist and licensed acupuncturist, responded:

> For me, seeing Mark was like seeing a light. He had such a kind and clear presence. But getting together took a while because I wasn't ready for a relationship. I felt too wounded from various life experiences. After Mark's party, our first date was to go cross-country skiing and attend a Sufi whirling-dervish performance. At that point I still didn't have any defined feelings for him. But something happened while we were skiing. Mark was way ahead of me. I could feel his presence, and suddenly I became interested. All we did the next few times we saw each other was talk. Communication was on a very high level and deep. We talked about God and those kinds of things, a free-flowing appreciation. That was it. Without saying it, we knew we were in a relationship.
>
> Right away we established that we wanted a connection with God even though we didn't know exactly what that was. With my previous partners there wasn't an interest in spiritual matters, so Mark's concern in that area made a difference to me. Before we met Ammachi we used to visit the Christ in the Desert Benedictine Monastery near Abiquiu, New Mexico, and we'd spend a lot of time in nature. These were our main forms of spiritual expression.

Meanwhile, the beginning of Dawn and Mark's relationship was not always easy. Dawn explained:

> I had a lot of mistrust. I was burnt from a series of relationships, including my relationship to my father, who was alcoholic. So I would literally test Mark. For example, we'd get really close and then I'd disappear for a few weeks. Or

while we were together, I'd be very distant and unreachable, as if we'd never been close. If I'd have been him, I'd have just said, "Forget it." But Mark stuck it out.

Mark's expression while gazing at his wife revealed the intensity of his feelings—there was the sense that he was fully absorbed, that nothing could distract him from his love for her. "I just hung in there until the difficulty passed. I knew her moods weren't the reality of our connection. It was worth the wait."

Dawn smiled knowingly at Mark, then described some of the qualities that made their relationship meaningful:

> After my testing period was over, our connection became very strong. For example, we could be getting ready for a camping trip and for hours we wouldn't need to say anything. We'd always know what the other was feeling or thinking. The same happens while riding in the car. We can be with each other for hours without talking. It's pretty incredible. The silence is totally moving.

Mark added: "There's a sense of merging that is so extensive, but since we're not enlightened, we still perceive each other as individuals. Yet at the same time we see ourselves as a unit. It's hard to explain. And because our connection is so strong, it's extremely difficult to conceive of existing without Dawn."

Dawn expressed her appreciation for Mark's devotion to her:

> I've never had anyone in my life, or perhaps in lifetimes, who is so totally there for me on many different levels—emotionally, physically, mentally, and spiritually. Mark cooks

for me. He's always thinking of ways to take care of me even though I can take care of myself. Sometimes I feel a little selfish because I'll put all my efforts into work at the hospital and the clients in my treatment room here at home, to the detriment of my family. All the time he's serving me. He even gets up early in the morning to make tea for me every day. He does simple things, yet it feels really profound.

At this point Dawn looked at Mark and said, "Kind of like that Shiva and Parvati story, I feel like you do take care of me like you would take care of a guru, a spiritual master."
Mark rejoined:

We have a lot of the model of the guru-disciple relationship, yet we don't think of each other as each other's teacher. We've learned a lot about how to be in a relationship from our connection with Ammachi. Ammachi captured my heart with so much longing that I've wanted to be around her as much as possible. But after some time that's not practical. So what do I do when I have an experience of love like that for only a few days out of the year? The other three hundred sixty days I'd have to be miserable. So I bring that love into my home, to our daughters, Aurora and Amber, and to Dawn.

Our love is not a selfish love. It's a love that is fed, cultivated through service. We do things for each other that incrementally deepen our love for each other. What we do for each other is really an extension of our love. It's not with the idea of getting something from the other. I get more joy out of serving Dawn than in being served. Dawn's incredibly independent. She doesn't need me to do things for her, but I love to. I think about her often while I'm at work. I think about what I can do for her and what she will like. Being in each other's presence is so uplifting and renewing that when I'm away from Dawn, there's an angst, a longing to be together.

Dawn described how Mark's affection changed her:

In my practices I was always more comfortable with formless spirituality, and with the more austere paths such as Buddhism offers. I could easily live alone in a cave and be happy there. I'm already soft, but in this lifetime I need more softness and to be loved and treated with kindness. Mark's tenderness has opened me to love in a way that I don't have to do anything in return. Both my relationships with Mark and with Ammachi have expanded my ability to receive.

In the beginning, in the first years after we'd met Ammachi, I couldn't relate to all the longing most devotees had for Mother—their yearning for her presence, her smile, her laughter, her feet. All that physical stuff was not my style. Now I like being close to Ammachi's physical form. I've become more human about love. Now I understand the importance of being in a human body. It's a similar feeling that I have for Mark that I now feel for Mother.

Recently I was with Ammachi in Australia. I was doing a lot of *seva*, selfless service, and was exhausted. I fell asleep somewhere and when I woke up I realized I'd missed the whole night with Mother. I raced to the *darshan* line. There were only two or three people left in line. Usually with so few people remaining I wouldn't go up to her. But this time I went right up and fell into her lap. Inexplicably, I began to sob. For me that was a huge breakthrough. That incident broke me open more than any other experience I'd ever had with Mother. Now I can see some of the similarities in being in a relationship with Mark and being in a relationship with Amma. My heart is opening up.

After a long silence, Dawn looked at Mark and asked, "What did I do for you? You helped to soften me, to build trust in you and to appreciate your tenderness, but I don't get it. I don't know what I've done for you."

Without a moment's hesitation Mark answered:

> Your gift to me has been more on an energetic level. There's a perspective that you add to my life that wouldn't be there if I lived by myself. You bring beauty and grace into my life. Without you I would probably have a grungy house, ugly clothes, and my life would be much less interesting. You've added a lot of appreciation for things of beauty, including yourself. Also, you have an amazing intuition and understanding about people that I think has enhanced my own latent intuition and understanding of others. I'm enriched by you in that sense. The experience of serving you has given me patience and endurance. It's enhanced my ability to serve in the world. These may seem like odd gifts, but I consider them as gifts. . . .
>
> Dawn's career has been one of service: occupational therapy, acupuncture. The way she approaches people and what she does in the world is all service-oriented. Whereas my profession has been more mundane. I see my life as one of service, but not in an overt way. So there's been a lot of learning through observing Dawn and the way she lives and goes about what she does. So how do I serve when I'm sometimes afraid to talk to people or relate to people? I just watch Dawn and she teaches me how. It enriches my whole life.

Dawn had been listening intently: "Because we're so appreciative of our marriage, we came to the realization that relationship is our path. I used to compare myself to the renunciates in Mother's ashram in India. I kept traveling there alone, without Mark. He actually helped me go. While I was

there I'd think that lifestyle was the only way for me, that
there was nothing back home. Then I'd realize that wasn't
the case."

Mark clarified that Dawn's departures helped him learn
about surrender. "Every time she'd go off, I'd have to really
let go."

Dawn shed light on the difficulties her inclination toward
renunciation presented in the marriage:

Eventually my experiences with Mother, especially during
that trip to Australia, showed me how to get back into my
heart and out of my head. I was very drawn to Buddhism.
Somehow Mother helped me see that I already knew that
path really well and my desire for it was like an old habit.
When I came back after being at Bodhgaya, where the Buddha attained enlightenment, I started a very strict and serious
practice. Mark was a little scared.

Mark rested his chin in his palm and muttered: "It's true."
Dawn continued:

I didn't care. I'd go into our meditation room here at our
home in Santa Fe and wouldn't come out. Our daughter Aurora would knock on the door and I'd get really irritated. Or
Mark would want something and I'd get mad. The phone
would ring and I'd get furious. I'd have to go to work and I'd
feel resentful. One day I got the wake-up call that this was
making me an irritated person. I realized I couldn't lock myself up in the meditation room forever. My extreme approach
to my spiritual practices was making me too austere. The ascetic path wasn't helping me serve people. It wasn't teaching
me about being kind and living my path on a daily basis. I
realized I wasn't really living my life.

Mark's steadiness and always just being there were

important for me in these kinds of situations. Also, the way he walked his talk. Mark is extremely honest. He always tells the truth. Sometimes he'd have to think about something for a while, but when he did speak, what he said was truthful. He'd tell me about myself in ways that were caring and supportive and considerate. Because of the way he'd tell me, I wouldn't bolt and run away. His humor is helpful, too.

I always felt like I had so many flaws. Coming from an alcoholic and Catholic background, I didn't feel I was good enough. I was forever trying very hard and falling short. All the parts of me that I didn't want anyone to see, Mark saw. And I kept testing him: Okay. You want to see another one? And another one? He'd just be there. I couldn't believe it. I began to love myself more.

Mark was drawn into philosophical reflection:

Because I'm not self-realized, I'm identified with my body and who I think I am—how I look, what I'm known for, all wrapped up in a package. I used to think my personality had definition. When I met Mother, she began to break down my old perspectives. Through her I started to bleed out beyond my self-definition and into her. I think what Dawn and I have experienced is the same thing, but with each other.

The senses hold out the promise of fulfillment. Most of us are constantly striving for personal satisfaction through physical pleasure. Mother has used this example: You can have the most incredible gourmet dish in the world, but once you are full, eating more of it is sickening. In the same way, Dawn and I have found that sometimes expressing our love in a very physical and sexual way is too much overstimulation.

Dawn added: "In Buddhism they talk about not being too attracted or averted. I'm getting much more neutral with many things. Going out and buying things for the house, or plants—I'm watching myself more. I think, Well, maybe we don't need these flowers or that vase."

Mark presented a slightly different angle:

One of the illusions I've had about enlightenment or growing on the spiritual path is that my desires would just go away. Maybe that is the case ultimately. But I suspect that's not quite the way it is. I still feel incredible attraction and desire for Dawn, but I also know that trying to express that or trying to fulfill that through wanting to be close to her through sexuality isn't going to do it. For us, physical love has become kind of a hollow avenue of trying to come together. Even though we don't make love very often anymore, we don't feel deprived or that we're missing out on anything. When we do choose to share our love physically, it has become more conscious.

Dawn explained further:

Mother put it so well last year when she said, "Celibacy is more than refraining from lovemaking. It's refraining from hatred and jealousy as well." I feel that is true. Especially coming from a Catholic background, I don't want to make detachment from the senses happen because of all those "should dos." To say we shouldn't do this or that, or should not have sex is repressive. Then the shadow seems to emerge more fiercely.

Mark and I have had some funny things happen. One year when Mother was here, I woke up one morning and announced, "I think we should stop making love." Mark looked at me as if to say, "What?" We did pretty well with celibacy for about six months. But I began to wonder about my idea. I was so close to Mark, who'd been so warm and tender and exquisitely appreciative of me as a woman and as a person. I began to think, This is nuts. We shouldn't do this. We love each other. This is ridiculous. So we started making love again. It was fine and I didn't feel any weirdness about it or that we were bad, slimy people in the way Christianity implies.

Later we were considering the idea of celibacy again. We'd even written a letter to Mother in India requesting to take *bramacharya*, vows of celibacy. She never wrote us back. Next time Mother was in Santa Fe, we went up together as a couple to get *darshan*. She did something funny: she put her arms around us in a headlock, like a yoke, and rocked us back and forth, all the while she was laughing and laughing, like there was some big joke that only she understood.

Mark concurred:

Gradually the sexual aspect of our relationship began to seem irrelevant or extraneous. It wasn't necessary, yet it was wonderful at the same time. Eventually we found we even could make love with some detachment because sex wasn't essential to expressing or fulfilling our love for each other, nor was it critical that we remain celibate. There's a strange dichotomy in having a desire to merge on the physical level, yet knowing we can never really merge physically, at least not in the way that we can on the spiritual level.

Dawn said,

Yet Mark's physical presence is important to me. One of the hardest lessons for me is thinking about him leaving before me. I've thought about death and about God a lot since I was a child. Now, having created, with Mother's help, such a wonderful life, the test will be being able to detach during the

death process. I don't want my last thought to be Mark or my
kids. The test is to love and be loved so much that at the moment you are ready to make the transition and go to God, you
can let go.

Mark: "I fantasize that we'd merge and come back together in one body if we had to reincarnate."

Dawn: "Or that we'd come back and both be on a spiritual
path. I often wonder if Mother's swamis might have been
husband and wife in past lives. I want to come back and
serve. For me, being in a state of bliss is nice, I'm sure, but I'd
like to help out and be around a mahatma like Ammachi."

Mark:

Dawn has given me exposure to Buddhist teachings, and one
of the things I've taken as a personal meditation is the bodhisattva[3] prayer:

I seek the supreme enlightenment for the benefit of all
sentient beings. May all beings be free from suffering
and the cause of suffering. May all beings experience
happiness and the cause of happiness. May all beings
have peace of mind and equanimity, free from attachment and aversion.

I can't imagine simply going into bliss when I die and
leaving everyone else behind in suffering. It seems so selfish.
There's no question in my mind that I wouldn't feel comfortable if I were given the choice. I'd want to come back and
serve. And if I were going to do that, I'd have to be with
Dawn. I don't know if I can make such a negotiation with
Mother, but that's what I'd like.

Dawn: "It's very painful. I think about it a lot—how difficult it would be for me if Mark went first. Perhaps the
pain of separation from him will be the force that drives me

further inward and helps me focus even more strongly on Mother and the spiritual goal."

Dawn personifies many of the aspects of Shakti, the feminine energy—she is moodier than Mark, more volatile, more unpredictable, like Mother Nature. As a healer, she is also like the Mother, nurturing, forgiving, and patient. Through her austere Buddhist practices, she aspired to the calm and quiet of the masculine energy, which she ultimately learned through Mark. Mark is naturally more like Shiva: tranquil, solid, steady, imperturbable. Like Shiva, Mark is also passionate and gentle, showing the elements of Shakti energy in a man. Mark's and Dawn's individual expressions of life demonstrate the dance of Shakti and Shiva within both male and female dispositions.

While Mark and Dawn's relationship characterizes the second stage on the Path of the Mother, the other stages are also evident. For instance, Mark exercised the third stage of discipline in the well-considered and caring ways he spoke the truth to Dawn. He also had uncommon patience. Shadow elements entered in when Dawn would start feeling inadequate or encounter inexplicable urges inside herself to hide or run away. Some of her methods of avoiding her inner pain included locking herself in the meditation room, disappearing for weeks in the beginning of their courtship, or having the impulse to remain at the ashram in India. The element of surrender was evident when Mark gave in to Dawn's distancing impulses. Dawn's surrender to Mark, and to herself, happened as he remained constant, always serving her and allowing, even encouraging, her independence. Ammachi offered the inspiration and the example of how to pass through all the stages.

The way Ammachi hugged Dawn and Mark—linked one

head in each of her arms as if held in a yoke—is reminiscent of Anasuya Devi, the Jillellamudi Mother's interpretation of the symbol of the yoke in the Hindu marriage ceremony. To her it indicated the equality of the male and female within the marriage, a perfectly balanced relationship in which the two walk unerringly together. Mark and Dawn's marriage exemplifies Jillellamudi Mother's notion of marriage as a state in which each partner revered the other as god or goddess. Anasuya Devi saw the matrimonial union as representational of a means through which one could attain higher levels of consciousness.

Perhaps I can take the liberty of interpreting Ammachi's laughter when she embraced Mark and Dawn in the yoke of her arms. Her mirth could have been communicating that the course of Mark and Dawn's relationship—the selfless service toward each other and world, the growing subtlety in their physical link, the all-absorbing love in their silent times together, their desire to merge into each other—is archetypal of the couple's journey into the heavenly abode of Shiva and Shakti, into the flowery meadows of the Himalayan Mountains.

For a person who lives in the world (i.e., a householder), to be able to live a full, productive life, he or she must pass through the passage of marriage with as much love, intimacy, caring and commitment as possible. Married life, if it is lived with the proper love and understanding, will help awaken the feminine within a man, and the masculine within a woman. This balance can eventually help both of them reach the final goal of eternal freedom.

—Ammachi

Part III

The Mother's Discipline

This disciplining is meant to teach the disciple detachment, self-surrender and acceptance, not only to the external form of the Master, but toward all of creation.

—Ammachi

Penetrating Deep into the Mind

This training serves to lift the disciple from narrow-mindedness to a higher level, allowing him to experience everything in a broader way. —Ammachi

A number of years ago, Ammachi established a regular meditation schedule at the ashram. Before this our meditation times with her had been more random and unpredictable. Now residents were expected to meditate on their own for four hours daily, and then together on the roof with Ammachi for most of the day every Tuesday. Some three hundred of us residents and long-term guests would sit, starting at six o'clock, after morning chanting. Away from the activity seven stories below, the roof was the quietest place and the least likely to have disturbances from visitors. Except for essential ashram duties and a silent walk downstairs to circumambulate the temple three times at around eleven-thirty, before lunch, we were not to leave our places. Lunch was lugged up in huge pots and served to us by Ammachi herself.

At around nine o'clock in the morning, Ammachi would climb the spiral staircase and sit cross-legged on her large benchlike seat covered with a lion skin. On the corner of her small platform, one of her disciples would place a pile of stones. Just in case we did fall asleep, or were plagued with a wandering mind, Ammachi would toss a pebble to wake us up. Then she'd ask us to stand in place for some time.

I always sat in the back on a chair about thirty feet away from Ammachi. At the time I suffered from swollen legs and painful hip joints, which made it difficult for me to sit cross-legged on the floor. I was certain I was too far back for her to cast a stone at me, and never expected her to notice whether I was asleep or bothered by a meandering mind.

On my first morning of this meditation practice, I had difficulty concentrating. I would open my eyes every time a straggler walked by, which was fairly often. Now and then, out of the silence, I would hear the *ping* of a stone hitting one of the metal supports for the plastic ramada. I'd open my eyes to watch the meditator scramble to her feet while Mother bubbled with laughter, babbling in her native tongue. Even in the midst of these amusing dramas, Ammachi expected us at least to pretend we were meditating by keeping our eyes closed.

After having opened my eyes countless times to watch the scene, all at once, out of the corner of my eye, I chanced to see Ammachi thrusting an imaginary stone at me, hard, an overhand throw like a baseball pitcher. I snapped my eyelids closed, amazed she had so effectively caught me in the act of peeking.

The next week, I didn't dare open my eyes. But after about an hour I was drawn as if against my will to open them. With a broad smile on her face, Mother was gesturing for me to stand. Not absolutely certain she meant me, I put on my glasses. She continued making the motion to stand, sweeping her arm, with open palm, upward. Still not sure she wanted only me to stand, I looked around to see if anyone else followed her instruction. No one did, so I stood and she stopped gesturing. I had not been aware I had fallen asleep, had only a vague memory that I might have been dreaming. I concluded I must have been sleeping and that she had awakened me at the very second I had drifted off. My heart swelled with love that she had noticed.

By the following week, my meditations had become deeper, more peaceful, and my concentration was more focused. The vast territory of my inner world had expanded beyond measure. I was pleased and thought she would be, too. As the hour approached when she would join us on the roof, I developed an intense craving for her to touch me as she walked by. Her path to her *peetham*, the platform in the front, went right past me, her garments always nearly touching me. I imagined her hand on my head would help me soar into still higher states of consciousness. Because of my experience in the previous weeks, I was convinced she would know my desire.

By the sound of rustling, of devotees scrambling to their feet, I knew Ammachi had arrived. Remaining true to my plan, I remained seated with eyes closed, waiting for the strategic moment. All at once I felt her swish by. She didn't put her hand on my head. I was stung. I opened my eyes, stood along with the others, and watched Ammachi settle onto her platform. She often ignores, I reasoned. This is just another one of those times. Oh, well.

As we all sat back down, within seconds I was struck with anguish. How could she not have known my desire? With tears streaming down my face, obedient to the training of the last two weeks, I closed my eyes and turned my thoughts inward. If the Mother on the outside had not answered my prayer, then surely it must be possible to find her inside. She must be there, mustn't she?

What happened next is difficult to describe. All at once, I was plunged into a desperate search inside myself. With my eyes closed and Ammachi sitting not more than twenty feet in front of me, I became like a lover separated from the beloved, lost, wailing in the dark. My mind was a vast, dense forest in which I searched, tearing through brambles, scrambling up hills, dashing from tree to tree. Now and then, when someone actually would brush by, I would swoon in ecstasy, imagining it to be Ammachi's sari touching me. Even the slight breeze caused by a passerby felt like Mother's breath caressing me. For over an hour, tears of yearning poured from me, sometimes in audible sobs. Strangely, in the pain of yearning I felt bliss and peace, bringing waves of rapture that I couldn't begin to explain.

Now we come to stage three along the Path of the Mother: The Mother's discipline. In Hinduism, many forms of the Mother depict her as holding a goad in one of her four arms, and a noose in another. The goad is an instrument used to poke an elephant so it will keep moving. It is a symbol that Mother also keeps us moving. The noose is what she has around our necks to prevent us from wandering too far away—she holds the end of the rope. These are symbols of how Mother guides us on our spiritual path.

In stage three we become willing to receive her discipline and her scolding because we feel an intimacy with the Mother in a very childlike and fundamental way. In addition, because we love her so much, we actually enjoy that she holds the rope more tightly than she would in stage one or two. In this stage, with a love greater than we've ever known, she grinds us down, removes the dust and dirt, the pain and suffering, and leaves us shining with love, setting us free.

Only later, after reflecting on the above experience, did I realize what Ammachi had done, how she had led my mind. First she captured my heart by showing me for two weeks in a row that in the crowd of three hundred, she knew my thoughts better than I did. By the third week I was wide open to receive her grace in a completely different way than I ever could have imagined. She seized upon the moment of my yearning to ignore my physical craving for her tap on my head, thereby leading me on a search for the Mother within. The results gave me an experience of joy more palpable than the physical reality of Mother's touch. I had tasted the bliss of yearning I thought was reserved only for saints.

During my second visit with Ammachi in India, I can honestly say that while my love for her was growing deeper and deeper, I was unaware of the intensity of my own feelings. I had kept my distance from her, and only communicated with her about my lofty spiritual interests; I was not interested in being as close to her as a mother is to a child, or a guru to a disciple. I even avoided such a possibility. When I did communicate with her in highly personal ways, it was from afar, in my mind, where I was not obviously connected to her intimate and very personal presence—until one day in the *darshan* hut.

Darshan literally means vision of a deity, a holy person, or a holy place. At the ashram in India, Ammachi used to give *darshan* of herself in a hut that was thatched with coconut palms and with a ceiling layered with palm branches. Situated not more than five feet away from one of the backwater washes where the ashram sewage is dumped, the small building could accommodate about two hundred adult bodies squeezed in, each person shuffling forward inch by inch while seated on the cement floor in the *darshan* line. One

Indian devotee sang devotional hymns while playing a *harmonium*, a keyboard instrument, accompanied by another devotee on the *tabla*, a pair of different-sized hand drums. Except for the quiet beating of the overhead fans, the soft music, and the sounds of Ammachi laughing and talking to Indian devotees, the room was quiet.

When invited to do so by Ammachi, or when a devotee by some chance of fate was lucky enough to find a spot, one could fit in among the eight people squashed behind the small platform where she sat to meet, one by one, with Indian and foreign visitors. There wasn't room to stay in the hut after receiving *darshan*, except in the back, or outside by a tiny window where it was possible to sit in the sand under a banana tree and catch glimpses of her in the dimly lit room—another form of *darshan*.

One day I had a feeling I might find a spot behind the platform. I went into the hut and saw a perfect place, not behind her but right next to her. I sank into a sense of deep contentment, realizing that on that particular day my emotional need to be near Mother knew no bounds. Suddenly a young American woman who often caused trouble around Ammachi pushed through to sit down next to me even though there wasn't room. Mother's attendant told her not to, but the devotee argued and would not leave. As a consequence, the frustrated helper asked me to leave instead, telling me to sit in front of her as she translated and kept the line orderly. To my utter dismay, the attendant blocked my view of Amma. Like a child who had lost its mother in a department store, I became almost hysterical that I could not see her. Burning with anger, tears welling, I tapped the Indian assistant on the shoulder and snapped, "Why did you make me move? I can't see Mother from here."

At that point Ammachi glared at the American woman, gestured for her to leave, and motioned for me to retrieve my place, which I quickly did, only this time I sat in the corner slightly behind Mother, not right next to her. My association with Ammachi was still somewhat new to me, and I wanted nothing to do with the painful consequence of loving too much. Since I had suffered instances of abusive love from my father, mother, first guru, and a couple of boyfriends, I did not want to subject myself to excessive feelings of love for Amma before I knew it was safe to do so. Maybe even never.

Once settled into my place, the boldness with which I had expressed ire at my seating displacement disturbed my sense of well-being. I said to myself, "It's not okay to love Amma so much that you make a fool of yourself right in front of her—just because you can't see her!" Yet try as I would to stop my surging emotions, gut-wrenching sobs welled up from inside of me. The more I told myself over and over and over again, "It is not okay to love someone this much," the more volcanic in nature my despair became. For some time my mind, my body, and my emotions were engaged in an inner battle, a war in which my very life felt threatened.

After perhaps half an hour, in the exact moment in which I was regaining a sense of calm, Ammachi turned around, flashed her eyes and scolded me in her Malayalam tongue, pointing and gesturing dramatically with her left hand. Although I was a bit surprised she chose this moment to reprimand me, something about it felt natural, a strange sort of healing balm. The only word I understood was *darshanam*, which, when mixed with the jumble of other words, seemed to have something to do with the actual act of visioning—a

verb, not a noun. I moved over a few inches as she had motioned me to do. Then, curious about the object of her concern, I looked behind where I had been sitting, in the
direction to which she had pointed. Sitting on a small ledge
were two small statues. Even though in the months that I
had been coming into the *darshan* hut I had never seen anyone made to move from in front of these figurines, I now
concluded that I was not to block their vision.

I contemplated the statues, easily identifying one as
Krishna, the dark, beloved, playful god who had been so important to Ammachi in her childhood that she had become
Krishna herself. Strangely, I became absorbed in feelings of
serenity, then felt drawn to pick the figurine up and dust him
off with my shawl. I felt an unusual sort of affection, like a
mother to a child.

When I lifted the second statuette off the ledge, I didn't
recognize her at first. I contemplated the stringed instrument
she held, turned the figurine round and round, wondering if
it was Goddess Saraswati. But all the symbols she usually
holds are not present, I mused. All at once I knew who she
was—Mirabai, the great woman saint of sixteenth-century
India, a wealthy princess who, for the love of Krishna, left
her palace and husband-king to wander the streets of Brindavan, to dance, sing, and sometimes suffer for her beloved
flute player. The minute I realized who she was, waves of relief poured over me. Amma's poignant and most subtle of
communications had become clear to me. Through my *darshan* with these two statues, Ammachi had answered my
question and calmed my original despair. It was as if she
was saying, "Just as Mirabai loved Krishna, so it is okay for
you to love me this much."

*   *

Loving someone "this much" is not all easy sweetness and rapture. Ammachi acknowledges that "when you are in the presence of a Great Master [Mother] . . . you are made to look at all your pain. . . . When the sun of the Master [Mother] shines, it penetrates deep into our mind, and in its light you see . . . the hidden hell that lies within you. . . . The Master's [Mother's] overflowing love and compassion will greatly lessen the pain. . . . His [her] intention is not to give you temporary relief, but permanent relief—forever."[1]

Who Is the Guru?

The guru is like the sun. He just shines. He
cannot be otherwise. He just shines and
whoever keeps the doors of his heart open
receives the light.   —Ammachi

In India it is taken for granted that if someone wishes to advance on the spiritual path, a preceptor is necessary. A guru helps guide us out of darkness into light. In the Western world we do not have the tradition of the guru-disciple relationship. When Swamiji Amritatmananda was wandering in the Himalayas and met a fellow spiritual aspirant, he was surprised that his new friend did not know who his guru was. Swamiji assumed that because his friend's spiritual practices were strong, surely he must have a guru.

In ancient India, the father and mother were a child's first gurus. From the parents, the son or daughter learned about spiritual life as well as practical, worldly affairs such as caring for the body, cleaning house, cooking, building, counting money, and getting along with others. Later it was expected that the children would go to a guru chosen by the family for further spiritual education, such as the study of scriptures, learning of rituals, and sitting in meditation. Once a young person was well grounded in religious practices, then he or she would learn a profession. The notion was that even professional life was to be governed by spiritual principles. Everyone was expected to hold God-realization as the ultimate goal in life. The profession, including motherhood, was the means through which one would ultimately be united with the absolute. All the diverse ways were considered to be of equal value and worth. While raising a family and earning a living, the parents had a family guru, a sage who offered worldly advice and spiritual guidance. Even in present-day India, in many households the custom of seeking the advice of a guru exists.

Relative to the stages on the Path of the Mother, the guru is essential every step of the way. For instance, in the discipline stage most of us don't have enough willpower or inner vision to follow through with the practices necessary to advance on the path. The guru gives us the encouragement and faith to continue when we get discouraged. Only the guru can see our true nature and thereby guide us according to our particular needs, as demonstrated in my story about meditation practice with Ammachi in India.

What is a guru? Since most of us have not been brought up with a guru tradition, we don't know exactly what the qualities of a real spiritual preceptor are. Ammachi describes a perfect guru as someone who nurtures and opens our hearts to innocent, divine love. She says that the circumstances created by the guru are so powerful, so precious and alluring, "that we will cherish and memorize every moment we spend with him." Even if we only have one meeting with a divine soul, we can gain the inspiration to continue on the path. If we stay in the presence of the guru or hold the memory of her image during our practices, we will start loving the guru with our bodies, emotions, and intellects. Our "love will flow both to the physical and the spiritual forms of the guru." When we come to know that our guru is the "very consciousness that shines within and through all objects," we will love everything.[1]

Ammachi explains that through the guru's words and deeds, he or she creates unforgettable moments and events in our lives. We literally become like small children when we are with the guru. The guru's love intoxicates us. Our "desire to love and to be loved by the Guru becomes like a blazing flame." Slowly, our love becomes so intense that our craving to be loved *by* her is replaced by a "craving to be in loving service" *to* her. To help us understand that "the Guru is not the body but the all-pervading Self," she creates circumstances for us to see her in everything and to serve her through every action. For this love to take place we "must empty the mind of all its desires. That is why Perfect Masters always insist on the importance of *sadhana* [spiritual practices]."[2]

Over the ages there have been many stories of both men and women who fill Ammachi's descriptions of the perfect guru. And there are many who remain anonymous. The characteristics of the Great Mother can manifest in male bodies or in female ones—Buddha, Krishna, Mohammed, Mary, Jillellamudi Mother, to name a few. According to Ammachi, "Although Jesus Christ was externally a man, internally He was a mother. Although love is abstract and formless, it took a concrete form in Him. He gave His life to love; He taught us how to love."[3]

What are some of the qualities of these great souls? Why do they come into human bodies? To help make clear the motivations of these beloved beings, Ammachi tells a story about Buddha:

Through years of *tapas* [literally "heat" and the practice of spiritual austerities], Buddha became enlightened. When he attained enlightenment, Buddha remained silent for many days. He did not want to speak. He just wanted to lose himself in oneness with consciousness. Therefore, he kept silence. Now, the celestial beings became very distressed. They grew anxious, wondering whether Buddha would speak at all. They knew that his enlightenment was a very, very rare gift. Thus they wanted him to speak so that the entire world and all its creatures would be benefited from what he had gained. If he did not speak, it would be a tremendous loss for the world.

So the gods came down from heaven and appeared before Buddha. Bowing down to the great soul, they repeatedly prayed to him to speak. They said, "O Holy One, please speak. Your experience is a rare incomparable one; therefore, be compassionate. There are many people who are suffering in pain and sorrow. One single word from you will give them hope. Your mere presence will give them peace and tranquillity. There are also seekers of Truth who need your help. Guide them to this state of Self-Realization. A word, a glance, a touch from you will be a showering of ambrosia upon them. Please speak, O Great One."

At first, Buddha, the Enlightened One, paid no heed to their prayers. Then after their continued insistence, he tried to explain to them that nothing he could say would fully express his experience of Truth. The gods continued to plead with him, "Think of ailing humanity. Have compassion for those who are in sorrow and despair, longing for someone to give them solace and peace of mind. Think of those seekers of Truth who are badly in need of someone to guide them to the goal. They need guidance. If nobody helps them, they may look back and think, 'I have been waiting so long to reach the state of Perfection. What if it does not exist? Maybe there is no such thing as Self-Realization, so why should I waste my time any longer?' And in that state of frustration and disappointment, they might even fall back into the world of plurality. Think, Holy One, think. Think of such people. Take pity on them. Feel compassion for them and speak. One look, one word or one touch from a holy person like you is sufficient for them to attain the goal. That attainment of a single soul is enough for the rest of the world to be benefited."

Gradually Buddha's heart filled with compassion. And so, after having experienced the highest Truth, after having been filled inside and outside, and having attained Oneness with the Supreme Being, he came down.[4]

You might be wondering, as I did for many years, how we could ever hope to have a Buddha or a Jesus as our guru. Many of us in the West have had difficult or negative experiences with gurus. It is certainly true that we must learn discrimination in choosing the master who will lead us to the goal. Since the guru tradition is not part of our culture, we are not familiar with how to choose. Because our minds are not clear, it is easy to become dazzled by someone with psychic or charismatic powers.

More than one saint from India, including Mother Teresa of Calcutta, has observed that Westerners are suffering from broken hearts. Many false gurus have taken advantage of our longing to love and be loved unconditionally. I have experienced one guru who was not self-realized and later one who is—Ammachi. One of the main differences between these two was that the first guru wanted something from me and Ammachi wants nothing. She only gives unconditional love.

Ammachi explains that when you are in the presence of a true guru, there is nothing to fear:

Seeing only his body, people judge the Guru externally. They project their own ignorance onto him. This is what makes them afraid to surrender. They think that the Guru will control them or snatch everything from them. They are afraid that he will take away their individuality and make them suffer. Because they see only the human form of the Guru, they fear that they will be tricked by him. The Guru is beyond the body; he is beyond being human. He is the embodiment of pure consciousness. In reality, he is formless and nameless. There is no person there. Only nothingness. How can the formless, nameless Guru snatch anything from you? How can he control you? He simply is, and you benefit from his presence. If you really want to use the Guru, then surrender to your own Self. Your Self is the same as the Guru's Self. Therefore, there is nobody who will claim, demand, argue or snatch. Surrendering to your own Self is for your own spiritual upliftment. It is not for the Guru, not for the Guru at all.[5]

How do we find such a guru? Some say we don't have to search; the guru will come. Yet, there is a paradox; we also must yearn for the guidance of a sage, as Rebecca in the earlier story began to yearn for a teacher and eventually found Ammachi. Our longing will bring a teacher to us. As illustrated in the story of Buddha, our desire for spiritual guidance causes holy beings to manifest on Earth, where we are drawn like magnets into their presence. Until our time comes to find a teacher, what can we do? We can focus on the images we've chosen for our altar. We can continue our spiritual practices and we can use our imagination; we can pretend we have the Mother in our presence.

≈

Adopting a Childlike Outlook

Have you watched children play? They can imagine that a small sand heap is a big castle. At one moment white sand is sugar for them, and the next moment it is salt. A rope with its ends tied together becomes a car or a bus. For them a rock can be a throne, and a leaf becomes a big fan. . . . This openness, the power to accept, is receptivity.[6]   —Ammachi

While spiritual practices should be approached with intense commitment and resolve, they should not be a cause for too much severity. When we adopt the attitude of a child, we become more open to the guru's love and his or her teachings, more open to receive a physical guru if we don't yet have one. I've heard that all true masters are bubbling with joy, always ready to laugh; this is certainly true of my guru, Ammachi. While I might be afraid of her discipline, I know Mother is always dancing with love.

Perhaps it would be good to start the childlike outlook practice with feelings of lightheartedness in mind. As Swamiji Amritaswarupananda said, underneath the serious face, underneath the disciplinary act, is always the smile, the smile that dances in eternity.

If you want to be closer to God, try to be like a child. A child's world is full of wonder and imagination and play. . . . There is a child within everyone.

Perhaps the following visualization will help stimulate your yearning for your guru or help you feel more lighthearted with your guru. The guided meditation sets a tone of levity and can be repeated any time you've found yourself getting too wooden in your approach. The child within you is an important link to the Divine Mother.

> Children, the wonder and the love that you felt as a child will never return unless you can again play like a child. Innocence is within you, hidden deep inside. You have to rediscover it.[7]

To begin, sit or lie down in front of your altar. Have some bubbly, meditative music playing in the background, such as Handel's *Water Music*, Carlos Nakai's *Cycles: Music for Native American Flute*, J. S. Bach's "Suites 1–4," "Sounds of Nature" by Sound of Nature Series, and "O'Cean: Flute and Sounds of the . . . [whales]" by Larkin.

Imagine yourself walking down a deserted beach along the Caribbean, Hawaiian, or Polynesian sea shore. Sitting on a rock, take off your shoes. Leave your shoes there and continue walking, feeling the sand between your toes. While you stroll, your feet get wet as waves wash gently onto the shore. You look out at the gentle rising and falling of the ocean swells and see dolphins playing and leaping in the waves. As they swim down the shoreline, you skip to keep up with them.

Then, in the distance, you see the Divine Mother walking toward you, wearing a white cloth. Her feet splash through the water. She walks out knee-deep into the waves, stretching her arms toward the dolphins, calling them to her. The Mother turns and motions for you to come near. There is a twinkle in her eyes. She splashes you playfully and chuckles. Then she takes you by the hand and pulls you deeper into the ocean, into the waves where the dolphins swim.

(Now let yourself be guided by your own imagination for

ten or fifteen minutes while you and Mother play in the water with the dolphins.)

When your swim finishes, wade out of the water onto dry land. Watch as the Divine Mother disappears down the beach and the dolphins become small specks swimming out to sea. Once again you are alone on the sandy shore, and you turn to head slowly back. At the rock where you left your shoes, sit down to put them on, and then continue walking homeward. As the image of yourself ambling down the beach dwindles, you become aware of your surroundings in your own home. Wiggle your toes, stretch your arms and legs, open your eyes, and look around the room. Take your time before getting up.

≈

Writing Letters to the Divine Mother

When you are a mother, you cannot help but love. You can only be compassionate; you can only forgive and forget. That is why whatever is loving and patient is known as "mother."

—Ammachi

Continuing with the childlike feelings that may have been aroused in the above visualization, you can begin pouring your heart out to Mother in the form of letters to her. If you have doubts and wonder how the Mother of the Universe could possibly be concerned with you and your letters to her, that is normal, especially in the beginning. Even after many experiences of Mother's omnipresence, I still find it difficult to grasp the concept.

Where is that place where Mother is not?[8]

In letter-writing practice, choose one of the pictures of the Mother on your altar to focus on. Allow yourself to communicate in every way, even ways that seem nonsensical, with Mother Mary, Lakshmi, Kuan Yin, Durga, Anandamayi Ma, Ammachi, Magdalena. If at any point you need to know that a living Divine Mother has received one of your letters, you may write to Ammachi in India (the address appears in Appendix II). She may not respond to you in written form, but the simple knowledge that she has received your letter can be very satisfying. She has said she receives our letters as we write them.

> Amma [Mother] remembers everyone! . . . How can Amma forget anyone, when the whole universe is within her? You are all parts of Amma. How can the whole forget the part? The part exists in the whole . . . when you remember that she is always with you, that she sees all your actions and is your sole protector and guide, you are remembering the whole—you are recalling your real nature and true abode.[9]

One time I needed to write Ammachi a long letter. I knew it wasn't allowed to take lengthy ones up the *darshan* line, so I asked Swamini Amma, her attendant, to read it to Ammachi in the privacy of her room. I felt vulnerable because it described all the ways I tended to be overly sensitive and, then, angry in response. After about three weeks, I became anxious for a reply. So, I went up the *darshan* line and asked the translator to find out if Ammachi had heard my letter. "Yes," she replied, but said nothing more. Still curious about it, a few days later I asked Swamini Amma if she had translated my letter to Ammachi. She said no. I told her Ammachi had said yes. Swamini Amma laughed. "She must have read it in her own way." While I had already had the sense that Ammachi knows and listens the moment we write our letters to her, this experience assured me that was so.

Ultimately, the Mother wants us to find her within ourselves, to know that in reality, she is us. Writing letters to her helps facilitate the unfolding of this truth.

> *Spiritual practice reminds you, "I am not just a part, but the part of the Whole—indeed, I am one with the whole."*[10]   —Ammachi

There are four parts to the practice of writing letters to Mother:

(1) introducing your early years to her, telling her what you were like as a small child;
(2) describing yourself as a teenager;
(3) going through the different decades of your life; and
(4) giving her information about who you are now.

In the first two sessions you will tell her how you would have liked her to have been there for you, especially in ways in which your own mother was not. The third session will include how you think she could have been present for you through all the decades of your life. In the fourth, you write and tell her what your relationship with her is like now, and how you would like her to be there for you.

Usually anything we start feels clumsy in the beginning. Let the letters express emotions, feelings, anticipation, anxieties, insights, and desires. Let them bring you into a very intimate and personal relationship with her. Tell her everything—events, feelings, desires, images, dreams, memories, difficulties, triumphs, sorrows, pains, emotional weaknesses—everything.

All your thoughts and actions pass through Amma [Mother].[11]

—Ammachi

Session #1. Allow forty-five minutes, with no interruptions or phone calls. Begin with repetition of the name for about five or ten minutes. Afterward, keep your eyes closed and let images or feelings from your childhood come to mind. If nothing comes right away, just remain open to yourself as a child.

When you feel ready, open your journal and write, "Dear Divine Mother, when I was little ..." Describe what you looked like, things you did by yourself and with your mother and father, brothers and sisters, pets, things you liked, things you didn't like. While you write, tell Mother how you might have liked her to have helped you in certain difficult situations. Tell her any emotions you feel as you write. Don't be surprised if tears come, both from sadness and love. Let the tears wet the pages of your journal. Ammachi herself used to cry and wet pages with her tears.

When you feel finished, end the session by closing your eyes and saying Mother's name a few times. Thank her for being with you.

If you want to write more about your childhood in other sittings before going on to the next session, continue to do so. Otherwise go on to the next and maybe come back to this one at a later date.

You merely forgot your innocence for some time. It is as if you suddenly remember something after having forgotten about it for a very long time. That childlike innocence deep within you is God [Mother].[12]

—Ammachi

Session #2: Once again, allow about forty-five minutes. Following the same format as in Session #1, sit and meditate for about five or ten minutes while you do the repetition of names. With closed eyes, recall when you were eleven, twelve, thirteen, or fourteen years old. Let a few memories or feelings of those (or these, if you are a teenager) adolescent or prepubescent times enter into your mind. Now, recollect specific significant events. It is important not to censor sexual images. Sexual thoughts and activities are part and parcel of these young years.

Begin by writing, "Dear Divine Mother, when I was a teenager . . ." Or, if you are a teenager, "Dear Divine Mother, I am now . . ." Tell her how old you are and what you look like. Who are your friends? What is your relationship with your parents and siblings? Take notice of any feelings of shame as you write. Let her know what you feel. Don't forget, she is the author of all, and there is nothing she does not know, nor is there anything she judges. You can tell her anything and everything.

If you need to close your eyes from time to time and become quiet again before going on, feel free to do so. Don't forget to let her know how you think she might have helped you in the past, or might help you in difficult situations with friends, parents, and siblings. When you feel you are finished, close your eyes and say Mother's name three times.

A child is born with pure consciousness, but society teaches him [her] to be unconscious. . . . He [She] becomes completely clouded and is made to forget his [her] real nature. He [She] is taught everything except how to simply abide in his [her] real nature.[13]

—Ammachi

Session #3: This session is divided into the decades of your life—twenties, thirties, forties, fifties, sixties, and so on. Decades often mark important times in our lives, whether it be a reevaluation of our lives at age thirty, a maturing of our values at age forty, or a confrontation with impending old age at fifty. It is recommended that you write about each decade in separate sessions.

Contemplate which topics were important for you during each ten-year period, including college, travel, relationships, marriage, child-rearing, profession, divorce, deaths in the family, personal crises, life-altering experiences, changes in lifestyle, moves to different geographical locations. Try to remember significant experiences that influenced the course of your life—the choices you made at critical crossroads. For example, how did a decision to marry rather than continue with college affect your life? What did having children teach you? What events seemed to happen by chance, not by your design or in your control?

Allow forty-five minutes, and, as usual, begin with a five- or ten-minute Mother meditation. Let yourself recall the particular decade for a few minutes before starting to write. Then write, "Dear Divine Mother, when I was twenty . . ." Or, if you are in your twenties, "Dear Divine Mother, I am now . . ." Tell Mother details of important events. Describe scenes in detail. How would you have liked her to help you? Don't forget to tell feelings, aspirations, and desires.

When you can dive deep into your own consciousness, you will
realize this innocence one day. At that moment you will discover
the child within you. You will experience the innocence, the joy
and the wonder that were hidden inside of you, and you will realize
they were always there.[14]   —Ammachi

Session #4: Allow forty-five uninterrupted minutes. Begin with the repetition of names. Then, keep your eyes closed. Become very aware of who you are now, today, how you feel, and what you look like. Try to remain present without going into the past or future. Just be with yourself as you are right now.

Write, "Dear Divine Mother, today I am . . ." Include your sense of how you would like her to be with you in difficult situations, relationships, job situations, or in attaining your life goals. If there seems to be an overwhelming number of situations that need attention, choose one for today and another for your next sitting. When you feel ready, close the session with Mother's name.

> *If you feel that Mother expects something, it is to take you beyond*
> *all expectations.*[15]   —Ammachi

Get into the habit of writing daily. Find a quiet time in the day, when you wake up or just before sleep, or after meditation. Make this practice an integral part of your day.

> *We delight in searching for the child within. When we were*
> *children, we had no worries or problems; recalling these days with*
> *love, we want to return to them. This desire is felt by all living*
> *beings.*[16]   —Ammachi

≈

Receiving Answers from the Mother

Listening is possible only when you are empty within.

—Ammachi

There may be times when you sit in front of your altar and you just can't feel a thing, or you are confused about some details in life. Worst of all, you can't find answers to problems, questions, or doubts that bother you. Even writing letters to the Divine Mother doesn't give the desired results. In this case, there are several ways to communicate with Mother. One of Mother's creative games is hide-and-seek. She sometimes uses this enchanting, often painful play to arouse our longing, to inspire us to search for her.

> *As far as Mother is concerned, everyone is her child. . . . Children,*
> *did not Mother come when you called? Thus did she not obey you?*
> —Ammachi

There have been countless times when I have been totally dried up, unable to connect with the Mother. I try everything and nothing seems to work. My experience tells me to keep at it. Don't stop meditating, don't stop writing letters to her, don't stop any spiritual practices, because one day, completely by surprise, there she'll be, even more powerfully than before. The Mother of the Universe comes when we ask, but sometimes, for reasons unknown, we must wait.

Many times we need answers to specific questions, or we long for spiritual guidance in worldly matters. The more you get to know Mother, the more she herself will show you how to talk to her. Many divining methods can be useful, including the *I Ching*, rune stones, Tarot cards, astrology, scriptures, and inspirational books. Again, it is helpful to approach these activities with the openness of a child.

> *In every person there is childlike innocence. Therefore we must*
> *again become like children, and only this will open the door to*
> *heaven within us.* —Ammachi

Using any scripture or inspirational book, simply open the book at random and read the paragraph in front of you. I've used *Awaken, Children! Dialogues with Ammachi*, by Swami Amritaswarupananda; the Bible; *Poems* by Rumi; *The Story of a Soul* by St. Therese, and many others.

I use one Tarot deck and guidebook on a regular basis when I feel stuck and can't hear the inner voice. I shuffle the cards while asking Mother's advice for a very specific question. Then I fan them out on the floor in front of my altar and pull one card. I've found that if I pull more than one, I get confused. If there are multiple choices, I make stacks for each choice (never more than three), and pull a card from each stack.

However, Tarot decks, astrology, and *I Ching* require interpretations and don't necessarily give us an answer that we can understand for certain. In this case, drawing straws for multiple choices can be useful. It is very precise because it is yes or no.

Still another method, developed by one of Ammachi's swamis, is to take three pieces of paper, all the same size and color, with no identifying marks. Write down three possible solutions to the question, one on each piece of paper. Roll the papers tightly into cylinders, mix the cylinders around while your eyes are closed so you no longer know which is which. Now pick one of the three papers for your answer. It is usually quite accurate. However, Ammachi says that if you don't like the answer, to ask again.

I have tried this method several times with good results. The first time was while I was in India. I had left Ammachi's ashram in Kerala to take a little rest by the sea in Mahabalipuram, a couple of weeks before returning to America. To my dismay I found myself in despair because of being separated from her. Since I was too far away to return to Kerala, or so I thought, I went to her small ashram in Madras to wait the seven days until my departure flight to the United

States. During that time, I became ill with high fevers and bronchitis, the beginning of the illness that was to return on my next visit to India.

The four days before going home seemed like an eternity. I couldn't bear it. I remembered that Ammachi was presenting a program at her small ashram in Trivandrum, a city three hours from her main ashram in Kerala. I had only about one hundred dollars and was hoping a roundtrip ticket to Trivandrum would cost only that. But, confused as I was, I also thought I could try to change my flight and go home early. So I prepared three pieces of paper. One said, "Go to Trivandrum and be with Ammachi." The other said, "Fly home early." And the last one said, "Stick it out and stay at the ashram in Madras." There were many enormous mosquitoes at the Madras ashram, and I was miserably unhappy, so I hoped that would not be my fate. I rolled up the papers, closed my eyes, shuffled them around in my hands, and threw them on the floor. My heart pounding, I picked up one of the cone-shaped papers. Slowly unrolling it, my heart leapt with joy when I saw: "Go to Trivandrum and be with Ammachi." I spent all my money and off I flew. All the coughing and perspiring from fevers did not suppress my delight for the entire three days.

The innocence and playfulness of a child exists in all human beings. . . . As we get older, we lose all enthusiasm and joy. We become dry and unhappy. Why? Because we lose our faith and innocence.[17]
—Ammachi

≈

Tapas

In the heat produced by tapas, the mind,
along with all its judgments and
preoccupations, will melt away, and you will
begin to function from your heart. For this to
happen the disciple must have a tremendous
amount of patience. —Ammachi

Even after doing the above practices of writing to the Divine Mother or receiving answers to questions, we may find it difficult to access our innocence, our childlike nature. Perhaps you've wondered, as I have, why the paradox? Why can't we just be innocent without effort? Why the need for commitment to our spiritual practices? Why can't we just be *in* love? The answer lies in our need to burn away the crustiness that keeps us from our divine selves. *Tapas*, meaning to burn through austerities, is one of the well-known ways to access our divine nature. Ammachi tells the following story, which illustrates the meaning of *tapas*.[1]

There was once an ignorant forest dweller who had never had contact with people who lived in towns and villages. One day, as he wandered deeper into the woods to cut down some firewood, he came upon a man meditating. The forest dweller had never seen an apparition such as this. He wondered why this man sat still with his eyes closed. The forest dweller walked round and round the man, wondering what in the world this man was doing. The forest dweller finally sat down and waited, hoping the man would open his eyes. After a long time, when the man looked up from his meditation, the forest dweller asked, "What are you doing? Why are you sleeping while sitting up?"

The man laughed at the forest dweller's lack of knowledge and said, "I'm a disciple of the great saint Shankara. I'm not sleeping. I'm meditating on my favorite form of God. Something you wouldn't be able to understand."

Innocently, the forest dweller replied, "Meditating? Your favorite God? What does that mean?"

"I told you, it's not possible for you to understand." With this, the man closed his eyes once again.

Every day the forest dweller passed by the meditator and eagerly waited to talk to him. After many meetings, the forest dweller asked, "Who is this God you are looking for?"

"I am contemplating my Lord Narasimha, the lion-man, an incarnation of the great Vishnu," he said.

The forest dweller became even more puzzled, wondered why the man whom he now referred to as "master" looked for a lion while sitting with his eyes closed. Above all, he couldn't understand how a half-man half-lion could be God.

As the months passed by, these two became good friends. The forest dweller noticed that his master was getting thin from not eating, and weary from not lying down to sleep. He was worried and became angry with his master's lion for staying away for so long. All the forest dweller could think about was that the lion's refusal to come caused his master too much suffering. One day the forest dweller decided he would look for the lion and bring it to his master. But first he would ask permission. The disciple of the great saint once again laughed at his forest-dweller friend's ignorance. To pacify him, he gave consent for the search.

The forest dweller set out on his journey, looking for the man-lion everywhere—under every bush, in every cave, on every mountaintop, and in every valley. On and on he pursued his quest for his master's lion. When he had hunted every corner, every inch of the forest without success, he began to call out, "My master's lion, come here, come here!" He became so focused on his search for the lion that he felt no hunger or thirst, stopped eating and sleeping, incessantly crying out, "My master's lion, come here, come here!"

Eventually the forest dweller's mind became silent, all thoughts disappeared, even the verbal calls stopped. His search had transformed itself into an intense inquiry that had purified his body and mind. All that was left within him was the burning fire of love that soared up into the heavens to the abode of Lord Vishnu. The forest dweller's meditations had become so powerful that the great Vishnu was compelled to respond. And so it was that the god of preservation took the form of Narasimha, the man-lion, and appeared before the simple forest dweller.

Delighted that he had found what his master was looking for, the forest dweller picked a length of vine off a tree, tied it around Narasimha's neck, and led the man-lion back to where his master meditated. This time, the forest dweller did not wait for his master to open his eyes. He called out, "Master, look, I have found your lion! Open your eyes!"

When Shankara's disciple came out of his meditation, he could not believe what he saw. He rubbed his eyes and opened them again.

As he fed the man-lion a handful of green grass, the forest dweller said to his master, "Come down from your rock. I have your lion. He's not dangerous!"

The man scrambled down from his meditation seat, prostrated in front of Narasimha, sobbed and cried out for forgiveness for his vanity and ignorance. The forest dweller was puzzled by his master's behavior until he heard Narasimha speak: "Stand up, my dear one," he said to the forest dweller's master. "Do not feel disappointed. I dwell both within and without. The prideful ego cannot exist where there is real love. And where there is real love, there I can easily enter and dwell."

Narasimha called the forest dweller to him, placed his hand on his head, and granted him final liberation. The Lord then consoled the devotee of the saint Shankara, told the now genuinely humbled meditator that he, too, would reach that ultimate state during his lifetime.

Both the forest dweller and the meditator were performing *tapas*. Both were destined to reach the goal of union with the divine beloved. The difference between them was that the forest dweller had an innate innocence that put him in a position of being fully openhearted. The meditator was egotistical, filled with self-importance about his spiritual practices; his heart was closed. He lacked a childlike attitude. While performing *tapas*, the meditator was filled with preconceived notions about it; his rigidity kept him from being receptive to his divine nature, and to the very form of God he sought: Narasimha.

However, the meditator's prayers were answered in the form of the innocent forest dweller. The meditator had done great *tapas*, but had not burned off enough of his crusty nature to reveal completely his divinity within. An enormous burning took place, however, when he was humbled upon seeing the ignorant forest dweller with Narasimha. The meditator's *tapas* brought God to him, but not in the way he had anticipated. He needed to cultivate more humility, more innocence before the divine could fully enter into him.

The forest dweller had to his credit a simple, humble nature. He was automatically receptive and innocent. He was not encumbered by intellect, or accumulated information. Additionally, he had the gift of only being concerned with present time, and in satisfying his curiosity about the strange man who slept while sitting. In the process the forest dweller developed a love for the man he came to call his master. The forest dweller had so much love in his heart that he was willing to give up everything to search for the lion-god—not for himself, but for his master. His selfless quest became his *tapas*. In the process, all of his forest-dweller ignorance was burned away.

About the above story, Ammachi says,

> This kind of person endowed with such a loving and compassionate heart is more dear to the Lord than one who meditates sitting in the lotus posture, proudly contemplating his scriptural knowledge and techniques of meditation and *japa* [repetition of Lord's name].[2]

Tapas can be performed in many ways. As a child, Ammachi performed *tapas* in her home—cleaning, cooking, milking the cows, and caring for her younger brothers and sisters. She used these activities as opportunities to imagine she did it for her beloved Krishna, for God. In addition, she meditated, and she danced and sang for Krishna. It was the same with the Jillellamudi Mother during her first years as a young wife. The difficulties she underwent at that time could be seen as a kind of *tapas*.

Ammachi explains the need for *tapas*:

Immense tapas (austerity) is needed for any new birth to take place. Take, for example, the birth of a child. A mother is literally doing tapas during her pregnancy. She has to be very careful with everything she does, the way she moves and acts, and even in the way in which she lies down. She cannot eat certain foods, and she must not strain herself by doing too much physical work. She may have to avoid certain kinds of situations where she could get nervous or upset.... If she makes a mistake it could harm the baby. The pregnant woman will constantly be thinking about the child she is carrying in her womb ... her awareness will be tremendous. Similarly, we ourselves should have the same commitment to the spiritual birth that is about to take place in us. This commitment is known as tapas.[3]

As seen with Ammachi, some of the activities in which it is possible to adopt an attitude of *tapas* include housecleaning, gardening, and doing office work. This kind of service is a convenient way to practice *tapas* for the average human being. It involves living in the normal world and doing tasks with which we are all familiar. Most of us would find it difficult to meditate for long hours every day because we must take care of our home and family, and we must earn a living. Like the forest meditator, we may idealize the notion of meditating for many hours, but in reality most of us are bothered by too many thoughts to gain much benefit by sitting still for extended times. Service is a practical approach, one that retreat houses of all faiths use in addition to prayer and meditation. In the ashrams I've lived in and Catholic monasteries I've visited, guests and residents spend many hours a day in selfless service, or *seva*, which usually includes such activities as gardening, washing dishes, cooking, and construction.

*   *

Steve Schmidt, a curly-haired, shiny-faced lawyer who is always smiling, is an example of someone for whom selfless service is his primary spiritual practice. He and his wife, Cathi, built the Amma Center of New Mexico. The Schmidts, married for twenty-five years, first met Ammachi in 1987. A friend had met Ammachi in India and knew the person coordinating Amma's first tour to America. The friend approached Steve and Cathi, asking if they would be willing to host a woman saint from India for a couple of weeks. Not fully realizing what lay ahead, they agreed. Steve, even before meeting Ammachi, saw a video of Amma and thereafter shed tears of devotion when he thought of her; he knew he was about to meet his guru. Cathi was more skeptical and preferred to wait and see. Within minutes of meeting Ammachi, both of their lives, and the lives of their two children, were changed. For weeks after Ammachi had left town, Steve, a meticulous worker, would sit in his law office, smiling, daydreaming about Ammachi. Cathi also was elated after the visit; at the same time she would often cry, yearning to be in Mother's presence again.

Cathi and Steve had been on a spiritual path for many years, and had been holding weekly devotional singing in their home. But their experience of Amma was beyond anything they'd ever known. Steve and Cathi work together building and maintaining the Amma Center in their own unique ways; they are individuals with different approaches, different temperaments. Steve is more practical in his devotion; Cathi, whose story I tell in more detail in Part VI, is more emotional. I would describe Steve as the father of the ashram; he is involved in all aspects of administration, including fund-raising. Cathi is the mother; among her many organizational tasks, she meets the emotional needs of the resident and nonresident community. In addition, she writes songs to express her love for the Mother.

Contemplating the service he performs as one of the main supports for the Amma Center, Steve said,

> I first started reading about spirituality in 1969. Putting concepts such as selfless service into practice was somewhat vague; I didn't understand how to be detached and not identify with what I was doing. Since meeting Mother [Ammachi], especially in the last six or seven years, these spiritual notions have become more concrete. Mother's given me an opportunity to contribute the fruits of my actions for building specific things for her. We've bought land and built a temple and an ashram.

Steve's sharp green eyes shone through his glasses as he explained that accumulating the land and buildings wasn't always easy.

> Even though it's a great blessing to be chosen for this task, it's taken its toll on my ego. We've encumbered ourselves with mortgages, which means paying for land and houses which aren't ours. In the beginning, my ego had a difficult time letting go of the concept of ownership—I'd think about the money being spent for something which wasn't mine. Even though I knew it was okay to be doing this, in the beginning it was somewhat uncomfortable. But now it really feels fine knowing that there's a good purpose to the mundane labor I do every day. I've not given everything away like some people do, but to the extent that I have been able to surrender, it feels good.
>
> At the same time, I have college-age children to take care

of, and I have to think about their future and our future, especially when Cathi and I get old. Now I feel less in control—a
deeper and deeper sense that Mother is the one who's in
charge. I've come to the point where I know that if I'm supposed to do something, Mother will tell me, and if I'm not
supposed to do something, she won't.

Steve recalled the earlier days when he and Cathi first got
wind that there might be more to their service to Ammachi
than hosting her once a year and holding the weekly devotional singing gatherings with other Ammachi devotees. "I
remember in 1990, when we first heard the rumor that there
would be an ashram in Santa Fe, I asked Mother about it. She
said, 'No, son. Something like that would present a lot of difficulties for you.' "

The first year during Ammachi's two-week visit, the Schmidts
held the programs in their home, a high desert setting among
piñon and ponderosa pines. The next year Steve and Cathi
rented a six-thousand-square-foot tent for the now four-day
yearly gathering, using donated oriental rugs to cover the
floor. After the Schmidts had been hosting Mother for a few
years, the Friday-night *satsang* group had grown out of the
family's small prayer room into their living room, then spilled
into the dining area. So, in 1992, the Schmidts built the temple.

Steve continued, "It wasn't because we had been planning to build a temple. I was sitting in on a board of directors
meeting in Boston. Since I wasn't really a part of it, I wasn't
paying much attention, but just watching Mother. At the end
of it, she said, 'Steve. Do you have any questions?' "

Wiggling in his chair, grinning like a child, Steve remembered his reaction.

I immediately felt like a little kid in class being reprimanded
by the teacher for not paying attention. I replied, "Oh, does

Mother have any advice for the devotees in New Mexico? What we should be doing?"

Mother told me: "At the end of Devi Bhava in Santa Fe, I had a vision that there would be a temple there. And, not immediately, but in the not-too-distant future, a larger structure attached to it." Mother then explained to us exactly where to build. So we did.

For the 1993 tour we were running out of parking spaces. It was a real problem because we had over a thousand people coming to each program. So I asked Mother if she would pray for me to help me buy some property to the west of our driveway; there were a lot of level spaces there. Mother said she couldn't pray for anything for herself, but that I shouldn't forget about the property on the other side, referring to the land where the ashram is now. I was really shocked Mother would mention this, because the only contact I'd had with that property was when I loaned my horses to someone else who was trying to buy it. I had only asked the owners, the Episcopal church, if I could purchase some acreage to buffer my thirty-five-acre lot from the prospective buyer's land. When we got back from Mother's tour, the bishop of the church told their land agent that I would be a good person to buy the parcel. I was surprised because I'd never had any formal contact with the church about their real estate. Negotiations got under way, and we closed just in time for Mother's next visit. We quickly had to get out there with backhoes and make roads and parking areas.

Steve laughed as he remembered the tricks his mind played on him after he'd bought the land.

Even though I knew I was buying the land for Mother, I kept saying, "Isn't this nice property, and wouldn't it be nice to do this or that with it and to pass it on to my kids?" Different parts of myself were attached, kept identifying with it as mine. Later, when so many devotees were approaching me about purchasing parcels for personal dwellings, Mother eased my mind when I asked her for suggestions about what to do. Mother said, "Mother will tell you what to do with it. Mother knows it's Mother's land."

From then on, it was embedded in me that it wasn't even mine to consider what to do with it. Mother's words helped me to become more and more detached, just serving Mother in the best way I could.

Then, in 1994, the rumors from her senior swamis about the ashram started again. Again I asked Mother, "Do you have further instructions for us regarding what we're supposed to do in Santa Fe?"

Mother said, "Yes. Build an ashram. The house should be about the same size as your house. Make it simple. Don't spend too much money. Mother will send a swami to live there."

That was all she said. Any further attempts at talking to her about it went unanswered. She'd told us what to do and that was it. We started construction in April 1995 and finished in June 1996, just before Mother's summer visit. Swamiji Dayamrita came to live in our house in November 1995 and moved into the ashram as soon as it was ready. Now there are rumors that there's still more to come. Mother's said Santa Fe is a spiritual place and that it will attract many serious seekers.

Backing up to a few years before the ashram was built, Steve said he had been getting tired of his law office, couldn't see any purpose in it anymore. Longing to do something different, he was feeling bored and frustrated with his work. So he asked Mother if he could retire. She told him he could rest briefly when he needed it and that she would tell him when it was time to retire.

Now, reflecting on Mother's words, Steve sees the wisdom in her advice. If he weren't working, his mind would be occupied with too many thoughts.

> Working is how I can focus and serve the best. If I weren't working, I don't know how I'd be serving Mother. There's a part of me that would like not to have all this responsibility, but there's also a part of me that knows I wouldn't necessarily feel better if I didn't. In my work I can concentrate, which is similar to meditation. Being focused on the details of my law practice helps reduce intervening thoughts. I'm probably the type of person who, if I did retire into the woods or had a low-key lifestyle, I'd probably be worrying about whether I was going to be buying bananas or oranges in the store.
>
> The truth about this land and the temple and ashram is that I never really had a dream or a desire to build a community or an ashram. Maybe it's good that I didn't have a desire to build an ashram or live in one because I don't have a preconceived program in my mind about it. If I'd had a lifelong fantasy about community, I'd probably have some set notions about it and how it should be run. It's ironic that I live next to an ashram, because when I asked about visiting Mother's ashram in India, she told me I could come for two days!

While Steve participates in daily chanting and meditation in the ashram or in his home, he has also come to see the value of charity as a spiritual practice. "Now when I'm at work I feel like it does have a purpose a little greater than just maintaining myself and the family and accumulating material things. And I'm no longer bored."

≈

Selfless Service

The beauty and charm of selfless love and service should not die
away from the face of this earth. The world should know that a life
of dedication is possible, that a life inspired by love and service to
humanity is possible.[4]

Selfless service is a well-known spiritual practice in all faiths throughout the world. Why? Because giving through donation or through physical labor can be a source of great joy. Whether we serve in big ways or small ways, it is certain to open our hearts.

I remember one of my first encounters with the joy of giving. I was about five years old. It was twilight on Christmas Eve. The stores were glowing with colored lights, decorations, tinsel, toys, music boxes, and Santa Claus faces. My mother was not far away, but in this moment I was alone. I was on my way down the street to buy something for myself with the twenty-five-cent piece I had in my pocket. Outside the store that I was about to enter, a Salvation Army volunteer was ringing her bell. I knew why she was there. Without hesitation, I pulled the quarter out of my pocket and dropped it into the big black bucket. I vividly remember the warm feeling that came over me from this small act of charity. Helping others became a way for me to feel the love within.

Acts of service can be done in many different ways; the practice does not have to be regimented. The purpose of it is to fill our hearts with joy and love. It can involve anything from isolated and spontaneous acts, such as putting coins into a Salvation Army bucket, to giving large sums or volunteering for a local charity, or, like Steve Schmidt, to dedicating the bulk of our lives to a spiritual cause.

The Indian saint Anandamayi Ma explains more about cultivating an attitude of service:

> Make the interests of others your own and serve them as much as you can by sympathy, kindness, gifts and so forth. . . . Whenever you have the opportunity, give to the poor, feed the hungry, nurse the sick. But if you are incapable of doing anything else, you can at least cultivate goodwill and benevolence toward all and pray for their welfare.[5]

At the same time, we must approach any charitable activity realistically. Even when we are working together for a good cause, there can be interpersonal difficulties that make us angry or sad. While these pitfalls can be aggravating, they offer yet another opportunity to view the shadow and observe our negativity. Ammachi tells us that working together is like polishing stones; at first we will experience our rough edges, and eventually we become shiny and smooth. Amma explains ways to overcome the problem of unpleasant encounters while doing charity:

> Along with doing selfless action, one should also find enough time to contemplate, meditate and pray. As you try to perform selfless actions, friction and conflicts are bound to occur. It is inevitable for these things to come up, especially when you work in a group. Friction and conflict will sometimes cause your mind to be agitated. This, in turn, might cause your enthusiasm and vigor to diminish, and you may feel less inspired by the ideal of selflessness. Anger, hatred and thoughts of vengeance are bound to arise. In order to remove all such negative feelings and in order to keep yourself always in the right spirit, you must meditate, pray and contemplate. You should not let any thoughts block your spiritual growth.[6]

One of the most dynamic examples of selfless service comes to us in the form of Mother Teresa of Calcutta. Her devotion to help the poor and the dying set an example for the whole world.

Poverty is not a natural situation willed by the Creator. If wealth was shared by everybody, poverty could be removed from all over the world.   —Ammachi

Mother Teresa demonstrates how simple the act of service can be. Rather than being overwhelmed by the enormity of her mission, we can be inspired by some of the uncomplicated ways she helped others. After she left her job of twenty years teaching the rich children of Calcutta, her first effort with the poor involved setting up a school outside on a patch of ground among shacks and cardboard dwellings. With a stick, she wrote the Bengali alphabet in the dirt. One by one children came and watched. Eventually, starting with nursery rhymes, the little street urchins learned to read and write. Later, when the Sisters of Charity began to gather, Mother Teresa understood the importance of staying connected with the divine while working. She instructed her nuns to pray and meditate, and at the same time she taught them how to care for the sick and the dying. These two activities always went hand in hand.

Mother Teresa counseled, "Let there be kindness in you. Kindness in your face, in your eyes, in your smile, in the warmth of your greeting. For children, for the poor, for all those who suffer and are alone, always have a happy smile. Give them not only your care but also your heart."[7] Her advice is useful to us no matter how we choose to serve—helping a blind person across the street, letting a mother and baby in front of us in the checkout line at the grocery store, or helping to feed the homeless on a weekly basis.

Mother Teresa's mission included all faiths, all creeds. When she set up a home for the dying next to a Hindu Kali temple, there were protests. The police commissioner who had been called to drive out Mother Teresa said, "At the back of the place is a black stone image of the Goddess Kali, but there, inside that Home [for the Destitute Dying], is the living Kali."[8] Once Mother Teresa picked up a priest of that same temple who was dying of cholera. She carried him inside, nursed him, and nurtured him while he died. When the priests and devotees realized she was not trying to convert Hindus, there were no further problems. Mother Teresa aspired to see God in every human being, regardless of faith, and she taught her nuns to do the same.

> *This attitude of selflessness has a beauty of its own. As you feel the bliss and joy of selfless action more and more, you enter deeper and deeper into a state of selflessness and meditation. So in the beginning, just feel inspired by that very ideal. Love the ideal; be inspired by it. In the beginning it is a conscious and deliberate attempt. As you feel more and more inspired by the ideal of selflessness, you start working from your heart. By the very performance of the work, a joy will spring forth from deep within you. Eventually it will become spontaneous.*[9]   —Ammachi

≈

A LITTLE MORE ABOUT TAPAS

The tapasvi, *the spiritual seeker, who practices austerities and*
conserves energy is in due course . . . transformed into an
inexhaustible power source.   —Ammachi

What is it that draws us to do *tapas*, whether it be through
selfless service, meditation, or living more simply? At the
same time, why is *tapas* a frightening notion? Most of us long
to be truly happy, but we're afraid to give up certain ways of
being. That's where the misunderstanding lies. It's not that
we can't have things; it's not that we can't have loved ones.
What is needed is to release our dependence on them, to do
away with our notion that they are the reason for our happiness. When we seek inner satisfaction from outside means,
we lose contact with the wellspring of divine love, the true
source of power. Ammachi describes the problems involved
when we cling to our possessions too much:

> We are deeply attached to . . . [TVs, cars, houses, computers]
> and to the small comforts they offer. If they are damaged or
> destroyed, we hastily engage ourselves in repairing them. Yet
> we do not realize that it is actually we who are most urgently
> in need of repair. For we have lost faith in ourselves. We have
> lost faith in the heart and its tender feelings.[10]

For most of us it is difficult to see exactly what keeps
us from inner peace and happiness, what it is that keeps
us clinging to outside objects for contentment. Eventually
our life experience shows us that it is not people or ideas
or things that give us pain; it is, as Ammachi suggests, our

entanglements with them. Ammachi further explains that "people who live in constant indulgence, with never-ending expectations, dreams and hopes, build castles in the air. They drain all their energies and finally break down." It is at this juncture that some of us might approach *tapas* eagerly.

Tapas will help clear away inner debris to help us see more clearly, so we can relax and become more receptive like a child. As we come across obstacles along the journey, we will need the help of a masterful hand, one that carries a sword to cut away our blind spots. The guru at this juncture takes on the qualities of Goddess Kali, for it is she who supports our efforts to gradually let go of our attachments. Kali is the Black Mother who appeared on the battlefield to vanquish the evil king. She is the Mother who sustains us and nurtures us as we perform *tapas*.

Kali[1]

When the Universal Mother becomes angry,
it is a dazzling sight—like billions of suns
ablaze at the same time. Who could bear such
a thing? . . . Only consciousness in its pure,
motionless form can bear it. The anger of the
Universal Mother is a violent tempest of
consciousness. . . . It can only be
counterbalanced by an energy that is
perfectly motionless; and that is Shiva lying
prostrate, while Kali dances out all Her fury
on top of Him.
          —Ammachi

Mother Kali's infinite compassion and patience is equaled by her capacity for wrath. She represents the divine principle of fierceness that annihilates our negative and false sense of self. For most of us of the Western world, Kali's image is so foreign, so conceptually incomprehensible, so terrifying, that it can be difficult to relate to her.

Often we take for granted our secure position in the world and have no reason in the moment to remember our ephemeral state, especially if flowers are blooming, the sun is out, and there is a slight cooling breeze. Then, one day in midsummer, black clouds appear overhead and thunder rumbles in the distance. The wind blows fiercely, lightning strikes nearby, and the drum-roll sounds that were once far away are now cracking with ear-shattering force. Maybe the

lightning breaks a tree limb, starts a raging forest fire, or kills a person who didn't heed the distant warning sounds. Kali is both the benign weather and the tempestuous.

In some of her more ferocious appearances, she is a volcano eruption in Hawaii, an earthquake in India, a tidal wave in Japan, the fallen meteor in the Nevada desert, a supernova bursting into a new star, or the violent explosion of our own sun when our solar system was born.

Her devastation is synonymous with creation. The volcano forms a mountain, the storm brings water for life on earth, and the earthquake splits the ground into an enormous crevice, a phenomenon of beauty. Our own birth is at once a creative and devastating experience. Fifty pounds of pressure on our tiny heads expel us from the womb, along with the blood, urine, and feces that can accompany birth in natural settings. This creative force is also Kali.

The rapture you might experience while lying on the ground on a summer night, gazing at ten billion stars shining from above, represents still another aspect of Kali: her night of eternal peace.

Even in our wildest imagination it might be difficult to envision a beautiful young woman as the author of all that is. Wouldn't it be more understandable for a female who causes the creation, preservation, and devouring of the entire universe to come to us in an awe-inspiring, maybe even terrifying, form?

Mother Kali is portrayed as naked, black, with red tongue hanging out, three-eyed, full-breasted, and with long, unruly hair flying free. Often she is depicted as standing with one foot on top of a reclining, white, and peaceful-looking Shiva. In the middle of a battlefield, while holding the severed head of the evil king she had pierced with her dart, Kali remained filled with infinite rage. In her tempestuous fury she didn't quit her annihilistic course. To prevent her from destroying the entire universe, Shiva lay down in front of her. She stepped on him, felt his infinite calm, and stopped. In this classical pose, Kali represents perfect union, her active primordial force and his inert pure consciousness. In her supreme state, she is both Shiva and Shakti.

In Hindu culture, black represents the feminine and white the masculine. Black is that color into which all colors go and out of which all colors come. Yet black is also a paradoxical symbol. The great Indian saint Ramakrishna tells us that Kali looks black only because we see her from a distance and lack an intimate knowledge of her properties. He says the phenomenon is like looking at the ocean; from far away it looks dark, but when we come closer and dip into the water with cupped hands, we can see that it is crystal clear.[2]

In her most intense darkness, the Mother is a densely concentrated light, not vibrant but imploding like a black hole in outer space, out of which she creates the worlds and sends forth a million billion shining suns. Since both the masculine and the feminine reside within her, out of her alone everything is born. Through her everything is nurtured and protected, and into her everything is devoured at the end. Over and over and over again, an eternal cycle of creation, preservation, and dissolution continues. To know the numbers of these cosmic seasons would be like counting the stars on a moonless night.

Within the Mother's created world exist the polar opposites of male and female, light and dark, good and evil, birth and death, demons and angels. Kali presides over all these polarities that make up the vitality of the world and are the natural order of our life force. She makes no distinction or judgment between these opposites; they just are—they are the nature of creation.

Ammachi, thought by many to be an incarnation of Kali, explains:

> Among all the gods, Kali is the only one who didn't marry. Eternal virgin . . . eternally celibate! Whom should Kali marry? Who can marry Her? Shouldn't there be two people in order to marry? Where is that second person? How could Kali's marriage happen? Kali is neither man nor woman. She is both. She is Pure Consciousness as well as Primordial Nature. She fills both outside and inside. Kali is the compassionate Mother of the devotee who longs to see Her as well as the fierce Bhadrakali who kills the ego of the egotistical. Kali is everything.[3]

Those of us who truly desire to free ourselves of cumbersome and inhibiting egotistical ways can meditate on Kali and get her blessings quickly. Why is this so? Ammachi explains that our minds are easily fixed on Kali's fierce aspect, since that is what predominates in our own character. Most of us are of a highly active and easily distracted nature; we want excitement, adventure, romance, danger. Kali's form is suitable for this kind of passionate mind.

At first sight, Kali, complete with blood dripping from her trident and out of the corners of her mouth, is repellent. But contemplating the significance of her form further reveals a more expanded and realistic view of the Mother of the Universe. Her nakedness tells us that she is without illusions or veils of ignorance to cover her. She is clothed with the sky, with the universe itself. Her full breasts epitomize her ceaseless act of nurturing, her eternal state of motherhood. Her disheveled hair represents her boundless freedom. Her protruding tongue symbolizes the passionate nature of the feminine force and her insatiable appetite. With her tongue, she

stimulates us to act out both our attractions and our re-
pulsions. With her teeth, she cuts off our intense longings
and aversions, devours our ignorance, and leads us into
liberation.[4]

Most people all over the world prefer not to entertain the
inevitability of suffering or death as an aspect of life and of
creation. Yet death is certain, and so is birth. Kali is the har-
binger of both life and death, and of joy and suffering. She
represents the most extreme potential of all creation. All the
good in the universe is contained within her left side; all bad
is within her right side. She is the giver of all and the destroyer of all. She grants us the gift of life—its joys, its pain,
its beauty, and its ugliness. And after we've become totally
immersed in her creation, entangled in her enchanting
world, we fear the inevitable, which is her power to take it
all away. In the end, she ushers us into her eternal black
night in which we become endowed with absolute joy beyond compare. We become supreme reality. We become resplendent. We become her.

> She is the great destroyer, forever swallowing up all She has
> created in order to fashion it within Herself and send it forth
> in new births. Her dance of death is that of a life constantly
> renewed. Like the gods She has light, like the demons She
> has force, but more divine than the gods and more terrible
> than the demons, She can conquer all. This is why She is de-
> picted showing opposing tendencies like beauty and beastli-
> ness, terror and tenderness, because they can and do co-exist
> within us. Sometimes She enchants the world, at other times
> Her frightening dance makes the world tremble beneath Her
> feet. She bewitches with Her charm and instills fear. Yet be-
> yond these, She wields a power in which all oppositions melt
> away.[5]

Even though I adore Kali beyond comprehension, I am also in awe of her, afraid she might take away something I'm attached to before I think I'm ready to have it removed. Yet each time she swings her sword, I'm left with a greater sense of her infinite love. My personal experience of Ammachi as Kali inspired me to write the following poem:

Mother, please forgive
my feeble understanding
of your grace.

Your divine fire
scorches putrid sores,
sears age-old
crusts of disillusion.
My mind recoils,
quivers
like a wild beast
caught
in an iron trap.

Oh, my dear Mother,
how easy it is to forget
my urgent prayers
requesting you to remove
all impediments
blinding me to your love.

Oh, yes,
I welcome suffering
at the onset, Mother,
and then
your light
shines on
some rotting treasure
I've clung onto

for centuries,
one of the thousands
that had seemed to give me
golden wings
for flying free.

Like a small child
refusing to let go
of its soft and furry
but stiff
dead kitten,
I weep,
pleading for you
to restore my illusion.

Over and over again
I call
your name.

After the coals of your skillful devastation
die down,
you float in,
filling charred, empty spaces,
with the fragrance
of lilacs,
the sweetness of your unfathomable love.

Part IV
The Shadow from a Spiritual Perspective

The diverse and contradictory nature of life is a delightful play for one who is aware of life's ever-changing nature. He can smilingly welcome both the negative and positive experiences of life with equal vision. But for those who do not have this awareness, life becomes an unbearable burden, filled with sorrow.

—Ammachi

Forgotten Secrets

Through the exhaustion of both the seen and unseen vasanas *[latent tendencies], karmic bondages [results of past actions] are being dissolved.... A real seeker is trying to dissolve his mind and go beyond the intellect and body.*   —Ammachi

Since I was a teenager I had been plagued with tendencies toward rage. After engaging in spiritual practices and in various therapies, I would be convinced the causes of my pain, and subsequent angry expressions of it, were healed, only to be devastated by continuing displays of temper. My confidence was whittled down to nearly nothing. My emotional uprisings seemed to have a life of their own, living within me like insidious parasites, robbing me of my inner substance. I was haunted by the possibility of unforeseen outbreaks.

During my third visit to India, I began to experience a series of uncontrollable eruptions of anger. After anguishing self-inquiry with no tangible results, I wrote Mother a long letter about my problem. I described my emotional venting in detail. My eyes were red after hours of crying when I handed my three-page letter to Mother's attendant. For days I waited in anticipation of an answer, but I received none. My fear and agitation escalated to the point of paranoia.

Now I was afraid to approach Mother in the *darshan* line for fear she would expel me from the ashram, a measure that had been taken against me at my ashram in Pennsylvania. After several weeks I couldn't bear the suspense. I had someone translate another note into Malayalam, Ammachi's language, which simply said, "Mother, what do you advise me to do about my anger problem?"

I gazed at my paper, at the squiggly alphabet I couldn't read, all the way up the *darshan* line, unfolding it, looking at it, refolding it, over and over again. As I came into her lap, I handed her the letter. She held my face tightly against her breast during the silence while she must have been studying my plea. I was still a little frightened when all at once I felt her body quivering as she bubbled forth with loud, mirth-filled laughter. "Savitri!" she said, nearly shouting. It was the first time she had ever called me by my name. Joy poured out of her body, filling mine. I joined in her contagious and mysterious celebration, reveled in the glee that momentarily dissolved all my concerns about anger. Swept away into her abandon, I was glowing inside. With a big smile on my face, I looked at her sparkling, dark eyes, shrugged my shoulders, and held up empty hands as if to say, What am I to do?

Through the translator she gave—as is often the case—a quite unexpected response. She said, "Throw your Amma doll."

Since I didn't have one, I immediately bought a miniature Ammachi doll. It had black wool for hair, brown jersey for skin, and a piece of Mother's own old, white sari for clothes. I threw it once just to try her suggestion, but preferred to hold it as a symbol that Mother loves me even when I am angry. Still, I spent the next months frightened of my volatile nature, terrified of hurting others because of my hidden pain.

My last day in India was a Tuesday, the one day a week

when Mother gives *darshan* only to residents and long-term guests like me. I got in line to say good-bye. One of the residents, the mother of a teenage girl, had been summoned and was standing near Ammachi. It seems the mother had not made certain that her daughter attend school and Ammachi was in a rage about it. In her Malayalam tongue, Ammachi yelled at the woman while we all inched forward in line. An American woman in front of me got disgusted, did not want to witness Ammachi's drawn-out anger, and left. I had seen Mother angry before and was aware that she is not the least bit identified with the emotion. It moves through her with ease, and only when needed. I have seen her smiling brightly fractions of seconds after such expressions, as if they hadn't occurred.

As I knelt next in line, I gazed into Ammachi's eyes while she raved. I was transfixed, drawn into the blackest black I had ever seen in her eyes. For me, in that moment she was Kali personified. All at once my turn came; Ammachi drew me into her arms. To my astonishment she pushed my head so that my mouth was thrust onto her throat while she stormed on. I cannot begin to describe the sensation of my lips pressed into the vibration of her neck while she bellowed. As she let me loose from her neck, my temporal mind nagged at me, wanted to see her smile, to tell her that this was my last day. "I'm going," I said. But her lashing didn't cease. "I'm leaving," I said, more urgently. She interrupted her rage with a punctuated grunt. "Uh!" she said and let me go. I was to be left with a deeper truth rather than with the emotional satisfaction of the normally acceptable vision of love from the Mother.

In the shadow, stage four of the Path of the Mother, the Mother's light reveals old, forgotten secrets, ones that probably arouse pain and fear. The inevitable outcome of doing *tapas* is set into motion. Our denuded inner ugliness can cause us to feel like running away, but by this time we love her too much to run away. We have seen that her goad and her noose have served us well. With some sense of trepidation, we accept Mother's guidance through the shadow to purify our emotions, our mind, and our negative tendencies. Feelings of innocence and helplessness are particularly useful at this stage, because we might need to run to her like a child.

However, during this stage we might harbor doubts and ask, "How can the Divine Mother really love me if she allows painful occurrences?" Or, "How can the Great Mother be omnipotent and at the same time let these events or feelings take place?" Perhaps you've survived the death of a loved one, fallen ill, or lost your home. Even seemingly insignificant events such as mine in the above story can bring to our consciousness a deep sense of frailty, loss, or betrayal.

Some of us may respond so negatively to the purification process that we don't ever want to have anything to do with the Mother again. But in stages one through three, our love has become so strong that this is not likely to occur. If it does, however, it is a necessary part of the journey, and an essential wavering.

Still, rather than facing the cause of your pain, you may think you'd prefer just to let her fade out of your life forever. In this case, often there is a deep spiritual or religious wound that is the main cause of the suffering and pain. When you recognize this possibility, your awareness of it can be a major turning point in your spiritual quest.

At some point in this fourth stage you realize the real problem lies within you, so you look inside and ask, "What is the Divine Mother trying to teach me?"

"The Inner Mother, whose true nature is infinitude and silence, manifests visibly through this [external] body so that her children can have a glimpse of the Mother who is deep within."

"What are the greatest qualities of a Mother? Love, forgiveness, and patience."

"I could see nothing as different from my own Formless Self, wherein the entire universe exists as a tiny bubble."

"Love is a sudden uprising in the heart . . . an unavoidable, unobstructable longing for oneness."

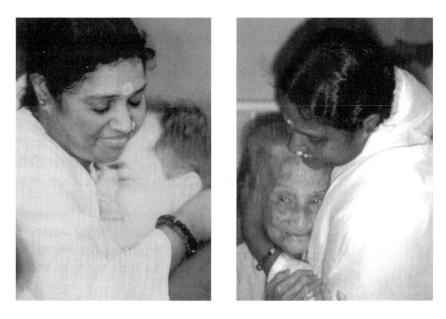

"Whoever comes into the river of love will be bathed in it, whether the person is healthy or diseased, a man or woman, wealthy or poor."

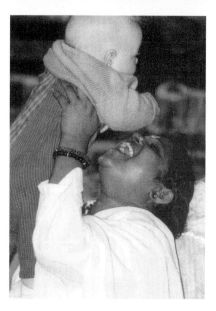

"As far as Mother is concerned, everyone is her child. . . . Children, did not Mother come when you called? Thus did she not obey you?"

"The innocence and playfulness of a child exists in all human beings."

"Amma is not a guest. She is your Mother. . . . Whatever you offer with your own hands is like ambrosia to Amma."

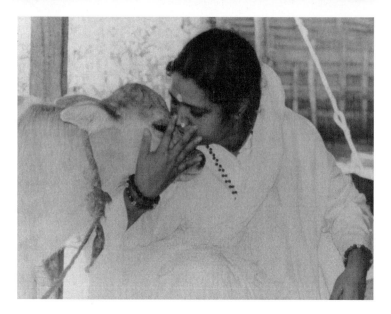

"By loving and serving Nature, we are worshiping God Himself."

"Even when you meditate on the name or the form of a God or Goddess or Mother, you are, in fact, meditating on your own self, not on some external object."

"There is an unquenchable thirst to drink in the beloved, an unappeasable hunger to eat him up, and an immeasurable intensity to become love."

"Everything is pervaded by Consciousness. It is Consciousness that sustains the world and all the creatures in it."

"When you see life, and all that life brings you, as a precious gift, you will be able to say yes to everything."

The above story is one of my many anger stories. I return to this particular manifestation of stage four over and over again. Anger is one of my greatest teachers. Sometimes I feel as though I've made no progress. However, over the years my bouts of fury, rather than being long and drawn out, with their repercussions lasting sometimes for weeks or months, are shorter, less explosive, and over in a day or two.

I've made countless educated guesses as to the source of my anger. For many years, through my teens and early twenties, I didn't even wonder about why I would become infuriated; I just accepted it. In my late twenties, I began to ponder my temper but concluded I was justified; someone had said or done something disagreeable, therefore I had good cause for my volatile outbursts. In my midthirties, after I moved to the ashram in Pennsylvania, I was faced with the fact that acting with outrage was not acceptable monastic behavior, and, worse, it hurt others. I began to experience the consequences of anger; reverberations adversely affected my meditations and my relationships with fellow ashramites. Worse, my remorse would cause me pain for weeks or longer.

In my early forties, after I had left the ashram and started my own yoga and meditation center, I was horrified that I still suffered from angry flare-ups on occasion. During this time I experienced more tangible evidence of the consequences of such behavior: it interfered with my associations with the people I worked with and therefore with the success of my efforts to run an organization. After all, wasn't I supposed to be an example of the peace and contentment I was teaching others?

So I began to delve into my mind through various therapies: investigations into my relationship with my family, and transpersonal explorations, discovering the influences of spirit world, past lives, and other nonordinary realms. These musings, these psychological probings, shed some light, but they served to pacify me only for short periods. My conclusion about anger at this stage in my reflections was that hurt feelings were usually the cause.

Then I met Ammachi. As shown in the story introducing this book and the above story, I was shocked to discover more pain stuck inside of me breaking loose. After being with Ammachi for a while, I began to get extremely discouraged and to wonder if my problem was getting worse instead of better. After several years of being with Ammachi, I heard her say something that gave me hope. She said it takes a long time to get to the bottom of our anger, that we must have a lot of patience. "One day," she said, "we'll just wake up and know, like waking up to the light of day after the dark of night." The moment I heard her words I had a flash of understanding. I decided my fury was the result of an absence of love, that if I felt love all the time, there would be no way to become hurt or angry.

I've seen Ammachi express anger enough times to wonder what it's like to be infuriated and not feel fury. On that afternoon when I witnessed Ammachi's rage, I didn't know why she put my mouth on her throat while she was yelling at the truant teenager's mother. Rather than experiencing the scary, trembly feeling I usually get when someone else is angry, I was awed and inspired. I speculated that she was trying to tell me it was okay to be angry as long as I didn't want something, as long as I wasn't attached to the feeling or to the outcome. When Ammachi is enraged, I can feel her love. When I'm enraged, I feel only the terrible sting of it.

I know my desire for control over other people and events is one reason for my temper. I suspect the feeling of an absence of love is the root of attached anger. However, a perfectly clear view of what lies in my own shadow is still hidden.

Another experience I had in the beginning of my second year in India with Ammachi further illustrates stage four:

Just when I would settle into a sense of deep love and interconnectedness, something would happen that would shake the foundations of my spirituality and my relationship to Ammachi. My trust rattled, I would wonder how she could allow certain events to take place. At first I wouldn't understand. I would feel hurt, sad, angry, disappointed, even betrayed.

For instance, one time when Ammachi was in America, I wrote her a note through the translator, asking if I should go to India on a certain date, and if I would get the funds in time to do so. I was bubbling with joy when she answered both questions with one yes. Without a shadow of a doubt that anything could go wrong, I left postdated checks for all my major and minor bills, and managed to borrow enough money to pay for a one-way ticket. After a couple of weeks in India, I found out that the balance due on a house I had sold had not come through as expected. No money to pay bills or to buy an airline ticket home! It was as if I was held captive with no escape.

I was afraid to tell Ammachi how deceived I felt, but even greater was my terror that she would withdraw her love. I was certain she would abandon me forever if I were to confront her with my belief that she had advised me poorly. If Ammachi is omniscient and omnipotent, how could she have made such an enormous error?

Before this incident I did not suspect that the security of money had carried such grave importance for me. Even more amazing was my discovery that I had more faith in money than in a Father or a Mother God. Instead, I believed the Mother had betrayed me on all levels. Hidden in the depth of my shadow lay the fact that money represented freedom, trust, and empowerment on all levels. I was incensed. How could the Mother of the Universe pose such an enormous obstacle to my source of independence?

Full of despair, aching inside, I ran to her in desperation. All the way up the *darshan* line my heart was beating wildly; my throat was in a knot. I was certain she would know exactly why I was so distraught and would deliver me from my financial mess. When I reached her lap, I was not comforted. Even as I lay in her lap, I could not feel her with me. To my surprise, she didn't let on that she knew my plight. Instead, with a twinkle in her eye, she asked, "Problem?" Since I felt irreparably separated from her, I said, "I can't feel Mother with me."

Through the translator, she replied, "Child, I am always with you."

I blurted, "But I can't feel Mother with me."

With a soft light in her eyes, she said, "Sometimes I hide so you will come running to me like a small child."

This encounter pacified me for a few days, but it didn't bring the needed money, which I naively had thought it would. Surely she knew my predicament and could fix the situation! Ultimately, my mind became so tormented by this event that I reacted by becoming ill with fevers and bronchitis. I was too confused to understand how to approach Ammachi in a more direct way. The angry and hurt part of me wanted to stomp my feet like a child and demand to know how she could have counseled me so poorly, but a wiser part of me knew that there was an important lesson in it.

Since I really needed to know what to do and badly

wanted her to help me as a mother would a child, I eventually mustered the courage to seek further counsel. I took her a letter telling her the details of my financial entanglement.

"Ask again," she told me.

Even though her answer didn't make sense according to the financial particulars, out of some tender spot in my fossilized hope for faith, I did exactly what she said. I called my friend in America and asked her to call again the individuals who owed me the balance on my house.

The process of waiting stirred up muddy, dark images of myself. Had Mother really known what she was talking about when she told me to ask again? Feelings of fear and unworthiness pervaded my being. I concluded that I must have done something terrible to have deserved so much inner torment. I remembered the story, recounted at the beginning of this book, of when I'd sat behind Ammachi while she was giving *darshan*, when my shadow side seeped into my consciousness, and hoped she'd again love me in spite of my crusty woundedness. I received relief from her nurturing presence, bathed helplessly in her love, as I sat with her while she hugged the thousands who came to her daily. Over the next couple of months, through fevers and gut-spewing coughs, my distress began to melt away.

During that time, an intuition as certain as the flow of tributaries into a river seeped into my consciousness: I knew Mother had foreseen my financial delay and wanted me to be in India with her rather than in America with no job, no money, and no place to live.

With the dense fog clearing out of my mind, it gradually dawned on me that this monetary drama had at least one purpose. It exposed a few of my inner demons. Through it, Mother drew out of me archaic pus from lifetimes of injuries having to do with loss of trust, feelings of betrayal by the supreme. When I saw that my fear of unpaid debts was a surface manifestation of a much deeper wound, my heart softened into her love. I now knew that, instead of money, faith in Mother was my key to freedom and security.

One warm evening as I sat on the stoop of my thatched hut, gazing at the stars through the coconut palms and listening to the ocean waves beating against the shore, I received a phone call from my friend in America. The sum owed to me had been deposited into my bank, and all of my debts had been paid.

Demons Within
and Without

*All their darkness needs to be removed. It is
not only this dirt that you see on the surface,
the dirt you are aware of; it is also the dirt
that you cannot see and are not aware of. So
when you start the process of purification,
approaching it with an attitude of self
surrender, naturally all this dirt, both seen
and unseen, both the manifested and
unmanifested, will come up.* —Ammachi

What is the shadow? How does it figure into our spiritual
path? As defined briefly in the introduction, the shadow
often refers to the hidden place where we store denied
aspects of ourselves—positive and negative qualities as well
as divine and demoniacal ones. When we collect these qualities and shut them away, close off their usual expressions,
they grow another kind of life of their own and ooze out,
taking on undesirable, unrecognizable forms. They become
like demons. The story about my anger and the story about
my financial plight are examples of the hidden nature of the
shadow.

To describe the shadow in another way, imagine you want
to build a house, grow a garden, and raise a few pets. At
some point, you decide the local bear with her cub is a

potential risk to your safety. Rather than trying to understand the bear's nature and how you can live in harmony
with her, you block her cave so you can get around to important gardening tasks. Even though your intention is to close
it off only temporarily, you forget. Later you inadvertently
remove the barrier and find that warm, cuddly, nurturing
mother bear in a terrifying rage. Now she's dangerous. Now
she's a demon. So it is with the contents of the shadow; over
time they can become hazardous from neglect, lack of awareness, rejection, and absence of healthy expression.

For many of us the word *demon* might conjure up images
of many-headed, misshapen creatures with long teeth, wild
hair, furry feet, and perhaps only three claws on each scaled
hand. No matter how we may describe them or envision
them to be, they have played complex and critical roles in
probably every civilization of the world and in all ages. Ex-
planations of their reason for being are no doubt as varied as
are the different cultures around the globe.

All of us on spiritual paths are bound to encounter personal demons at some point or other. They are an inevitable
aspect of inner growth. They are part and parcel of Mother's
creation. Whether they appear as creatures out of our sub-
conscious minds or as events in the world around us, we
need to define them in order to see clearly how these shadowy imps affect our lives.

According to *Webster's New World Dictionary*, "demon"
means: 1. a daemon; 2. a devil; evil spirit; 3. a person or thing
regarded as evil, cruel, etc.: as *the demon of jealousy;* 4. a person who has great energy or skill: as, a *demon at golf.* In the
same dictionary, "daemon" is defined as: 1. *in Greek mythology,* any of the secondary divinities ranking between the
gods and men; hence, 2. a guardian spirit; inspiring or inner
spirit; 3. a demon; devil.[1]

I was fascinated to learn that the dictionary's definition of demon is not laced in black-and-white moral religious concepts, but covers a wide range of possibilities, both good and evil.

Throughout Hindu mythology, demons are portrayed as integral aspects of creation. They provide the necessary polar opposite to good. Just as in any engaging theatrical script, demoniacal beings supply the dramatic tension that is needed to have a believable, enchanting, gripping, and sometimes violent and painful world within which we perform our unique roles. Without the evil ones, the Great Mother's *lila*, as the divine play is called in Sanskrit, would have no interest, no goal, no sense of purpose, and no way to measure good. Demons furnish a living dynamic that is an integral part of life.

In one of Hinduism's many creation stories[2], the first act was to create demons. Brahma, the creator, out of the quality of darkness, out of his thigh, brought into existence the demons, who were known primarily for their evil and aggressive qualities. After this was accomplished, the great and eternal Brahma discarded his body. Like a giant ink spot spreading throughout the sky, Brahma's cast-off body became the night. He then took another body and out of his mouth he produced the gods, in whom the quality of goodness was predominant. Brahma once again abandoned his body, which expanded as if from a million beacons of light and became the day. And so it was known that demons are powerful during the night, and the gods are strong by day.

In still another incarnation, the lord of creation became like a father and out of his goodness he created the ancestors. Once again Brahma cast off his body. As the reflection of the setting sun disperses infinite soft lights dancing on ocean waves, his body became the dwindling light of dusk, between day and night. Out of Lord Brahma's fourth body, which was of the essence of passion, was born the human race. Now Brahma's deserted body became the passion of humans and is associated with the early light of morning, the emergence out of night into day. Therefore men are considered to be the most powerful at dawn, and ancestors gain strength during twilight.

Building upon the basis of these four embodiments, Brahma continued the process of creation. Out of passion, hunger was born, then anger, then emaciated beggars and deformed cripples, then more kinds of demons, then two kinds of snakes, then more anger, then eaters of flesh. When Brahma sang, the "drinkers of speech" were born. He made the birds from his own youthful energy, the sheep from his breast, goats from his mouth. The grasses, fruits, and roots were born from the hairs on his body. On and on Brahma continued the creation process until all the beings, plants, flowers, creatures, and crawling things were born.

Qualities that defined demons underwent extensive changes over many thousands of years. One of the characteristics that differentiated gods from demons in early times was that gods renounced deceit and falsehood as weapons, and the demons renounced truth. Yet in later myths, the gods used as much treachery and deceit as the worst of demons. Paradoxically, the demons became strong and rich as a result of speaking falsehood, and the gods became weak through speaking the truth. But in the end, the gods always overcame the demons.

It is a common belief that the Hindu stories of wars between the gods and demons are symbolic of an internal battle that goes on in every human being until enlightenment or final liberation is attained. While the battle between gods and demons is a central theme throughout Hindu mythology, most Hindus believe that these two are ultimately the same. The wars between them are mere illusions since everything they do, like puppets on strings, is in the hands of Mother or God.

In Judeo-Christian biblical stories, the concept of the demoniacal underwent interesting evolutionary developments. Initially, certain angels appeared in adversarial roles as servants of God. The Hebrew term *satan* referred to any of God's angels who were sent to block or oppose humans from engaging in forbidden or harmful activities. While humans often experienced *satans* as undesirable obstacles, the angels' functions were to teach and protect individuals from evil ways.

Later, *satans* became more than just servants of God. They began to provoke him. For example, a *satan* challenged God to test Job's faith by insisting that God take away all Job's possessions and his family. Job's love of God remained strong. The Great Lord showed his pleasure by restoring Job's lost wealth and his dear ones. In further stories, *satan* angels took on characteristics that were sinister and malevolent. Instead of working as God's helpers, *satans* began to function as opponents of God and were invoked to characterize any opposition to Jewish law or custom. Jews who had assimilated or adopted other cultural and religious practices, such as the Essenes or the goddess cultures, were seen as evil, as having been seduced by the *satan* in defiance of God's will.[3]

At this critical juncture, during the turn of the first millennium, Satan had become a being unto himself, an opponent of God, no longer a humble servant. The most famous story of the origin of Satan is that of the once-devoted angel

Lucifer ("light-bearer") who aspired to be better than God and ascended into the heaven above God, only to be punished, brought down into darkness, where he became the embodiment of evil, another well-known synonym for Satan. Of the many stories on the origin of Satan, there is one point upon which they all agree: "That this greatest and most dangerous enemy did not originate, as one might expect, as an outsider, an alien, or a stranger. Satan is not the distant enemy but the intimate enemy. . . ."[4]

While some groups within Judaism and Christianity recognized the fight between good and evil as a metaphor for an internal battle, the prevailing belief within these traditions was that of an external war. The kingdom of Satan and his allies was seen as an ominous and insidious oppression, an equal adversary to the kingdom of God and his believers.

Originally, for both Jews and Christians, Satan had no specific form, and was known primarily through believers' immoral behaviors or lack of adherence to doctrine and dogma. To appeal to the lively imagination of Christians of pagan heritage, during the Middle Ages Satan evolved into a recognizable symbol, the half-goat half-man of Greek mythology. Pan, who once was celebrated as the god of joy and sensuality, became known as the devil. Pagan converts were baptized as Christians only after confessing that their revered deities were demons who contended "against the One God of goodness and justice, and against his armies of angels."[5]

So you see, there are a lot of different ways to look at demons. Whatever your definition, it is important to realize that these gnarly beasts are as much part of the Great Mother's creation as are the beautiful or righteous ones. They add stimulation, struggle, and suffering to our lives.

The dark creatures of our inner realms can teach us to be vigilant and discriminating in all of life's encounters. Like the knowledge of impending death, demons remind and challenge us on all levels of the spirit's journey.

When asked about sorrow in the world, Ammachi responded:

> What? Do you mean that happiness alone is enough and there is no need for sorrow? There is everything in creation. Even a small needle and a blade of grass have their own purposes. Nothing is a waste in creation. Keenly observe. It is sorrow which helps our growth. Human beings will not work and move forward if there is no sorrow. . . . There must be everything in creation, both good and bad. Having one without the other is not creation. To understand the place and importance of each and every object is our duty. Everything has its own place in life. Just give things their proper place, their proper due, neither more nor less, then everything will be all right.[6]

≈

Accessing the Shadow Through Collage

It is better if one can transcend both happiness and sorrow. That means to accept them equally, understanding this to be the nature of life.   —Ammachi

Like storm clouds hiding the luster of the full moon, the shadow conceals our divine essence. The shadow by its very nature tends to elude. You may be aware of something vague, some putrid festering in some small corner inside that keeps you from experiencing inner peace. However, you may find yourself in a quandary trying to access the blockage with words or thoughts. Feelings, symbols, and images related to your hidden nature are often easily available through visual expression: in this case, collage.

The intuitive connection between the heart and the hand brings us in touch with our emotional nature. The connection to Mother is deeply intertwined with our ability to feel. However, the very thought of creating something visual can cause the mind of even the most practiced artist to churn in anticipation or fear. It is a normal response. For this reason, the simple visual methods used in this section can be attractive to individuals of all ages and abilities. No artistic skill is needed. Yet even the least artistic among you will be surprised by how alluring the results will be.

As you enter the underground passageways to your dark side, there can be many fears—of entering the unknown, of living in endless pain and suffering, of being inherently bad, of losing loved ones, or of the lurking potential for evil. These and other doubts or apprehensions are normal and healthy responses when embarking on a journey through unfamiliar territory. It is important to know that the surgeon will not stop before the operation is finished. Nor will Mother abandon you in the middle of the process. She won't let you run away, either. At least not very far.

Even as we travel through the dim light of the shadow, Ammachi assures us:

> Once the final breakthrough happens, that is, once you transcend the limitations of body, mind and intellect, once you reach that state, there is no return. The bliss is forever. And it is infinite. But for this to happen you need to pay [make the effort] accordingly [through spiritual practices] . . . in spirituality, once you attain the highest peak, all pain and tension disappear.[7]

General guidelines: Instructions for making a collage are followed by suggestions for putting together "demon" and "self-portrait" collages. Your artwork could be inspired by any of the topics in the shadow section, and could include "family or ancestor" and "religious" collages. Feel free to begin with whichever subject lures you. Your creative endeavors do not have to be done in any particular order; whatever inklings bubble to the surface of your conscious mind are signals that something is ready to be revealed.

Please note: If the process of making any of the shadow collages brings up issues that are too difficult to handle on your own, please do not hesitate to consult a qualified and reputable therapist—this could be one of the ways the Mother helps you.

Before you start your artwork, invite Mother to be with you. Sit in front of your altar, close your eyes, breathe deeply, and ask her to guide you through every detail. She is the essential personage whose unconditional love is an integral part of your journey. Repetition of her name is the thread that will keep you connected with her throughout. Treat the process of creating a collage as a sacred act, a form of worship, a spiritual art form.

Instructions for creating a collage: Collect magazines such as *National Geographic, Zoo News, U.S. News, Yoga Journal, Common Boundary, Life,* and *People*; art magazines, museum and book catalogues; old calendars, junk mail, newspaper clippings, and old photographs. You will need a large variety of pictures to choose from. As you work, you will find yourself continually enlarging your palette of evocative images. It is important to have a lot more than you need.

The following materials are available at your local art store, craft shop, or department store:

poster board, 18" × 28" (five or six pieces)
rubber cement
scissors
newspaper

As you gather clippings together, imagine that the magazine photographs and selected headlines from different publications are like the letters of the alphabet in a game of Scrabble. Knowing the dark also means knowing light—the contrast of beautiful must be there to see the ugly. Therefore collect shadowy as well as divinely inspirational material. Your visual expression will include everything from light to dark, sacred to profane, masculine to feminine, depths of despair to spiritual heights, so expand your collage palette with this in mind. As you cut out pictures, you may want to use manila envelopes or folders for categorizing pictures according to the exercise topics.

Allow yourself several days to make each collage. Lay out different cutout images on the poster board before pasting them down. At first it is best to cut the pictures larger than you think they need to be. You can always cut them down and reshape them later. Cut pictures into different shapes: rectangular, triangular, hexagonal, round, or irregular. You can even cut some all the way around the image, creating a silhouette. Don't worry too much about the cutout shapes at first because you will overlap pictures with other pictures— that's part of what makes a collage unique and exciting. Actually, there should be a lot of overlapping pictures. Don't be afraid to leave blank white poster-board spaces. Every inch does not have to be covered, and sometimes it's best when it's not.

To begin, consider what you would like at the top of the

picture, what feels best at the bottom, and what feels like it belongs in the middle. Maybe what you put at the top could represent heaven, the bottom, hell. Perhaps some fallen angels drop from a phony heaven, and the real heaven is down below on the earth amid the lakes and trees. Let your rigid concepts of how things ought to be disappear. It is best to give your intuitive mind full rein. If some crazy idea comes into your consciousness, use it. If you want to make your design childlike, feel free. You may design your collage diagrammatically with symbols, sort of like a Kabbalistic tree of life or a family tree.

Put the unpasted assemblage near your altar. Let it sit for a couple of hours or even a couple of days. (If you are afraid it will become disarranged, put some wax paper over it and hold it down with a book at each corner.) Look at it. Contemplate it. Move the pictures around or cut them into different shapes and add still more pictures.

It is helpful to notice your emotions as you work. How does the collage feel? Do you love it? Does it sometimes make you squirm, make you want to hide again? All of the above are signs that it is working, signs that your secret self is emerging.

When you are ready, and you feel good about your collage, paste everything down, one piece at a time, so you don't go crazy trying to remember where everything goes. Or, trace the outlines of some cutout shapes with a pencil in order to place each picture exactly where you want it.

Start by pasting the underneath pieces first. Turn the first cutout piece upside down onto the clean sheet of newspaper. Brush a thin layer of rubber cement over the backside of the whole piece, letting the paste go onto the clean piece of newspaper. Quickly (rubber cement dries fast) pick it up and place it where you want it on the poster board. If you accidentally get paste where you don't want it, don't worry; it will rub off when it's dry.

The final result will end up slightly different from the unpasted layout. Don't worry whether or not each piece is in the precise place you had it in the original plan. That's part of the artistic process—it's always changing. Let the changes take place easily before your eyes, almost as though you haven't any choice in the matter. If one spot doesn't turn out as you thought it would, paste another picture partly over it. You can paste and paste, make all the mistakes you need to, and always be able to change it. Collage is wonderfully forgiving.

As you work, give yourself over to the process. If you feel awkward or inadequate at any time, focus on the childlike feelings that come up. Be aware of mistakes as being exactly right. See the wisdom in blunders. What hidden secret did that error reveal? Rather than attempting to have control over the procedure, let it have control over you.

Above all, cultivate a strong sense of total immersion in present time and space with each step you take. Suspended in slow motion, work as if you had all the time in the world to make this collage. Let it be a form of meditation and contemplation.

The demon collage: Surround yourself with all the magazine images that represent the demoniacal, including ones that reflect the most agonizing aspects of a difficult world, and including your own emotions and experiences. As mentioned in the collage instructions, contrast will make the scene more powerful, so you might also put in elements of beauty and light along with demons, goblins, the devil, creatures, Lucifer, ghouls, volcanic eruptions, Satan, gargoyles, ghosts, thunderstorms, lunatics, vultures, animals killing other animals, images that represent hell—all the visionary symbols that you associate with demons. The opposing images might include sunsets, mountains, rivers, oceans, light coming through clouds, deer, swans, whales, eagles, and saints.

Since demons tend to represent a chaotic realm, it is okay to be disorganized while working. Let yourself work spontaneously without careful planning. Glue pictures haphazardly, not knowing what will come next. Maybe paste several photos down today in a spurt of inspiration, and then wait until tomorrow to do more. Let the unfinished piece sit by your altar and catch your eye before and after meditation. Give yourself ample time. Let it incubate in your dreams.

> *What is hidden within must become manifest sooner or later, no matter how much one may try to do otherwise. It is just a question of time.*[8]   —Ammachi

Be particularly aware of the events throughout the day, relationships, wildlife, weather patterns—you never know when something seemingly ordinary will inspire you. Maybe during a trip to the grocery store a magazine will catch your eye, one that contains just the few more pictures you need. Maybe you'll see a cloud formation that reminds you of an image that needs to be a part of your visual expression.

Let the intuitive feeling-mind guide you, not the intellect. Contemplate the finished piece. Maybe take it to some lonely place, a beach or desert or forest, where campfires are allowed. Gaze at it in the firelight. Sing to it. Sprinkle water on it as a blessing.

At some point when it feels right, you may want to do a

releasing ceremony in which you burn this collage as a statement of your intention to move through the negatives that keep you from your divine self.

Self-portrait collage: Find images that tell the story of who you are—your desires, dreams, aspirations, spiritual nature, sense of humor, and your negative qualities. Since we are dealing with the shadow, it is important that the self-portrait include images of your deepest, darkest secrets. Since the shadow holds secrets even from you, don't stop when you are drawn to some shocking or surprising photograph to include in the collage.

Maybe a photograph of a growling tiger reminds you of your angry nature. Maybe a mountain climber characterizes your spiritual aspirations. Perhaps a picture of a mother with her baby depicts the essence of your nurturing self. Maybe dolphins leaping through ocean swells remind you of your sense of freedom. Maybe a documentary photo of a wounded, screaming child in war-torn Bosnia reminds you of your own childhood. Perhaps a close-up of the face of a charging football player or an animal killing another animal reveals the essence of your aggressive tendencies. Maybe a photo of a tortured woman reminds you of feelings about the Spanish Inquisition.

Don't forget this process is a visual meditation. Spend time contemplating it, both during the process and when it's finished. Let it fill you with the beauty of who you are. Put it on or near your altar or on your refrigerator or in a special place where you can view it.

≈

The Religious
Shadow[1]

*Religion contains the essential principles of
life by which egotism and narrow-
mindedness are eliminated. But sometimes,
due to lack of proper understanding, the
same religions become a breeding ground for
these negative qualities.*

—Ammachi

"*Spirituality* is the real name of religion," says Ammachi. "Religion is the outside and spirituality is the inside."
Understanding the relationship between spirituality and religion sheds light on the shadow. Ammachi defines these
terms:

Religion can be compared to the outer skin of a fruit and
spirituality, then, is the real fruit—its essence. Spirituality is
the true essence of religion; in fact, they are one and the same.
You cannot differentiate between religion and spirituality, but
it needs proper discrimination and understanding to penetrate the outer skin and dive deep into the true essence.[2]

The reality of religion is something far beyond people's
concept about it. The so-called intellectuals of all religions
have taught people about a religion that they themselves
have created ... which has little to do with true religion. ...
They fool the people by making them follow only the external aspect of religion, and never the internal. If the internal oneness of religions were to be revealed, their own

importance would be greatly diminished.... Since they, themselves, are stuck in their own intellects, they cannot assimilate the real principles of spirituality; and if they have not imbibed those principles, how can they teach anyone about spirituality?[3]

Since the time of Adam and Eve, many of the teachings in the Judeo-Christian tradition have contributed to our confusion about the relationship between religion and spirituality and, therefore, about *dharma*. Dharma, loosely translated as righteousness, is a Sanskrit word that refers to every human being's unique path to the ultimate goal of enlightenment. Dharma is a highly individualized process for each person; it includes our professional and family lives, or any activities relating to our sense of purpose in life. It is different from the Judeo-Christian meaning, in which we are considered righteous when we act according to the laws, doctrines, and dogmas set forth by the religious fathers. Dharma, however, is not an artificial rule, but a principle of right living in which we intimately participate in the eternal and immutable principles "which hold together the universe in its parts and in its whole."[4] It is a vital dynamic of universal truths that is inseparable from all people, all plants, all creatures, and all things.

When we follow our dharma, we are striving to know our own nature well enough to maintain our inner balance with respect to that of the universe; we are seeking to understand our own tendencies toward good and evil; we do our best to follow the spiritual practices and to become more aware.

In Hinduism, there is no beginning and no end. There are four ages, or *yugas*, that endlessly repeat themselves. Each *yuga* is such an enormous measure of time—hundreds of thousands of years—that the meaning of time collapses. There is only the continuous change from perfection to decline, from perfection to decline, again and again. In the Hindu view, each *yuga* as it appears over and over in endless time is preceded by a period of twilight that serves as a transition between ages. In every twilight before the *Kali Yuga*, in which we now live, the Path of the Mother is revealed as a guide to help maintain dharma throughout the difficulties of this time. (Mother Kali appears in *Kali Yuga* to help maintain righteousness. These two "Kali" words have very different meanings, as defined in Note 1 under Kali, on page 392.)

In the first *yuga*, as Ammachi describes:

> There was only Truth, one hundred percent. This was the Golden Age. People in this age were completely selfless, living amongst each other with faith and mutual understanding, abiding by higher values. Perfect harmony existed between humans and nature in such a way that there was one hundred percent yield for crops sown. People would simply sow the seeds and then would have no need to return to the field until the time for the harvest. No fertilizers had to be used and no weeds interfered with the growth.[5]

In each of the succeeding ages, harmony inevitably decreases until we reach the *Kali Yuga*, the "Dark Age of Materialism." Ammachi explains the qualities of this age:

> There is a lot of chaos and confusion. Meditation, being very subtle, is difficult to practice. The atmosphere is completely polluted with negative sounds and vibrations. Human minds have become very gross. . . .[6] The harmonic relationship between human beings and nature has disappeared so that no matter how hard people have to work, production is always insufficient for our needs.[7]

The *Kali Yuga* sounds much like the world into which Adam and Eve came after their expulsion from paradise. The story of Adam and Eve's fall from innocence is the Judeo-Christian answer to the great human question, How did life come to be so difficult? The concept of *yugas* is the Hindu version of how life came to be so hard, a dispassionate view in which there is no blame, only the endless turning of time.

In the Western view of things, after God created the heavens and the earth, the light and the dark, the dry land and the seas, the plants and their seeds, the sun and the moon, the years and the seasons, the sea creatures and the birds, the creeping things and the beasts, he then created a man and a woman who were called Adam and Eve. God planted for the man and the woman a garden with fruit-bearing trees, with a river running through, and then he gave them cattle and other beasts. After Adam and Eve were happily settled in the Garden of Eden, God told Adam that he must not eat of the fruit of the tree of knowledge in the middle of the garden or he would die.

One day, while Eve walked alone in the garden, she encountered a serpent, a known symbol of the Goddess, who told Eve that she and Adam would *not* die if they were to eat the fruit of the tree of knowledge, but that their eyes would be opened and that they would become like God and know good and evil. "So when the woman saw that the tree was good for food, and that it was a delight to the eyes, and that the tree was to be desired to make one wise, she took of its fruit and ate; and she also gave some to her husband, and he ate."[8] After they ate, they realized they were naked, covered their genitals with fig leaves, and hid from God among the trees.

Suppose for a moment that the wisdom to be gained from

eating the fruit from the Garden of Eden's tree of knowledge represents the Hebrew equivalent to the Hindu practices that were to have been revealed during the twilight period before *Kali Yuga*. Imagine that the wise council of the serpent was the first in a series of mystical lessons that would have given Adam and Eve the practical spiritual instruction needed to enter the coming age equipped to handle the difficulties. Suppose that after eating the fruit they experienced a new vulnerability or "nakedness" that impelled them to cover their genitals with fig leaves because they now knew that sexuality could be the potential source of both their downfall and their exaltation. Consider the possibility that the information gleaned from the so-called forbidden fruit would have provided them with the secrets of life that, when followed well, would have made them like God, or self-realized.

If the serpent's intention was to reveal important teachings, then why would the scribes of Israel represent God as disapproving? Since the incipient age is one in which jealousy, power, and arrogance were likely to have prevailed, perhaps the scribes and priests fell prey to the potential egotistic qualities characteristic of the *Kali Yuga*, a phenomenon predicted for priests of all religions.[9] Perhaps many of the rabbis preferred to forget they were mere instruments of the divine, and in their pride seized upon the situation in order to gain power.

To have followed Eve's example, to have continued to learn the lessons from the tree of life, might have meant that certain religious practices would focus on the Mother and all human women who embody her. Such a notion would have gone against the newly developing ideas that the Mother God could not serve equally with the Father God. To have continued following the advice of the serpent also would have meant that individuals would have had a self-empowering source of knowledge upon which to base their lives and a path to follow that would help them along a spiritual path, to taste the real fruit.

Hebrew priests were remythologizing the Old Testament as late as 400 B.C.E.,[10] so there is no way to know if the story of Adam and Eve remains unchanged. Even if it has come down to us in its original form, it is possible that its implications were either misinterpreted by the authorities, or that the religious leaders of the time chose not to reveal the full wisdom of it. Instead, they might have decided it was better to operate under the male God who, as the story continues, was described as having issued severe punishment to the serpent for communicating to Eve about the tree of knowledge, to Eve for following the counsel of the serpent, and to Adam for eating of the fruit of knowledge that Eve offered to him.

From that day forward, the scribes tell us, God commanded that the serpent was to be treated as the lowest of the low; women were to suffer unbearable pain in childbirth and be ruled over by man; and men, because Adam listened to his wife and ate of the forbidden fruit, were to suffer in sometimes vain and painful toil because the ground they walked on was cursed. It is interesting to note that in spite of all the trouble Eve seemed to have caused, Adam had named her Eve and acknowledged her as "the mother of all living."[11]

The story continues when the God of Israel, who often is strikingly reminiscent of a few of the gods in the Hindu pantheon in his tendency toward vengeful passions, lost his patience and expelled Adam and Eve from Paradise into a difficult and frightening world. The scribes imply that the earth now would be a harsh place because of Adam and

Eve's unrighteousness, not simply because of the inherent difficulty of the encroaching age.

Adam and Eve are portrayed as being foolish for having made the choice to eat of the fruit of knowledge; their decision is cast as one that became known as a sin. Rather than encouraging Adam and Eve to use the wisdom taught by the serpent, the scribes depict God as having punished them for the innocent desire for knowledge and instilling into man and woman the emotion of shame without hope of release from it—an outcome that might be considered the true original sin.

In Hinduism, sin, *papa*, is defined as doing something destructive to our own selves or following a path of action that goes against our own dharma. The opposite of sin is virtue, *punya*, when we take a course of action that agrees with our dharma, makes us happy, brings us closer to our inner sense of love and interconnectedness to the divine. Neither *punya* nor *papa* is related to set doctrines or rules, but is changeable according to our particular circumstances and relationship to the world around us. Anything we do that contributes to the sense of interrelatedness of all people and all things, anything that supports our spiritual attainment, is *punya*, virtue. Anything that hinders the individual soul from attaining a sense of unity with all things is *papa*, sin. In both Christianity and Judaism, sin commonly is considered anything that is in violation of doctrine and dogma or man's interpretation of "God's will."

The Genesis story ends by telling us that after God evicted Adam and Eve from Paradise, he blocked the tree of life from access by any other person so that no one could become equal to God by taking the fruit of the tree of life in order to "live forever." In the story of Adam and Eve, the God of Israel was portrayed in a humanlike attitude, a tangible form rather than the formless supreme. Therefore, this act could be interpreted as a prideful one, bearing still another similarity to the gods of the Hindu pantheon, most particularly Indra, who, as in the earlier story, is constantly confronted with his pride and resultant vengeance. Among their many tasks, the Hindu gods serve as role models for humans who also tend toward arrogance and forgetfulness. In Hinduism, when a god who has momentarily forgotten the absolute can successfully be reminded and humbled by another representation of the supreme soul, as Indra was reminded by Devi, humans are more likely to follow the example.

The difference between the Genesis story and similar Hindu stories is that we never see the Hebrew God humbled for his arrogance. If there was originally another ending to this story, we may never know about it. Instead, according to the present-day rendition of the Old Testament's Book of Genesis, the initial act was set in place for religious authorities and their followers to act out of anger and arrogance rather than out of patience and humility. If that is the case, those few but influential Hebrew priests who fostered this trend could be seen as having hindered dharma. Adam and Eve were cast out of the Garden of Eden without the complete instructions from the serpent regarding the tree of knowledge, causing them to lose their way back to innocence, back to the supreme Father and Mother.

In addition, during the time of Genesis, Hebrews were establishing a monotheistic religion. Originally, like the other Mediterranean cultures of the time, the God of Israel had a wife.[12] Perhaps her presence in the Garden of Eden was symbolized by the snake who seems to have been a representation of Mother Kundalini Shakti. Is it possible that in the story of Adam and Eve the scribes purposely omitted obvious mention of God's female counterpart? If so, perhaps her exclusion benefited a few self-centered scribes and priests. As the story is told, the bewildered children of Paradise were sent into an arid land without the moisture from the heart of Mother. The split between the genitals, now covered with fig leaves, and the mind, now impregnated with shame and judgment, were set in place at this time. With Mother hidden from view, the subjugation of matter was begun.

If Mother is the creatrix, how was it possible for her to agree to accept an inferior position? Why didn't she assume the terrible form of Kali and destroy the prevailing arrogance and pride? If love and patience are her qualities, we must assume she had her reasons. Maybe certain events had to come to pass before she would come out from behind her veils. For Mother, five thousand years is like a grain of sand on the ocean floor in the great scheme of things. Possibly she preferred to accept both the burden and the grace of carrying humanity's lost humility when God cursed her and said: "Upon your belly you shall go, and dust you shall eat all the days of your life." [13]

As the story is written, God clothed Adam and Eve, cast them out of Paradise, and placed "a flaming sword which turned every way to guard the way to the tree of life"[14]—an act that might be interpreted to mean that no one was allowed to follow a path to enlightenment.

The Family Shadow

The family house should not be a place where a group of individuals live together in conflict, always fighting and arguing. . . . That makes family life hell. It will cut your personality to pieces. Family life such as this is equal to death. —Ammachi

In many cultures the world over, in times long ago, family life was centered around a large community in which religious practices and daily life were inextricably intertwined.[1] Today evidence of families living in harmony with nature and devoting themselves to spirituality exists only in rare indigenous groups scattered in isolated areas around the globe.[2] Ammachi describes an ideal family:

> A family is not merely a group of individuals who live together. As they live together, this "group" can learn to understand many things. . . . Just like the spiritual guru, who treats his disciples as his own children, the father and mother are the gurus in this case, and the children are the disciples. . . .[3]

The history of many cultures all over the world tells a story of family life that is fraught with nightmarish abuse to women and children. Ammachi's family was a typical example, as was Jillellamudi Mother's early years of her marriage.

Most of the world's great religions fostered a belief in the inherent inferiority of women, Hinduism, Christianity, Islam, and Judaism included. Old Testament customs are well known for the subjugation of the feminine half of humanity. From Genesis to Zachariah, women are minimalized and exposed to unequal and unjust laws.

Christianity inherited many of the social dynamics not only of Judaism, but also of Greece and Rome. Original pagan beliefs in the sanctity of all creatures and all things became distorted during classical Greece and in Rome. Cruel treatment of wives, children, and slaves was commonplace. Infanticide, which included the brutal murder of most female babies, was common. This custom continued, though not openly condoned, in Christian times. In Greece and Rome young boys frequently were sexually abused by men, often by the household teacher. A pervasive practice was to keep slave boys in the home for adult homosexual entertainment. Boy brothels flourished in every city.[4]

Aristotelian and Platonic beliefs supported the subjugation of women, babies, and young children. Philosophical and spiritual practices included the notion that a man's seed was believed to be superior to the ovum and the womb. It was believed that only through men's bodies could one evolve spiritually. At a young age women were to assume the only attitude that was socially acceptable—shame.[5]

Philosophical views of the Greco-Romans were carried over into Rome's Christianity and eventually were to spread throughout the Western world. In the centuries that followed, infant cruelty, child beating, and other forms of parental tyranny were commonplace. The compulsion to abuse came from the belief that children's fresh and innocent minds were susceptible to the power of the devil. To instill the fear of God and Satan into young ones, "adults regularly terrorized them with a vast army of ghostlike figures, from the Lamia and Striga of the ancients, who ate children raw, to the witches of Medieval times, who would steal bad children away and suck their blood."[6]

As if it was not sufficient to frighten a little boy or girl with monstrous stories, in still later times it became a common practice for adults to make costumed dummies to ensure that horror would strike their hearts lest they succumb to evil ways. According to one English writer of the 1700s:

> The nurse takes a fancy to quiet the peevish child, and with this intent, dressed up an uncouth figure, makes it come in, and roar and scream at the child in ugly disagreeable notes, which grate upon the tender organs of the ear, and at the same time, by its gesture and near approach, makes as if it would swallow the infant up.[7]

The question might arise in your mind, as it did in mine, where was motherhood during all of this abuse? How could a mother stand by and accept the murder or the physical and sexual abuse of her own child? How could anyone, man, woman, or child, believe in or accept a Father God or a male-dominated philosophy that fostered cruelty in the name of divinity and perfection? How did we lose the love and compassion upon which all of our traditions were based?

In addition to the speculations presented in the Adam and Eve story, Swamiji Amritaswarupananda's examination of Ammachi's upbringing sheds light on the above questions.[8] Although Ammachi's family was from a remote fishing village, her mother and father were typical in many ways of Western society's historically problematic approach to family life. Ammachi's mother, Damayanti Amma, was representative of many cultures the world over in the sense that she acted out of her limited understanding of what it meant to be a devout religious person. She was well known for her pious nature: performing her daily prayers, chanting her morning and evening rituals, and raising her daughters in a disciplined and virtuous way according to her understanding of Hinduism. It was no secret that Damayanti Amma was conceited about bringing her daughters up well and finding suitable husbands for them when the time was right.

Damayanti Amma's religious devotion, however, was not based on spiritual truths. Using Ammachi's fruit analogy of spirituality and religion, we could say Damayanti Amma partook of the peel of the fruit and not the fruit itself. She did not comprehend the concept of trying to see God as dwelling in all beings. Her brand of devotion, common among most worshipers in all world religions, was based on the wish to fulfil her own desires through satisfying God. She wanted to receive the benefits of her worship. Her view of religion had nothing to do with becoming a better person or of modifying her negative tendencies. Her objective was to pacify her fear of committing accidental or intentional sin and to act in the manner taught by her forefathers. The true meaning of dharma, of having self-realization as the goal of life, had been forgotten in her family for generations.

Damayanti Amma therefore felt justified in her cruel disciplinary measures toward Sudhamani during her childhood days: she corrected Sudhamani out of fear of God and to improve her own and her daughter's social standing. We can imagine she reasoned that harsh measures would form her daughter into a more desirable match for well-bred suitors. If Sudhamani was very pious, well behaved, and skillful in household matters, perhaps these qualities would make up for the fact that Sudhamani's skin was dark.

However, Sudhamani was no ordinary child—dancing in

ecstasy for Krishna, sitting in meditation, stealing food for the poor. In addition, many instances demonstrate her fully aware state since birth. When Sudhamani was five months old, her father was frustrated by her weeping, lost his patience, and threw her onto the cot. Not long ago, Ammachi reminded her father of his brutality. For a few minutes he couldn't remember, and then was astounded by his daughter's memory.

Even in the remote coconut groves of southern India, some of the methods used for taming children were similar to Western society's horror treatments described earlier. In Ammachi's village there was a woman whom parents would call to frighten their small children if they became too mischievous. Damayanti Amma hired the woman to scare Sudhamani. The woman covered her head with a sack and jumped up and down near the window making frightening gestures. Sudhamani said to her, "Go away. I know who you are. You are that Appisil Amma. Don't try to frighten me!"[9]

We can imagine that through her childhood experience Ammachi was forming her views about family life. I imagine many of us would be able to identify with the abusive conditions in Ammachi's home. In later years Ammachi used her inner storehouse of information to help others:

The child learns his first lessons of love and patience through his mother. But she cannot simply talk about love and patience and expect her son or daughter to adopt those qualities. No, that is impossible. She has to set an example of love and patience by putting those qualities into practice in her dealings with her child.

A child can be very adamant and uncompromising, of course. But that is the nature of most children since their minds are not fully developed. Caring only about their own needs, they can be very selfish and stubborn. But, that is permissible, for it is not contrary to nature or to the laws of nature. But if a mother becomes stubborn and impatient, that is something very bad. That will create hell. A mother must be patient—patient like the earth.

A father is just as deeply involved in rearing the children as the mother. A father, too, must have patience. When a father grows impatient, that is the end of the child's innocent and trusting life. He or she will grow up to be impatient and adamant, never having experienced what it meant to be patient since nobody had shown them what it was. Socially they will have a difficult time. We cannot blame them for that. . . .

But you can turn your family into a haven, your house into a home, an abode of happiness and bliss, a place of peace and love. There definitely is effort involved; it can be a kind of *sadhana* [spiritual practice].[10]

From Swamiji's analysis about Damayanti Amma's motives in child rearing, we have some clues as to the ignorant driving force of many parents today and over the last four millennia. Most of our forefathers themselves have been victims of a lack of the motherly qualities of love, forgiveness, and patience in the home. Most parents don't know how to convey their unconditional love behind a disciplinary show of anger. Given the modeling in the foregoing interpretation of the story of Adam and Eve, we have the example of a God who also lacked patience and forgiveness. Even if God's wrath was done out of fatherly concern, the scribes of the Old Testament, as already suggested, do not show us how God was patient and forgiving after the expulsion. As if to dig in the message of acceptable parental procedure, the events in biblical chapters beyond the Genesis Adam and

Eve story are filled with tales of vengeance and abuse toward men, women, and children and people of other cultures. While extreme behaviors and events are part and parcel of creation, and while they symbolize our own inner battle with our minds, the outcome of the horrors of generation after generation of abuse might tend to leave most of us with a feeling of hopelessness. Over time many of us are likely to conclude that religious or parental authority does not contain the edible fruit of love and forgiveness.

To add to our contemporary dilemma in Western times, violence within families no longer seems to be the direct result of a desire to instill the fear of God and Satan into the hearts of children, at least not for most people. Physical and emotional abuse of men (yes, men!), women, and children now seems to occur out of a senseless, existential habit, perhaps only vaguely based on religious and philosophical assumptions. Even the consequences of philosophical or religious convictions about the superiority of the male sex no longer are filled with a conscious Aristotelian logic or Platonic idealism. I doubt one could find many misogynists who truly understand the reasons for their behavior, nor a child abuser who knows his or her impulses toward violence could stem from ancient ancestral beliefs.

As a dying animal quivers and shakes in its last instinct for life, it may be that humans' atrocities toward other humans continue because of lingering imprints in the genetic memory. The Bible does tell us that the sins of our fathers will continue for seven generations. Like ghosts from the past, habitual negative tendencies often prevent families from living lives focused on the present. Present-day abusive habits are like an ancestral disease unwittingly causing injured souls, both men and women, to thrash out at invisible forefathers lurking in the shadows.

To examine the question of how our ancestors' philosophical convictions influenced our spiritual life in our individual families is like panning for gold: a lot of sifting is needed. As Ammachi advises, we must ultimately transcend our difficulties and recognize that sorrow helps our spiritual growth. "There must be everything in creation, both good and bad."[11]

The Personal Shadow

Spiritual realization is the highest type of
happiness that can be attained, and therefore,
the price that you have to pay for it is also
very high . . . to seek spiritual attainment is
to die and to be reborn.   —Ammachi

As our relationship with the Divine Mother grows more intimate, her intense light shines in, revealing the source of our
suffering—age-old attachments, crusty wounds, unrealized
desires and talents—all clinging and waiting to be set free. A
common mistake for many of us is to pretend, or at least
wish, that no demoniacal fiends lie within our being, that it
is dangerous even to contemplate such possibilities. In my
own experience, I discovered I had a tendency to scratch
only the surface because I dreaded what might skulk in the
deepest mud at the bottom of my unconscious. Yet I never
could avoid the thorny creatures that hid in the shadow. In
order to pursue my path with authenticity, I knew I had to
confront my own dark side. It was the unavoidable result of
doing *tapas*.

To uncover shadowy material has been a delicate task for
me. Before I understood the nature of the spiritual burning
process, in the beginning I feared that an exploration of
demons could metamorphose into an unmanageable, seduc-

tive fascination, one that could have the potential to lure me away from my spiritual pursuits. However, even before I met Ammachi, I discovered it was far more dangerous to assume that my negative qualities were nonexistent, since the potential to be evil is inherent in our very existence. When I would try to push down my diabolical inner creatures, they had an almost predictable habit of growing larger or multiplying like the monsters in a bad dream, until I could no longer ignore their existence. It was tempting to wallow in unfinished encounters with negativity and instead to watch helplessly as my hidden inclinations bubbled out of me in distorted and self-destructive ways.

To enter into and move through my encounters with inner demons has been an integral part of my spiritual purification process, one that enables me to come closer and closer to Mother no matter what my life condition. I found that just as I bathe my physical body daily, I also must purify my mind constantly.

Purification symbols are used in religions the world over. Hindus bathe in rivers before entering temples; Moslems bathe before entering mosques; Roman Catholics splash water on themselves before going into churches. These external actions represent an internal process. As was so with Damayanti Amma, large numbers of people perform these sacred activities without being conscious of their meaning. However, true purification leads to the truth and is not a rote practice. Ammachi says, "Purification is heating up the mind in order to remove all impurities, and this process inevitably involves pain . . . spiritual pain uplifts you to the abode of everlasting bliss and peace."[1]

For me the shadow is so muddled and murky that bathing in the most sacred of rivers created only a small beginning toward fully cleansing my inner vessel. To embark on the long purification journey, perseverance has been essential. My concentrated spiritual endeavors often drop me down into what feels like uncharted waters, an unfamiliar abyss filled with both the numinous and the frightening. As shown in my personal accounts throughout this book, many surprises have awaited me. As a small boat surges through rapids into a silent pond, I continue to cascade over precipices, then slide, amazed, into a strange and wondrous convergence with joy and bliss.

The consequence of entering Mother's mystery and pursuing divine adventure with Ammachi as the guide has altered my view of fear and suffering. After tumbling my emotional body over and over again in various whitewater confluences, I have found that the spiritual path is a continuous plunge in all the hallowed rivers and tributaries of life.

In a true seeker this [pure, innocent] love becomes like a forest fire,
yet it is even more intense, more consuming. His whole being will
burn with the intensity of that fire of love. In that blazing fire he
himself gets consumed and then comes the complete merging.

—Ammachi

For most people the probing of the spiritual shadow and the clearing of the emotional and physical channels to the divine is a sensitive and subtle endeavor. To show how the inner purification process burns away shadowy material—including visual, emotional, and physical experiences beyond the realm of our Western culture's understanding—stories of two contemporary women, Irina Tweedie and Bernadette Roberts, follow.

The Russian-born Britisher, Irina Tweedie, in her book *Daughter of Fire*, documents her emotionally charged spiri-

tual path with a Sufi master in India.[2] She records her encounters with her shadow and her purification ordeal in
eloquent detail. After studying theosophy for many years,
the fifty-two-year-old widow went to India to meet a spiritual master who would lead her close to her goal of self-
realization. A friend introduced her to the guru who would
serve in that capacity.

Daily, Irina would walk the short distance down the dusty
road from her rented room to sit with the master in his courtyard for a few hours each morning. Although he was not
well known, he had a stream of devoted disciples who
would visit regularly, sit at the foot of his cot, and imbibe his
wisdom. Often, while Irina was in his presence, her heart
would swell, filling with a love beyond any she had ever
known.

In the beginning her guru spoke to her frequently,
instructed her, asked about her progress, and probed the
details of her dreams. As time went by he seemed to ignore
her, paid more attention to what she judged to be inferior
or lowly visitors, a situation that plummeted her into feelings of jealousy and anger. Her agonies, when confronted
with these inner demons, were to crop up with regularity
throughout her studies. Like waves on the ocean, broken-
hearted feelings of abandonment and subsequent rage would
emerge, then sink once again as if into the water's depths.
There she would melt into states of inner peace, love, and acceptance that were beyond comprehension.

Occasionally, she would spend days experiencing inner
calm while she sat in the courtyard with her guru. During
those times her heart would seem to enlarge in order to accommodate his radiant love. However, she often had difficulty accepting that he loved everyone equally. During her

more volatile periods she would spend sleepless nights, tossing and turning, waking with confused dreams and harboring doubts. While she knew her guru was always with her, even when she was alone, she tended to be too caught up in her passions to comprehend why he seemed to neglect her. Intense feelings of being cast aside, coupled with her own judgments of others, blinded her. In the midst of her temperamental episodes, she was unable to grasp that his dispassionate, unconditional love for her enabled her to enter into the purification of her emotional body.

Her difficult experiences demonstrate why most of us need a guru to shed light on our inner demons. As we must look in a mirror to see a sore on our face, we need a person of divine light to help us witness our self-destructive tendencies. Our most subtle and most denied negative characteristics are often too insidious for us to recognize on our own.

One day in the fenced courtyard, her guru sat on his cot conversing with a few English-speaking devotees. Many months had passed. Irina sat on her chair in her usual spot, alone, well behind the others. They were talking about Kundalini, merging, and surrender. She was perplexed by her guru's comments, especially about physical surrender, and pleaded for an explanation. He told her that certain things should not be discussed until it is time, and then proceeded to say:

> The surrender of the body can be achieved much deeper, more intimately and more completely than in the sexual union. In sexual union there will always be two. How can there be oneness? But it is done and it can be done.[3]

She was aware that he watched her struggle with this concept. After some time, many people had arrived and gathered around, enjoying the master as he laughed and joked. Suddenly he turned to Irina and asked:

> Suppose there are four doors leading into the Spiritual Life: one of gambling, one of drink, one of theft and one of sex. And supposing you are told that you have to pass through one of them in order to reach spirituality; what would you do?[4]

Irina panicked, couldn't answer at first, then said, "I suppose that if I have to take the door of gambling, I will have to gamble first, in order to pass through it; if it is the door of drink, I suppose I have to get drunk; if of theft, I have to steal something, and if . . ."[5] Here she hesitated, partly because she was aware that many men sat quietly waiting for her answer, partly because she was frightened, puzzled as to what he was driving at. Since her path included total commitment to her guru, she might have wondered how sexuality could be an issue in the midst of her celibate lifestyle.

"And if it is the door of sex?" he asked with a wicked little twinkle in his eyes and just a suggestion of a smile.[6]

She stifled wild breathing and said quickly, "Well, I suppose I will have to do it, too."[7]

That night she passed through what she described as the most terrifying night of her life in which she was "flooded with a powerful sexual desire." The experience began with a strange sound vibration and a sensation of fluttering, whirling, or tickling localized between the anus and the genitals. She recognized what transpired in her body, knew that her guru had activated Kundalini Shakti.

Irina Tweedie describes her unique purification process, one that exemplifies one kind of Kundalini awakening experience:

Never, not even in its young days, had this body known any-thing even faintly comparable, or similar to this! This was not just desire—it was madness in its lowest, animal form, a paroxysm of sex-craving . . . a wild howling of everything fe-male in me, for a male. The whole body was SEX ONLY, every cell, every particle was shouting for it, even the skin, the hands, the nails, every atom . . . the inexplicable thing was that even the idea of any kind of intercourse was repul-sive and did not even occur to me . . . [yet] I was biting my pillow not to howl like a wild animal. . . . And it went on for hours. I was shaking like a leaf . . . a mute, helpless trembling jelly, carried away by forces completely beyond any human control. A fire was burning inside my bowels. The sensation of heat increased and decreased in waves. And I could do nothing . . . was in complete psychological turmoil.[8]

She was to pass countless nights, with each experience more extreme than the last, facing the relentless purification fire of Kundalini Shakti. For Irina the burning was in the form of inner sexual demons that had probably been hidden away in the secret corners of her unconscious mind for life-times. The cleansing of her suppressed sexuality flooded her being:

The most hideous things, or beings, leering, obscene, all cou-pled in sexual intercourse, elemental creatures, animal-like, performing wild sexual orgies . . . with dogs, humans, men and women, horses, the most ghastly spider-like creatures obscenely exposing their private parts, a grotesque ritual all moving around, all leering at me, dancing, gray shadows . . .[9]

In the midst of her gruesome visions, Irina's analytical mind reasoned, "It [the sensations and images] must have been *in* me. I was sure I was going mad. I never suspected that anything like this darkest vice could be experienced by a human mind. . . ."[10]

Irina had not been aware of the existence of such demoniacal creatures at any time previously, a fact that characterizes the shadow, and the power of the guru to shed light on it. The anger and jealousy that came to the surface while with her guru, coupled with her intense love for him, was the catalyst to provoke full exposure of the source of her pain and suffering. The agonizing periods she had spent perceiving her guru as avoiding or distancing himself from her, the external observations that plummeted her into rage, might have been related to the strong sexual imagery of the internal drama of her spiritual ordeal. The physical sensations of fire and heat accompanying her visions and confused emotional feelings clearly identify her unique experience as an aspect of Mother's skillful devastation that must occur before complete union with the divine takes place.

Irina was ashamed to go to her guru about her nightly experiences but was forced to do so because she had become too emotionally weak to tolerate it. Her guru had revealed patterns hidden even from her and, in the process, burned them away with his love. When she finally submitted to her guru and confessed what had been happening to her, her heart opened to the next levels of the guru's guidance. The above experience clearly marks one of the major turning points in her quest. Afterward she was ready to catch glimpses of the blissful states of union that accompany enlightenment.

However, Irina's journey was not over. With painstaking honesty, she recounts her continuing bouts with feelings of abandonment and anger. Each time she viewed her shadow, she was able to enter into more and more feelings of peace and a sense of union with all things, only to be thrown into darkness over and over again. Her story is an excellent example of the step-by-step spiraling of the stages on the spiritual journey in which we seem to experience the same problems over and over again.

After two and a half years and the death of her beloved guru, Irina Tweedie retreated to the Himalayan Mountains to contemplate her dramatic spiritual sojourn. In her quiet time alone, in the nine months before returning to England, she documented what she referred to as the distillation process. Her descriptions of beauty and peace are equal in intensity to her accounts of pain and suffering. At the end of her journal she wrote:

> I know that there is nothing left TO DO for the devotee who has surrendered himself. For from then on He takes over and the will of the devotee becomes the will of the Beloved. . . . Love for the Unlimited is also unlimited; that's why our hearts have to be broken and become nothing to be able to accommodate the Unlimited. . . . All this I know. My life is offered to You. You take over. . . . And may God help me. . . .[11]

Irina Tweedie's story introduces the realms of possibility. While her case serves to show us what could be encountered during spiritual purification experiences, the intensity of our awakenings will vary according to our spiritual readiness and according to divine grace. Irina's quest demonstrates the importance of the presence of an enlightened master. Her guru guided her safely through demoniacal struggles, and ultimately to unveiling aspects of her inner divinity.

Many times in her guru's garden, after the above encounter with the burning of Kundalini Shakti, she tasted spiritual bliss: "I reflected on the feeling of oneness. Here we are, two different physical bodies. Not even sitting near each other. There was a bodily difference, of course. But already on the mental level there was some intimate feeling of belonging. And somewhere, deep, deep down, there was absolute oneness."[12]

Later, in the Himalayas, she wrote: "Like a perfume rising from the innermost center of sweetness is this still joy. . . . All stillness, all peace ... And the heart keeps singing His Name, singing as though to infinity in utter tenderness."[13]

Bernadette Roberts, in her book *The Experience of No-Self*,[14] illustrates the loneliness that can be encountered when there is no physically external or embodied spiritual guidance present. The following account also supports the notion that when we are committed to a particular spiritual discipline, one we've used for many years, we are more likely to trust that we are guided by an invisible divine hand.

Bernadette Roberts was raised in a family in which she was encouraged to question doctrine and dogma, and to keep the Catholic faith even when agnostic or atheistic questions would arise in her mind. When she was a child, her father would engage her in philosophical conversations that helped her form a unique, yet profoundly Catholic spirituality. As a young adult, she became a Catholic nun. After many years, she left the order to marry and raise a family. She hints that her spiritual aspirations as a monastic had been fulfilled.[15]

While she led a secular life, devotional activities remained an integral part of her existence. She always considered herself first and foremost a Catholic contemplative. She would attend retreats not far from her home in Carmel Valley, California, and often went to a nearby chapel to contemplate and pray. One afternoon, when the nun came rattling keys to lock the door of the sanctuary, Bernadette couldn't rouse herself from her profound altered state of consciousness. Try as she might, none of the usual "tricks" would bring her back to "normal." Because it was time to lock up, she forced herself to get up, go to her car, and drive home. Still she was unable to find her "usual self."

In Hinduism "Self" with a capital "S" refers to the absolute, all-encompassing divinity, but to Bernadette Roberts, there was only the self with a small "s," the one that described her personal ego-identity. For her, the concept of being without a self had nothing to do with divinity, not yet. The only way Bernadette could explain her experience was that she had lost her "self." From her point of view, she no longer possessed a self with which she could identify. Search as she might in the best of libraries, she was unable to find anything within the Catholic contemplative literature that chronicled an experience of what she called "no-self."[16]

She was familiar with the many mystical accounts of exalted states of union with God, in which the self temporarily melts into oneness with the divine. However, Bernadette found no maps to describe the irreversible state of permanently transcending the sense of a personal self. She found nothing in the Catholic writings or from priests, monks, or nuns that was useful to her as a guide into no-self, or how to connect to God without a self.

Initially, Bernadette drove home from the church on that memorable day thinking the experience would subside, and that she would find herself once again with a self. So unfamiliar was she with her new inner life that she often became disoriented. While preparing dinner for her family she would have to remind herself, "Now I am cutting carrots, now I am pouring water." She was accustomed to there being an ego-identity that would take her through the day's chores, but now that was gone. Often she would forget to comb her hair, or take care of herself in the usual ways. One day a woman came up to her in the grocery store to ask if she was sleeping, when in fact she had slumped onto her grocery cart in a trance state. She struggled to recall why she was in the store in the first place, pulled herself up, and reminded herself, "Now I am pushing the cart, now I am buying potatoes." Simple activities that she never before had to worry about had become enormous undertakings.

In the dim access she maintained with her controllable mental faculties, she wrestled with her experience. One of the most distressing aspects of her newly developing state of consciousness was that she no longer experienced herself as separate from God, therefore she no longer felt love of God as other. She was unable to reconcile with her lack of feeling for God. She missed the exalted experiences of divine union, which she hints had been integral to her spiritual life. She was well acquainted with the grace of rapture described voluminously in Catholic mystics' writings.

Her inability to extricate herself from her new state of mind, or no-mind, led her to seek refuge in the Sierra Mountains from early spring to late fall. There she lived with a sense of peace, joy, and bliss beyond any she had ever known. She had hoped that the time alone would bring her back to her customary relationship to God, or at least bring an understanding of how to integrate her experience of no-self into her Catholic belief system. However, her inner spiritual process was to take its own course. Sometimes, while she would sit on top of the mountain looking in a certain direction, there was a foreboding sense that something or someone lurked, waited to come after her.

When she returned to Carmel, she was unable to avoid the ever-present demon. One day while she walked on the beach, the "thing," in its "icy, ominous presence," came after her so menacingly that she was impelled to run for her life. Never before had she been so terrified. From that day forward, she moved through life with the apprehension that the demon would come after her and perpetrate some horrible, unknown act. Her spiritual trust, her faith in God, and her deep understanding that everything was God's will kept her alive and willing to move through her lonely, frightening, and painful process. Her experience supports the notion that when we have been immersed committedly in a spiritual discipline for many years, we are more likely to trust that we are guided by an invisible hand.

Much as she would have preferred to stay in the company of her four children, who distracted her by occupying her full attention, she had an appointment for a retreat at a monastery. While she feared the quiet time would bring her back in touch with the dreaded demon, she felt that a discussion about her spiritual dilemma with the monastic brothers would be fruitless. She assumed they would interpret her fears as insanity, and she concluded that she would have to undergo facing the terrifying entity on her own.

Bernadette describes the inevitable confrontation, another kind of Kundalini awakening:

> On the afternoon of the third or fourth day the icy fingers came back, and in a moment of bravado I decided it was time to have it out with whatever it was. I could not keep running from this thing all my life, I had to get it out in the open, face it head-on and deal with it, because I could no longer stand

its continual lurking around every corner of my day. I decided to go outside, sit on the hillside, and stare it in the face until one of us gave way—or went away. . . . This thing I had to stare down was simply a composite of every connotation we have of "terror," "dread," "fear," "insanity," and other things of this order. In a word, it was a mental, psychological killer. Although I knew this whole drama was only in my head, my thinking mind was all but numb in its presence; but for this reason, the thing seemed wholly on the outside so I could personify it as icy fingers, which were like darting tentacles of light. Though it was unlocalized, it was easy to stare at because it was all around me, there was no place else to look.

The longer I watched these fingers the closer they approached . . . later my head grew hot, so hot, in fact, it felt like it was on fire, and visually all I could see were stars. Then I felt my feet begin to freeze with the freezing sensation spreading upward to encompass all but my head. Finally I fell back against the hill in a convulsive condition with my heart beating wildly.

I knew I was going to crack, crack wide open, but never having done this before I had no idea what would happen. . . . It seems that the body had been left to bear the brunt of an assault which neither the mind or the emotions could take part in. . . . But so bad was my physical condition, I never doubted for a moment that only a miracle could save me; yet, I never expected one, didn't even hope for one, nor could my mind have formulated the simplest prayer. All I wanted to do was get it over with—to die if necessary.

I was not aware of the moment when the dreadful thing departed, for the next thing I was aware of was a profound stillness wherein there was no physical sensation at all. After a while, something must have turned my head because I found myself looking eye-level at a small, yellow wild flower, no more than twelve inches away. I cannot describe that moment of seeing, words could never do it justice. Let us just say it smiled—like a smile of welcome from the whole universe.[17]

While it would seem that this experience marked the end of Bernadette's journey, it did not. Afterward, she went through what she considered the most difficult stage of her unfolding, one that she calls the Great Passageway. In it she felt nothing, was "completely cut off from the known," was unable to relate to the objects of the world in a normal way. Instead, the usual objects of the mind and sense were seen in a global sense, which made for some tense moments, particularly when driving or shopping in a market.[18] In the passageway she experienced a constant void, an emptiness, a heaviness, a cloudy grayness that offered no meaning. Any traces of joy or humor had disappeared from her life. It was an ordeal beyond despair, beyond insanity, and it endured for four devastating months.

On a few occasions Bernadette experienced what she calls "divine relief":

[The burden of] its apparent endlessness, the fatigue, the pressure behind the eyes, the precarious state of sanity, the total lack of understanding . . . suddenly became overwhelming, and under its monstrous weight, something collapsed. Whatever remains without a self disintegrated, melted away like the thinnest veil to the infinite. It was the obliteration of all but the joyous, humorous smile of the divine. . . . Its most poignant, immediate word of description was "melting"—a veritable melting in which God was all that remained.[19]

One day, Bernadette sat on the banks of the river near the beach. Daily she would meet her son there, and they would stand and watch the debris float down the river. Her son would throw stones at logs. While she waited for him to arrive, something unusual happened.

> With neither reason nor provocation, a smile emerged on my face, and in the split second of recognition I "saw"—finally I saw and knew I had seen. I knew: *the smile itself, that which smiled, and that at which it smiled, were One*—as indistinguishably one as a trinity without division.[20]

We could say that in this simplest and most undramatic of moments, Bernadette knew herself to be one with God. It was not an experience filled with flashing lights or rapturous union with the divine, after which she would return once again to a sense of a self. Hers was a quiet, permanent crossing over into a state of consciousness in which she would never again have a sense of a self-conscious self. She had become the deep silence within all. In this seemingly ordinary second at the river, Bernadette realized that she was in a state of consciousness that in Hinduism is called *sahaja samadhi*.[21] I would venture to say she attained a level of self-realization.[22] She knew she was one with all things at all times and no longer experienced anything or anyone as separate from herself.

Bernadette insists that her experience was a natural outcome of the Catholic contemplative life and therefore, above all, was a Catholic experience. Up until this point she had followed the frame of reference outlined by the Spanish mystics, whose model often describes the rapturous state of the personal self's union with God, or the unitive state.[23] However, Bernadette's journey marked a road beyond this map. She permanently transcended the ego-self, or any identifiable self, had no self that could be in union with God, but rather *was* one as God.

Until that second at the river, something inside of her waged a Herculean struggle against letting go into the no-self state of consciousness. The traditions or dogmas defining the mystical path of the Catholic contemplative apparently shadowed Bernadette's ability to recognize that she had transcended the ego-self. Her laboriously concise documentation in her books, *The Experience of No-Self* and *The Path to No-Self*, opens the door for many Catholic contemplatives to expand their hearts and minds, to be aware of the potential for similar journeys in themselves and others.

Bernadette found some hints of her experience in St. John of the Cross and, later, Meister Eckhart, but in mainstream Catholic Christianity, Bernadette did not find any writings about a state beyond what she calls the unitive state. She was well aware that any announcement concerning her no-self experience would have been considered heretical throughout most of Catholic history. While Bernadette makes no claims to this effect, her journey beyond the unitive state might be comparable, or at least close to, the state of consciousness that Jesus knew. However, as the tree of knowledge in the Genesis story was guarded from access by all people, so was the path to enlightenment excluded from the Catholic tradition after the Gnostic Christians were banned as heretics when Rome ruled over the Christian church.[24]

Bernadette suspects St. Thomas Aquinas had entered a state of no-self when he stopped writing, but that the Spanish Inquisition would have made it dangerous for him to speak about it. I assume Bernadette's experience was known by many saints, but not documented. Some Gnostic Christians understood that God is within and without.[25] During the more liberal twentieth century, Bernadette has been able to enter her story freely into the Catholic archives as an experience of no-self.

In the midst of possible controversy, Bernadette warns of the importance of maintaining a balanced perspective when confronted with any spiritual experience:

> It cannot be emphasized enough that the sole value of experience is not experience itself, but rather, what is learned in or through experience—the Truth, in other words. Experiences do not last, they are not eternal; only Truth lasts and is eternal.[26]

Even with the knowledge that Bernadette went beyond the icy fingers and the Great Passageway to experience the peace of union with all things, we might ask: Why continue our spiritual practices if we have to go through what might be a scary purification ordeal? There is no doubt that when the Mother begins to awaken us to our inner divinity, there can be many frighteningly alien encounters. So why open Pandora's box? If we have tasted even a little of Mother's divine honey—moments of peace, feelings of rapture, longing for the beloved—these precious times can serve as sufficient reminders to urge us forward. It is certain, however, that the journey of spiritual purification needs to be approached with gentleness and wisdom.

Without a doubt there have been times when I have felt that I am wandering through a dark labyrinth, bumping into walls, tripping over boulders, lost, with no sense of direction. And, because of my lack of familiarity with the process of divine union, I instinctively resist. As with Irina Tweedie and Bernadette Roberts, the struggle with the unknown can turn into a battle between our will and the Great Mother's will in an encounter of epic proportions. The process might make us feel we are going crazy.

How can we tell the difference between spiritual awakening and insanity? In dealing with our own spiritual shadow and the subsequent purification consequences, it is important to note that Irina, Bernadette, and others who talk about equivalent experiences knew they were not mentally deranged. Even though they describe their encounters as madness, they understood them to be aspects of divine unfolding. I would guess that at least one reason why they characterize their awakenings as insane is because insanity, not Mother's fire, is a realm with which we are the most familiar in our society. Even Ammachi often laughingly referred to herself as a "crazy girl," not because she thought she was, but because others viewed her that way. We do not have a word in the English language to describe the process of entering the selflessness of our divine nature. Referring to the experience as madness is the only context we know that comes close to defining the omnipotence of complete transformation.

However, the realm of spiritual awakening, including the difficulties we are likely to encounter while going through it, is not a psychological issue in the end. It is a spiritual issue. The primary characteristic that psychology and spirituality share in common is probing the secret self and healing inner wounds. While psychological delving undoubtedly overlaps with the beginning stages of spiritual growth, most psychologists and alternative therapists are not equipped to comprehend the depth of penetration necessary to assist in irreversible metamorphosis.

Helping professionals might support us through invaluable regressions, powerful abreactive experiences, and certain aspects of spiritual purification. These experiences might break through the tip of the iceberg, heal portions of our inner injuries, and give us glimpses of a reality beyond our normal understanding. However, like most of us, these well-intentioned health professionals are limited by their own minds, their own wounds and past-life dispositions. How can they know all of our innermost tendencies, all our past lives, or the extent to which we are enmeshed in life's intricate web?

Ammachi says:

> No doctor or psychotherapist can heal those wounds. They cannot penetrate that deep into your mind and remove your wounds. Your wounds and tendencies lie deep within you; they are very old and have slowly started gnawing you from inside.... As long as they [doctors and psychotherapists] themselves have not penetrated into their own minds, how can they penetrate into others?... They too have deep wounds and strong tendencies, just like you.... Only a true Master, who is completely free from such limitations and who is beyond the mind, can penetrate into your mind and treat all those unhealed wounds and remove all your strong tendencies and old habits.[27]

Some therapists might think our pain comes from family upbringing, the birthing process, broken relationships, unfulfilled desires, a loved one's death, or physical and emotional trauma. While these probings can be helpful, from a spiritual point of view, the root cause of our suffering is not externally created. It comes from deep within. It is extremely subtle and has to do with our temporal desires, our attachments, our bondage to forming attractions and avoiding repulsion. Spiritual purification brings about not only healing but total eradication of our inner wounds. It is a gradual process of completely eliminating the small self and becoming free forever.[28]

Once achieved, enlightenment is a supremely—perhaps the only—sane state. Within the literature of enlightenment it is documented again and again that once past the difficult death of the small self, all the difficulties with torment, fear, and rapture cease. Ammachi offers a definition of enlightenment:

> Self-Realization is a state of perfect mental balance by which one can face all the situations of life without weeping over the painful and rejoicing over the pleasant. Welcoming both pleasure and pain while abiding in peace, and going beyond them, considering them as the very nature of life, this is Self-Realization.[29]

≈

Honoring the Dark: The Mask

The sufferings and problems that you may witness in the life of a person who is trying to become a true disciple or devotee are actually speeding up his or her process of purification.   —Ammachi

One of the ways I used to help myself through my darkness was to honor it by making masks. Much later I realized my coverings over the divine are indeed merely masks—scary facades sheathing the reality that lay beneath them. My mask-making could be likened to going through one of the doors Irina Tweedie's guru talked about: gambling, drink, theft, or sex. For me it was with emotions such as jealousy, anger, and pride. Hinduism names six main obstacles to spiritual growth: *kama,* lust; *lobha,* covetousness; *moha,* delusion; *mada,* pride; *matsarya,* jealousy; and *krodha,* anger.

Others include intolerance, attachment, hypocrisy, and repulsion. All negative emotions usually entail the fear of loss, or the threat of someone getting ahead of us in positions of power or romance.

For two and a half years I explored the nature of my shadow through the creation of woven masks, a different media from the more easily created papier-mâché mask-making process described below. (I am a tapestry weaver, so weaving was the most obvious way for me to satisfy this creative expression.) At the time I had not yet met Ammachi. I was discouraged with my mental state even after so many years of spiritual training, so I went to therapy. One time, during a Gestalt session, a being called "Dark" appeared out of my unconscious mind and told me to "honor the dark." It was a positive force, so I knew it was good advice, but I didn't know how to follow it. I had strongly suspected it was Kali who had come to me, because she was the only female deity I knew about who was black. I was aware of the Black Madonna, but she didn't enter my mind at the time. Since I had a strong spiritual practice from having lived so many years in the Pennsylvania ashram, I wasn't the least bit worried about this "dark" being; I *knew* she was benevolent.

In Pennsylvania, one of the disciplines followed twice a day was to read out loud a chapter from *The Bhagavad Gita* (a Hindu scripture) after morning and evening meditation. Whenever we got close to the Eleventh Discourse, "The Yoga of the Vision of the Cosmic Form," I would get excited in anticipation of hearing, once again, about Krishna's cosmic form. When we would actually read it, my body would revel in delight. I didn't know exactly why. Something about the warriors flying to their death like moths to a flame gave me a perspective on the source of my anguish. By envisioning the vastness of the universe, I saw myself as a tiny speck in it all, lending a sense of insignificance to my own inner problems. Maybe the terrible vision of Krishna creating and devouring the worlds reminded me of Kali, and in some way through the *Gita* I was meeting the Black Goddess face-to-face, imagining her long red tongue and the skulls around her neck, facilitating the death of my small self and leading me to freedom.

Then I began to wonder: Could it be that there was a purity beneath emotions of jealousy and anger? Most cultures have celebrations to honor the terrible. Western tradition has Halloween in America, Fastnacht in parts of Europe, Carnival in Brazil and Louisiana. But only once a year! What was I to do the rest of the time? So I began to explore the primeval beauty of the dark in the ritual creation of masks.

Since I didn't have a personal guru to guide me at the time (my first guru had died a few years earlier), I found mask-making to be an effective way to peer into the shadow. Even though people would remark how the images reminded them of Kali, I didn't realize I might be calling her to me. Soon after I was finished with the mask-making practice, I met Ammachi.

Creating a mask ritual: The papier-mâché mask instructions below offer you the chance to honor the dark in addition to the collages you have made. Yet a mask is more than something to contemplate, because you can put it on. I recommend taking your mask into Mother Nature and wearing it, dancing with it, climbing a tree with it, meditating with it, contemplating it, walking with it through the woods or desert. Celebrate around a campfire, with friends or alone. Or simply place the mask on your altar and meditate on it. Remember Mother throughout the ritual. Say prayers of gratitude to her.

Repeat her name. Praise the aspect of her creation that you have honored through the mask-making process.

Notice how the mask allows you to keep emotional distance from the quality you have brought to life, whether it be jealousy, greed, anger, pride, or lust. Through the mask you can see the essence of your emotion in a different light, thereby envisioning it as something separate from you, something perhaps primeval, or archetypal.

Your relationship with the mask can help you enter into a realm common to cultures all over the world for thousands of years. When you see your mask in this larger scheme, you no longer need to personalize or be attached to the quality which had given you so much anguish. Now what you see before you is an object of awe-inspiring beauty that allows you to view it while feeling inner peace.

Materials needed for the mask:
Celluclay (or another instant papier-mâché material), 1 lb.
Newspaper, 4 sheets
Board, masonite or cutting board, at least 16″ × 16″
Mixing bowl
Plastic wrap
Petroleum jelly
Masking tape
Water
Acrylic, one tube of the background color of the mask
Poster paints, set of 10 or 12
Muffin tin or artist's mixing tray
Paint brushes, add one 1″ brush to the ones you have
Small wooden or plastic mixing sticks
Magic Marker, black
Small bowl for water

Paper towels

One or two books with photographs of masks from different cultures such as Korean, African, Native American, Mexican, Indian, Tibetan, Balinese (find these in your library or bookstore)

To get in the mood, use this visualization: Allow yourself about twenty minutes or a half hour. Play music on an auto-reverse cassette deck, so you won't be interrupted by having to turn the tape over. Begin with a slow, soft drum beat— Native American or African drums, Gabrielle Roth's *Totum* or Glen Velez's *Handdance*. Thumb through a book with pictures of masks. Sit or lie down at your altar and do a breathing meditation.

Then invite the Mother of the Universe to guide you on a journey through time, a witnessing meditation. Ask the Mother to grace you with love and compassion for all you see. Let your imagination soar to the time of the creation of the universe: watch the explosion of suns and stars; experience the cooling of the Earth, then the creation of the waters, sea plants, single-cell creatures, jellyfish, sea anemones, fishes, ocean turtles, frogs, lizards, land plants, trees, snakes, furry animals, early men, and into modern civilization. Watch the constant flow of creation: calm, destruction, then calm again—all through evolution and the civilizations of man. Imagine people from native cultures wearing masks and celebrating creation while dancing.

When the vision finishes, bow down to the Mother, speak words of praise and gratefulness to her for taking you on this journey.

Allow yourself a few minutes to sit quietly. Then contemplate the darkest aspects of your personality. Choose one.

Now make a few sketches: Using crayons, quickly, without planning or thinking, sketch several images of masks onto newsprint. Meditate again, then scribble more sketches onto the page. When you feel satisfied that you have begun to penetrate into the core, beyond superficial anger and jealousy, to the archetype of the emotion, begin to make the mask.

Papier-mâché mask instructions: Let the mask be sublimely ugly or rapturously outrageous.

Prepare your working space. Have all the materials ready, including the board you will work on.

Mix a half pound of Celluclay or other papier-mâché mix. I recommend doing this outside to avoid having all the dust of the mix settle where you don't want it. Using your hands, mix with water until firmly squishy—stiff but not too stiff. Mix fully, no dry spots. Cover the bowl with plastic wrap to keep it moist.

To make the mask form over which you will apply the papier-mâché, take two full-sized sheets of newspaper and crumple them up into an oval ball. Take half of a third sheet and smooth it over what will be the front of the mask. Crumple it together at the back.

Secure newspaper with masking tape all the way around, lengthwise and sideways, just as if you were wrapping a package.

Take a quarter-sheet of newspaper (or less) and crumple it up for the nose. Attach with masking tape.

Turn mask form over.

Roll two pieces of masking tape, three or four inches long, into circles, with the sticky side out. Use these to tape the back of your mask form down onto the board.

Place form in center of board, right side up. Stick it down.

Cut off eight or ten small one-and-a-half- or two-inch strips of masking tape and have them available to tape down the cellophane.

Cut off a piece of cellophane that will go across the mask from ear to ear and all the way over to the edge of the board. Tuck it in slightly around the form and tape it onto the board at the upper left and right of the forehead and lower left and right of chin. Then tape down the part of the cellophane that extends past the mask form onto the edges of the board.

Cut a piece of cellophane to go lengthwise over the forehead and chin. Make it longer by three or four inches at either end of the mask form. Tuck in and tape in the same manner as above.

With a black Magic Marker outline the eyes, nose holes, and mouth.

Put a thin film of petroleum jelly all over the cellophane. Wipe your hands.

With wet fingers, take balls of papier-mâché mixture (golf ball–sized or larger), press them into flat shapes, and smooth onto mask form, approximately one-eighth or one-quarter inch thick. Don't make the mask too thick and heavy. Take your time. Smooth it down with wet fingers. You may combine smooth and lumpy to enhance the beauty (ugliness).

Keep eye holes, nose holes, mouth, and string holes open. Small holes at the temples near the ears will allow you to tie string so you can wear the mask. Eye holes can be pupil-sized. This would make it possible for you to paint in the rest of the eye after the mask is dry. Or you can make the eye holes the shape of the eye. Same with the mouth. You may want to make a large mouth or a very small mouth opening so you have room to paint teeth, tongue, and lips. You can make little holes at the top to tie hair or other decorations.

This is optional, as hair, etc., can also be glued down later when the mask is dry.

Make little (or big) eyebrows by putting more papier-mâché clay there. You can shape the nose, cheeks, and mouth in the same way. Sometimes rolling the clay between your palms can help you form these shapes. It's okay for the clay to be thicker in these small, accented areas.

Ears or other appendages can be extended out onto the cellophane; make sure they are well attached to the body of the mask. Smooth them into the clay on the mold so you can't see the seam where they were attached.

Don't worry if the mask isn't perfect. That is not the point. Feelings are more important. You are honoring the dark, so lumpy and crooked might be the perfect way to do that.

When you are finished applying the papier-mâché, clean up outdoors. The clay is not good for plumbing.

Let the mask dry for approximately fifteen to twenty-four hours, or until leathery.

Remove from form *very carefully* by undoing the tape and peeling off the plastic wrap. (If the appendages come off, fasten them down again with a little papier-mâché, or glue them later with Elmer's glue when they are completely dry.) Place the mask on a ball of crumpled newspaper (no cellophane). Let it dry until hard (it may take a couple of days, depending on how wet or thick it is or how warm your house is). If you want it to dry faster, put it in the sun. If it remains soft on the inside after twelve hours or so, turn it upside down to dry. If the mask is still leathery, make a little pillow of newspapers for the face of the mask to lie in while you dry the inside. Otherwise, if it is leathery, it will lose some of its shape.

Painting the mask: Once the mask is fully dry, it's time to paint. Place the mask on three or four layers of newspaper, and gather all your painting materials together. Jars of water, acrylic, poster paints, brushes, mixing tray, paper towels.

Sit quietly. Repeat Mother's name. Spread out the drawings you made earlier. Contemplate until a feeling or image comes into your mind. Don't worry if your idea is very clear or not. Some of you may work best intuitively without much planning. Others of you will want to have a very well-thought-out design. Both ways are good.

With a small wooden stick, mix your base color (acrylic) with a little water in the muffin tin or artist's mixing tray. With the large brush, paint the entire mask. Clean your brush with soap and water. Let the paint dry thoroughly (a half hour to an hour). Be sure the mask is covered entirely with acrylic before applying poster paints. If you are making a two-color mask, you can paint the whole mask with one acrylic color and then paint over the acrylic with poster paint. If you prefer to buy more than one color of acrylic, that is fine. It depends on your budget how you prefer to proceed. The important thing is that the whole mask is painted with acrylic before you apply any poster paint.

After the acrylic dries, you may begin to paint on designs using colors directly from your poster color set. You may want to mix colors with white or black to lighten or darken according to your vision. If you wish to mix colors in addition to adding white or black, remember that yellow plus blue equals green; yellow plus red equals orange; red plus blue equals purple; orange or red-orange plus black equals brown. In paint language, the primary colors are red, blue, and yellow. You can put together various combinations of the primary colors to create all colors. The secondary colors are orange, green, and purple. Contrasts to the above colors are chartreuse, turquoise, magenta, bright orange, bright yellow, and lime. They can be used as accents.

White, black, and brown are more neutral and can be used for contrast or as the main color. You will discover that when you mix too many colors together it turns into mud (that's one way to make a mud or brown color, if you want it).

Clean your brush every time you change paint color, or have more than one brush. One jar of water is for cleaning light colors, one for dark colors, and one for miscellaneous. Sponge the excess water off the brush by dabbing it on the newspaper (or paper towel if you prefer) before dipping into the next color. Keep your muffin tins and water jars clean.

Some coloring tips: use *primarily* one color and variations of it (lights, darks, mixtures) for most of the mask. Or use one main color for three-quarters of the mask and another one for the remaining quarter. Let the paint dry before applying colors next to other colors. Wait until colors dry before adding other colors on top of them. Too many colors can make your mask too busy. After the paint dries, you can change it or modify it.

Get ideas for how to use colors from the books you assembled.

You may highlight or decorate using significantly smaller amounts of many colors. For example, outlining eyes, eyebrows, and mouth; putting symbols (sun, crescent moon, antlers, triangles, circles, dashes, lines, geometric designs); shading cheeks, nose, or chin.

To add hair or other decorations, string those through the holes you made for that purpose, or glue them on with Elmer's glue.

Once your mask dries, it will be ready for creating your ritual.

$$\approx$$

Part V

Surrender

Like love, surrender cannot be studied or learned from any books or from any particular person or from a university. Self-surrender comes as love grows. In fact, the two grow simultaneously. . . . Pure and innocent love for God is what is really needed. The mind should long to become one with God.

—Ammachi

Releasing Gradually

> *Everybody is just being prepared to reach
> this final state of dropping all worldly
> attachment, all ego [limited sense of "I" or
> "mine"]. It must happen because that is the
> final state of evolution, you cannot avoid
> it. . . . The final destiny for all souls is the
> dropping away of every obstruction to peace
> and contentment.* —Ammachi

That second year in India when I was ill with bronchitis and asthma, I decided to try the services of Ammachi's newly established Ayurvedic clinic. In my early forties I'd developed chronic asthma, which didn't respond to natural approaches, making it necessary for me to resort to the regular use of an inhaler, a chemical medicine sprayed into my lungs. Ayurveda is the thousands-of-years-old traditional medicine of India. The Indian doctor recommended six weeks of *panchakarma*—a unique system of treatments that for me was to include drinking ghee, vomiting, nose oil inhalation, herbal massage, oil bath, rice pudding bath, purge, and enemas. I wasn't sure about the vomiting, but I'd been sick for four months and was willing to do just about anything to get well.

My program began with seven days of ingesting varying amounts of herbal ghee (clarified butter), then eating a watery rice dish in the late afternoons. To my astonishment, by the second day all traces of asthma had vanished; I no longer needed my inhaler. My face had completely changed, somehow more soft, more natural, more free, my eyes more luminescent. However, by day three, after drinking half a cup of green ghee, I felt as nauseated as a novice sailor on a stormy sea. The powdered ginger mixture the clinic had provided had not alleviated the feeling that I would throw up at any minute. The ghee supposedly was effective for clearing the liver, but I wanted nothing more to do with it. Since I was too weak to leave my dormitory bed, or so I thought, I called for the doctor's female assistant, also an Ayurvedic physician. I waited four hours, but she didn't show up.

With my body oozing with nausea, I made my way down the two flights of stairs to the clinic. I knocked. The doctor cracked open the door, frowned at my complaint, then shut the door in my face. A volcano inside of me erupted. Vomiting had been specifically prescribed for asthma; however, I believe my screaming and yelling that ensued must have been just as effective as any Ayurvedic vomiting. Swearing like a seaman, I hollered, "Stupid idiots!" and threw everything within reach—tin cups, plates, and plastic bottles. Now the doctor opened the door wide; I seized the chance to cast the last metal cup onto the floor at his feet, then stomped away. Now energized, I was headed back to the dorm when on the grounds below I saw several young male ashram residents running in my direction. Frightened and feeling like a criminal, I escaped, leaping up the stairs to the refuge of the women's dormitory.

Once back in my room, I was mortified at my behavior, convinced that when Ammachi found out, she'd have me thrown out of the ashram. One of Amma's long-time disciples sat to comfort me. I prayed for liberation from all sorrow. My insides moaned like a captive whale longing to swim free, to leap into the ocean waters.

Later the doctor's assistant, accompanied by Mother's translator, who happened also to be a nurse, came to check on me, and to bring me hot water for a bath. I told them I would not continue *panchakarma* without asking Ammachi.

A couple of days later Ammachi returned from her Australian tour. I took a note up the *darshan* line, written in her native tongue, telling her I'd had difficulty with the ghee, that I'd yelled and thrown things, and should I continue my treatment program? As Ammachi held me in her arms, I heard her talking in a serious tone, sensed she was receiving a more detailed account of the incident from the nurse/translator. My body began trembling with fear; I tried to pull away, to flee, but Mother held me fast, an iron grip. It seemed like forever. Finally I relaxed on her breast, and she loosened her hold. Then she lifted me, looked at me with eyes of a doe, watery and tender, and said, through the translator, "Child, you look so much better after only three days of panchakarma. Finish the program."

So I did. And at the end of the six weeks I was still asthma free, glowing and shining from undergoing the treatments that Ammachi has said is a kind of *tapas*, capable of working off lifetimes of karma. After a week or so I was feeling so strong and full of vitality, I wanted to celebrate by swimming in the ocean. After completing *panchakarma* we were to rest for at least three weeks—no travel, no windy or sunny places, no overstraining of any kind. Swimming seemed like a relaxing activity. I'd let it slip my mind that during the treatment we'd always washed with warm water, never with cold, and that at the ocean there'd be both wind and sun. I asked the doctor for permission, just to be sure. I think he took my request to swim in the sea as a request to take a shower, which in Indian languages is the same verb—to bathe means to swim or to take a shower.

The next day I came down with bronchitis. No Ayurvedic medicine would alleviate it. Very soon the sickness turned into asthma. I could barely breathe, wheezing, straining through locked lungs with every inhalation. In desperation I pulled out my old inhaler, which helped for only fifteen minutes at a time and soon made my condition worse. My body was new and tender from *panchakarma*, too sensitive for chemical medicine. The Ayurvedic doctor and his assistant, mystified that nothing helped, abandoned their efforts. Now I was in a panic, certain that if no relief came I would die.

In the dormitory, a psychic offered to help, and asked other women to join her. After holding her hand on my chest and back, the psychic assured me my condition wasn't deep, that the root cause had been released. That knowledge in itself calmed me. I knew lung problems were often related to a broken heart, and was aware that the loving attention of other women also helped to ease my breathing.

While struggling for breath, it was nearly impossible for me to lie down, so while everyone slept, I lit a candle, sat cross-legged on my bed, and stared at my Ammachi doll, which I had propped up so that she stood looking at me. For some reason, I had to urinate several times in the night. Physical effort tends to aggravate asthma; with trepidation, moving very slowly, I climbed the spiral staircase to the next floor, ambled down the labyrinth hallway to the toilets, then returned to the dorm with some difficulty.

Through the long night I felt more and more comforted as I imagined Ammachi in her room in the tiny three-story building next to the dorm. As the hours passed, my Amma doll took on a brightness, a life of its own, through which I could sense Ammachi's all-encompassing love. I had the definite impression she knew I was focusing on her. In the still, dark morning hours before dawn, Mother's love was growing more and more strongly within me, a warming light spreading through all my cells.

At four-thirty A.M., still breathing with great effort, I rose for morning prayers, pushed open the dormitory door that led onto the temple balcony, and was able to chant some of the response to the thousand names of the Mother. Usually one of Ammachi's newer disciples leads the chanting, but this morning for the first time I'd ever seen, one of her swamis, Swamiji Amritatmananda, led. The sound of his voice, like that of an Italian opera singer, resonated through the temple with a joy beyond description. Every pore, every hair on my body, was permeated with so much love I was certain I rested in heaven on a bed of rose petals. So full of love was I, I was willing to pay the price: If my heart and mind and body could remain filled with that much love, vast as the universe and bright as the sun, I was willing to live with asthma forever.

This brings us to stage five along the Path of the Mother: surrender. Usually an in-depth view of our shadow leaves us feeling tender and washed out, and often with a sense of failure. It might even leave us with a sense of disorientation as to who we are and where we are in relation to the world around us. In this state of not knowing, we are the most likely to have an experience of surrender; we are likely to have a glimpse of what it means to allow the Mother to enter in, filling us with her grace and her infinite love.

Most of us are terrified of surrender because we think it implies no longer being in charge, no longer being in control of our lives. In actuality, that is exactly the goal. A state of surrender means we no longer make claims such as "I did this or that" or "I accomplished this or that." Instead we recognize that everything we do is the result of divine energy moving in and through us.

Once we've experienced the grace of surrender, we are more willing to do the spiritual practice of surrender. As a practice, surrender does not necessarily come easily, nor do we necessarily experience it as grace. Instead, we now know it is desirable, so we practice it. We say, "Okay, I guess I'd better surrender to this or that situation." We invite feelings of submission; we encourage ourselves to experience the Mother as the cause of all our actions, our thoughts, and our feelings. We coax ourselves, bit by bit, into yielding. In this way, surrender is an act of will; it is a practice that ultimately leads to the real surrender. Usually it is a slow and gradual process taking place over many years.

The *panchakarma* story illustrates both kinds of surrender. In retrospect, it is easy to witness how I was being brought to my knees by my physical condition. I couldn't have tolerated being sick any longer. In the beginning, I was forced to take measures. Later, I had to surrender to my illness. Even though I'd had many glimpses and experiences of the real surrender, I didn't really understand.

Before this *panchakarma* program, I'd thought I had control over my body, or maybe the doctors did. So, I gave in a little bit and entered the treatment program; I even was willing to take an emetic and eat tons of watery rice for the vomiting remedy. But before any of that could take place, my mind entered in and decided it didn't like what was happening. I put up a very big fight. Then, another level of submission took place when Ammachi said to continue the program. Even during each of these periods of giving in, I was still under the illusion that I was in control; I was surrendering as practice, as an act of will, not fully as love or grace.

In actuality, it did take a certain amount of faith to do what Ammachi advised. Even the practice of surrender required me to believe it would help me toward the goal, which at that time had more to do with relief from physical suffering than with self-realization. Over the six or seven weeks of the extremely intense *panchakarma* program, my mind teeter-tottered back and forth, balking, then crying uncle, over and over again. In the end it was obvious—neither the doctors nor I were in command. All health methods had failed. My only refuge was opening my heart to the divine, to the genuine understanding that the only recourse was surrender. Then came the grace of unconditional love.

Ammachi explains more about surrender:

> We have no control over the things or objects that we claim as ours. We have no control even over our own body or existence. Then what can we say about other things? How can we say that a thing which is not under our control is ours? Neither the creation of an object nor its sustenance or destruction is in our hands. Yet, foolishly we think that it is ours. Therefore, dedicate everything to God. We should always feel, "O Lord, I am just a puppet in Your hands. You are the one who gives me power. Even a blade of grass will not move without Your Power." We should pray with a longing, "O Lord, where are You, where are You? Wash away my ignorance. Wash away my ego."[1]

It was in the sentiment of the above words that I decided to move to Ammachi's ashram in Santa Fe, the Amma Center of New Mexico. The story is an example of the gradual process of surrender, a practice sometimes filled with grace, sometimes with enormous struggle and confusion.

Long before I met Ammachi I had given up everything—my inheritance, a college teaching job, my possessions—to live in an ashram in Pennsylvania. The process threw me into great turmoil, but I didn't feel I had a choice. The love and peace I'd experienced in the spiritual setting was beyond any I'd ever known. I was afraid to lose it. My commitment to the community was either all or nothing, according to the guru I had at that time. Therefore, even though it looked as though I'd surrendered, I hadn't. Mentally I was still attached to all the things I'd given up. Nevertheless, the experience of forced renunciation had its benefits. The *tapas* of renunciation allowed me long periods of feeling free from desires, even from most worries. Then, seemingly out of nowhere, feelings of lack would enter in—I'd wish I hadn't given up my career; I'd wish I had a car and my own place to live. Sometimes my guru would take me aside and tell me to surrender, but I didn't truly understand what renunciation or surrender meant, as Ammachi explains so well:

> In fact, what you should give up is the attachment to the object. You can have the object and enjoy it—if you are not attached. We give up something externally in order to be internally free from the bondage to that object. Detachment is what brings peace and happiness. Real renunciation and detachment come only when we give up all thoughts and feelings about whatever we have renounced.[2]

I lived in the Pennsylvania ashram for about eight years over a ten-year period. For another ten years I ran a branch center in Tucson, Arizona. In 1992, ten years after my guru died, I met Ammachi, to whom I was drawn like a humming-bird to a flower. Yet I was not willing to take part in a false renunciation again. What a conflict! I was still under the impression that to be fully immersed in spiritual life, I had to give up everything. But forced surrender or surrender for surrender's sake was not Ammachi's way:

> Surrender is not something which you do to somebody else. It is to your own Self that you surrender. The Guru does not want anything from you. He does not have any personal interest, nor does he have anything to gain from your surrender. . . . The giving up is for your inner growth, for your own peace of mind and for your own bliss. It is for the unfolding of your little self into the big Self.[3]

Because of the Pennsylvania ashram experience, I had naturally let go of many desires for outside entertainment. Except for an occasional movie, time with friends, and a meal out, quiet time by myself had become my wealth. Nevertheless, I wasn't ready to give up what I did have, especially not my independence. I was happy living alone, owning a car, and being able to come and go from the ashrams in India and in Santa Fe as I pleased. The intense *tapas* I'd experience every year in India was enough for me.

Meanwhile, three years after meeting Mother, I inherited a little money from an aunt. I've always been a quiet environmentalist, so I bought an earthship home in Taos, New Mexico. The house was rounded, soft like the Mother. It was constructed with old tires, with mounds of earth piled up on the outside, smooth mud plaster on the inside, and a wall of windows facing south. The rain was my source of water, the sun provided electricity and passive solar warmth. There were huge planters with a hibiscus bush, banana tree, jasmine plants, an orange tree, and various herbs, and a solar waterfall. I used a composting toilet that churned out nourishment for my outdoor plants. I felt embraced by nature in that house, living closely with the movements of the sun and the seasons. It was like a little oasis in the desert.

After coming home from my third long trip to India, I was washed out, devoid of my usual ambition, drawn to meditate all the time or just look out the window. I didn't know what to do. I wasn't willing to submit to ashram life, so when Ammachi came to the United States for her summer tour, I posed a question about what would be good for my *sadhana*. In my note I mentioned a budding interest in writing something about Mother, the possibility of continuing tapestry weaving, or doing anything Mother would recommend. I was very nervous as I inched my way up the question line, terrified she would tell me to live in an ashram. As the hours passed, I gradually became completely willing to put myself in Mother's hands, yielding to whatever she would tell me. By the time my turn came, I felt as soft as a newborn baby. Mother barely looked at me when she said through the translator, "Write the book."

My home in Taos was the perfect setting to begin what Amma had bid me to do. Yet from time to time I was tormented by a yearning to give up my idyllic lifestyle to enter the ashram in Santa Fe. I longed for the feeling of freedom unique to the ways of spiritual community. One day in the meditation room of the Santa Fe ashram, two devotees were practicing on the harmonium and tabla. I felt an alluring sweetness to their devotion, as if I'd happened upon angels making music by an alpine stream. Struck by the peace of it all, I wondered what in the world I was doing living alone in

Taos. Why was I wasting my time? I decided to fill out the five-page application for residency. Back in Taos, I scribbled answers to the questions, about myself and my ability to live in a group, about my tendency toward anger. I was still afraid of hurting others during my outbursts. The paper sat on my dining table for days. I never sent it. I was too afraid of failure.

Another year passed. I was almost finished with one of the drafts of the book and my Old English sheepdog mix of sixteen years had died. No more good excuses not to move. What anguish! If I really wanted self-realization, mustn't I dive in and face my fears? I wrote a letter to Swamiji Dayamrita in Santa Fe. During my next visit, he advised me: "The reason we come to the ashram is to get rid of our *vasanas* [tendencies] and attain the goal, not because we've already attained it. Otherwise, why would we come?"

I felt reassured, prepared to enter ashram life at least as a spiritual practice, not necessarily as a permanent commitment. However, I wasn't convinced. I also wanted Ammachi's advice. On my next journey to India a couple of months later, I took Mother a note: "Would it be good for my *sadhana* to sell my house and move to the Santa Fe ashram?"

Amma cupped the small piece of paper in her hands, examined my one sentence for a long time, then held the note to her forehead, seeming to imprint something onto it, a prayer for me perhaps, and maybe a look into my future. It seemed like forever I knelt in front of her waiting for her response.

When she let me go and didn't answer, I felt a profound grace, a deep bowing down to her silence. Another time, I thought as I backed away on my knees, then bent to touch my forehead to the floor.

All at once the translator said, "What did Dayamrita say? Mother wants to know."

Still kneeling, a little bewildered, I blurted, "Yes. He said yes!"

In the same moment, while I was saying yes Amma also said yes.

While we can only guess the ways of Mother, among the many reasons why she might have hesitated, I supposed she must have foreseen the difficulties I would endure. Meanwhile, I sold my house within a month of returning from India and moved to Santa Fe in May 1998, settling on the two hundred acres in our little ashram of about ten residents, Swamiji Dayamrita, and Cathi and Steve Schmidt, who live in their own home some hundred yards up the hill. It is a New Mexico ashram in every way—the land of enchantment, a laid-back and relaxed air. Even institutional life in this high desert home isn't filled with the strong shoulds and should nots that generally accompany group spiritual ways.

At the Santa Fe ashram I feel Mother's presence palpably—in the air, the trees, the birds, the chanting, the devotees. We are free to come and go as we please, and, at the same time, everyone here has the same goal: to hold as much unconditional love in our hearts as we are able, to become detached, and ultimately to merge with Mother. To this end, we do the practices Ammachi suggests, including chanting the one thousand names of Devi every morning, devotional singing in the evening, meditation, and selfless service, or *seva*.

The close proximity of ten people purifying all together can be intensely challenging. My inner cauldron has bubbled over several times. The first two or three incidents, while far less intense than my history shows, were so devastating to me that I ran away for a couple of days, to the woods or to Ojo Caliente Hot Springs. I would wonder if my failure meant I should leave. After my most recent outburst I was terribly distressed. Cathi Schmidt took me to Starbucks. Over café latte she said, "Steve didn't build this ashram to house perfect people or saints; and cleaning up the broken cup was a small problem."

My heart softened. She was referring to the terra-cotta mug I'd smashed before I ran out the door to hide at a motel. Tears welled in my eyes as I listened to Cathi. Her permission when I'd expected reprimand eased my stress over my occasional but habitual lack of self-control. She reminded me we are all here to experience our weaknesses until the time comes when these shortcomings no longer disturb us. A week later, while writing this chapter on surrender, I opened one of the *Awaken, Children!* volumes to these words:

> It is when you have tried and failed that you are truly able to surrender. Though you fail time and again, you continue to try until, finally, there comes a point when you accept your failure; you fully experience and understand your incapacity to move forward. It is at that point that you surrender. So keep trying. That ultimate sense of failure must come to everyone, either today or tomorrow. . . . Unfortunately, we have a strong tendency to find an explanation for everything. Never accepting our failures, we find some reason or other to justify everything we do.[4]

The above words were sobering. Along with continuing my desperate search for the root cause of my negative thinking, I had started justifying my failures: "I was overtired," "I was ready for a break from the ashram," "So and so pushed me to my limit," "I had too many deadlines to meet," and so on. However, I don't think there are any accidents. I don't think I just happened upon Ammachi's words—it felt like a direct communication.

It had never occurred to me to accept failure. While I can't claim to have fully surrendered, like a little blade of grass in early spring emerging through the brown, perhaps I have an inkling about myself in a way I never had before.

The approach toward the death of my negative attitude about myself can be seen as one step on the path of surrender. It is not necessary for us to live in an ashram to undertake the gradual cutting away of habitual thinking. All walks of life and all situations can be fertile settings for the spiritual quest. No matter where we are, each time we truly give up something, as shown in all my personal vignettes throughout this book, we are certain to experience a sense of inner freedom. When we raise the white flag of surrender, we are acknowledging that we'd rather have inner peace than war. We are acknowledging that we have opened a little crack in our heart to let divine love enter in.

Developing an attitude of surrender can take place on a daily basis in the simplest of events. For example, recall the times when we've let go of an afternoon at the movies, a walk in the woods, a meal out with a friend. The more easily we were able to release our disappointment, the more quickly we were able to feel better. For the more difficult and seemingly insurmountable issues—such as the fizzling of a relationship, the loss of a long-time friend, the missed chance for a promotion, or the illness of a loved one—more time is needed sitting with the wound and gradually surrendering. Then we can soften into ourselves and experience the beauty of who we are without encumbrances.

Often the rather blanket and misunderstood term used for

our inability to deal with conflict and trauma, is ego. What is ego? As partially explained in Bernadette Roberts's experience of "no-self," in Hinduism the terms *self* and *ego* are often used to describe the sense of separation from the supreme, the Self with a capital "S." Bernadette used the term *no-self* because she no longer felt the presence of her ego or small self; ultimately she felt no separation from the supreme.

The split we feel between our personal desires and our desire for absolute identification with the supreme soul or Self contributes to the inner tension produced by the ego. When we refer to the ego we are talking about that part of ourselves that gets hurt or jealous, or thinks things should happen in a certain way, as in my story about asthma. In my account about my problems in the Santa Fe ashram, I was most miserable when I thought I should have control over my anger. When Cathi told me it was not a problem to clean up a broken cup, somehow I felt a letting go. I could relax and surrender to my weakness. According to Hindu philosophy, it was my ego that wanted to have my emotions respond in a certain way. At the same time, it was my ego that aroused me to anger.

While the ultimate aim is to sublimate the ego, paradoxically we mustn't fret too much about it. Ammachi assures us that it is not possible for us to live without expectations and without ego. She suggests we use our ego for constructive purposes. For instance, we can employ our will to put forth effort in our work, to gather possessions, and to engage in pleasurable activities. The ego can be the driving force that helps us do our spiritual practices. Yet we mustn't get led away from openheartedness, like the meditator in the forest-dweller story.

Ammachi warns us not to be blinded by our egos. We must not go against our own conscience or our own human nature, such as creating destructive technologies mentioned in Chandra Pillai's story. Nor must we engage in cruelty in parenting, as Ammachi's parents often did. With the ego intact, we can still have a loving and compassionate nature. "But," Ammachi says, "when you are blinded by the ego, you are completely blind."[5]

The gradual releasing of our attachments to possessions, people, emotions, and to ways of perceiving can bring us ultimately to the grace of detaching from our own death or from the passing of a loved one. Facing death is perhaps one of the most powerful tests to the process of letting go. One of Ammachi's devotees, Mary Noone, an Irish woman from County Donegal, shows us the way of surrender in a story about her father's last days. Mary, a hearty woman with dark hair, cream-colored skin, and a bright smile, was always anxious about her father's death: "In my whole life I was afraid of my daddy's dying. He would always be drinking and turning purple."

Her father wasn't well when Mary, a nurse, came home from a well-paying job in the United States to be with her father. On her way to Ireland, Mary stopped off in London where Ammachi was giving a program. From there Mary planned to go back to Donegal with her mother, back home to care for her ailing parent. But something happened when Mary got ready to leave: "I experienced the worst heartbreak I'd ever known. The thought of leaving Ammachi gave the most excruciating pain in my heart. For the first time I knew what it was like to be in love. I thought I surely couldn't live unless I was in her field."

So Mary phoned her father to tell him she wasn't coming right away, that she was going to go on Ammachi's European tour.

"Don't worry. I'll not die till you come home," her father told her.

In Zurich, two weeks later, Mary figured she'd better find out if her father was okay, since she'd been so rash about going off with Ammachi, abandoning all concerns about her failing father.

Mary's mother answered the phone. "Your daddy's not well," she said. "Even if you come now, I don't think you'll get home before he dies."

Mary exclaimed:

I couldn't believe it. Here was my life's task, my life's wish—to be with my daddy when he died—taken away from me. I didn't know what to do. I stumbled back into the hall where Ammachi was. It was Devi Bhava [the night Amma dresses like the Goddess, with a crown and colorful sari]. I was so distraught, rather than running up to her, I waited my turn in the long line. I didn't have the strength to run up.

When I finally got to Amma, I couldn't even speak it. Mother smiled, put my head on her knee, and held me there for some time. When I got up, to my amazement, Amma had completely removed my fear that he would die right now. I practically danced down from the platform, full of joy, completely secure in the knowledge that he'd live until I got home. It was incredible. I couldn't believe it.

For the next two weeks, I didn't call home or anything, and when I got back to Ireland, my daddy was very much alive. Everyone was so upset I'd been so carefree about staying with Ammachi when I knew my daddy was dying. But my daddy knew. When I went to him, he looked at me and said, "I feel her power when you're with her."

I knew from that, from what he said, that it must have been Amma kept him alive till I got home. Even though he'd never met Amma, only heard about her through me, he had a strong connection to her, probably because of his devotion to the Virgin Mary. My daddy never went to church or anything like that. But he prayed to Mary, kept a picture of her, one of those ones you always see where she's wearing a blue mantle.

About a year later, when it became obvious that my daddy's days were numbered, I wrote Amma a letter that he would die soon, that we needed her help and support. For three months there'd been a little robin pecking at my daddy's shed every morning at about six A.M., over and over again, pecking away out there. In Ireland we have a superstition that sometimes a robin will come to tell us someone is going to die. Since that bird was pecking at the window of his shed, my daddy understood it was letting him know he was soon to depart from this world.

On the morning of his death, he wanted to go out there to that shed. He'd spent most of his days in that dirty place, fixing all manner of things for people.

Mary wrinkled her nose, as she continued:

It was a wild, dirty old shack. It didn't make any sense why my daddy was so attached to that wreck of a place. I followed him out there, holding on to him, afraid he'd fall at any minute. Then he asked me to light a fire inside right in the middle of it. I was sure he'd burn the place down.

I yelled at him. "You're going to die out here and I can't carry you in!"

We hollered at each other, stubborn as can be. Finally he commanded, "Go get your brother!" My brother came running, used oil to start a fire in an old barrel, using all kinds of junk to burn. For two hours my dad sat quiet as anything, just looking at the flames. Every once in a while, he'd say, "That's great." I just watched him. Finally, he said, "Okay. That's it. You can take me in now."

I tried to make sense of it. I could only figure that the fire must have helped him get rid of his attachment to that rotten old shed. Now maybe he could go in peace.

Back inside our house, in the background I had one of Amma's devotional songs playing on our tape deck, over and over again. It was so peaceful. I knew Ammachi was giving him the courage to die. All day long I played that tape. People, friends and villagers, came by to pay their respects, people who owed him money, and others. He forgave them all, shaking their hands and joking. "I'm coopered [I'm finished]," he'd say.

Then my mother kept trying to get him to do confession before he died. But he kept refusing. Finally, he said, "I'll go for her [the wife's] sake." When the priest came, Daddy told him, "Well, Father, I committed every sin in the book." Finally Daddy said to the priest, "Go you home now, Father, before the storm. It's going to be thundering and lightning."

Mary wiped the tears from her cheeks and then went on:

At one point Daddy asked me to put my hands on his head, and when I did he said, "Now I know how you feel when you're with that woman." Then, he just lay there for a minute. "You've no idea how soothing it is for me," he said. "Too bad you couldn't put a blue mantle on her."

At the end, my dad looked into my eyes for a long time. He was in a lot of pain, and we had to give him a little sedative. So then he slept and just before he died, he opened his eyes and looked around, kind of like he was surprised, or something, and then he slipped peacefully away.

At the funeral the priest who'd come to take confession said, "What a privilege it was to be with him in the last hours." Then the priest who actually performed the service said, "There's something different about this death. It's like you don't know he's dead; you don't really believe it." He said this because it was like a celebration, a wedding, not a funeral. At our house we'd had eight weddings and only one funeral! My little niece said she saw a blue light come out of him. Ammachi'd been there; I'd no doubt.

The Song of God:
The Bhagavad Gita

*These bodies are known to have an end; the
dweller in the body is eternal, imperishable,
infinite. . . . Certain indeed is death for the
born and certain is birth for the dead;
therefore over the inevitable you should not
grieve.* —The Bhagavad Gita, 2:18 and 27

To apply the principles of divine surrender into our every-
day lives is one of the great spiritual secrets. How do we develop detachment? How do we become willing to give up
our lives for our divine principles? Or, how do we conjure
up the intense feelings that characterize a lover of God? One
of the major keys lies in the practice of *karma yoga,* a practical
spiritual approach. Like hummingbirds shimmering in front
of an array of flower blossoms, everything we do can vibrate
with love and divinity.

In order to accomplish this seemingly impossible task,
we must learn to become detached from our inner and
outer conflicts, and, in the end, from our fear of death. The
Hindu scripture *The Bhagavad Gita,* or *Song of God,*[1] shows
us how to experience dispassion in all our actions, how to
uncover our inner peace, and how to become aware of
the split second of present time in which divinity is revealed.

It provides us with a map for ways to surrender to divine love.

The nuances of *The Gita*'s sacred message are both simple and vast. According to *The Gita* "Everyone is made to
act helplessly indeed by the qualities born of nature."[2] In
every second of our lives, we are engaged in some kind
of activity. Breathing, walking, eating, eliminating, thinking, and sleeping all involve some form of movement. That
is the essence of Mother's creation. Therefore, all our actions provide the means to unveil the divinity that dwells
within.

As in many Hindu scriptures, the setting for the *Bhagavad
Gita*'s teaching is a battlefield. The ensuing war ushers in the
Kali Yuga, in which teachings of Krishna serve as a guide in
this age of materialism.

The Gita opens when the great warrior Arjuna is faced
with an imminent battle. He is overwhelmed with doubt and
inner conflict. He has been brought to his knees by his encounter with an evil cousin. From the epic called *The Mahab-
harata*, in which *The Gita* is placed, we know the long,
shadowy history that leads up to the initial scene in the *Song
of God*. For scores of years Arjuna and his four brothers had
been tormented and persecuted by this wicked cousin, the
son of a blind king. Among other things, the cousin was
so jealous of Arjuna and his brothers that he made several
clandestine attempts to kill them. At the culmination of the
cold war between them, before the clashing of weapons was
about to take place, Arjuna had harbored the hope that this
useless battle could be avoided. Nevertheless, preparations
had to be made, and the armed forces had to be gathered
together.

During the arrangements, Arjuna had been given a choice
between having Lord Krishna as his charioteer or having an

extra army of ten thousand. Knowing that divine guidance was more important than armies of warriors, Arjuna chose Krishna. As the war is about to begin, the blind king on the enemy side asks his charioteer to narrate the events of the battle. The one with eyes to behold tells the sightless king what he sees taking place in Arjuna's camp:

The opposing forces have gathered, sounded their trumpetlike conch shells, brandished their weapons, and established their positions. Arjuna wants to see those with whom he is about to fight and requests that Krishna drive his chariot out into the middle of the battlefield. Krishna artfully positions the chariot so that Arjuna faces his uncles, grandfathers, cousins, brothers-in-law, sons-in-law, and friends.

Upon beholding so many dear and lordly men who are about to kill one another, Arjuna is overcome with grief. He tells Krishna that he would rather die than have dominion over the earth by slaying his kinsmen in battle. He admits that his mind is confused and asks Krishna to advise him. With tears in his eyes, Arjuna sits down in his chariot, casts away his bow and arrows, and says to Krishna, "I will not fight."[3]

In this critical and vulnerable moment, the spiritual teachings of *The Bhagavad Gita*—in the form of a conversation between Sri Krishna and Arjuna—begin. As with Mary Noone when she learns about her father's condition, Arjuna's normal defenses are weakened. His heart is receptive, his mind wide open to listen. Ammachi explains the importance of Arjuna's position:

Only when Arjuna stopped speaking on the battlefield, did Krishna begin to speak to him. In the beginning Arjuna had countless misconceived ideas. He talked and philosophized endlessly. Finally, he was exhausted and felt utterly helpless. He dropped his weapons to the ground and stood quietly next to Krishna. His bow and arrows symbolize his ego—the intellect, the feeling of "I" and "mine," the attitude that "I" can fight and win.... His worldly knowledge, his royalty, his strength and skills as a great warrior couldn't help him now. He had no choice but to accept his total failure, and having done so, he exposed his sense of helplessness to Krishna. Only then did the Lord speak, because now Arjuna was open enough to listen. That silent stillness is the state of surrender. Only in the silence of surrender can you truly listen.[4]

While tens of thousands of warriors wait in a divinely suspended moment in time, the lord seizes upon the opportunity to teach Arjuna about spiritual truth and why he must fight. Lord Krishna says,

There has never been a time when I did not exist, nor you, nor these rulers of men, nor shall we ever cease to be hereafter. Just as in this body the embodied soul passes into childhood, youth and old age, so also it passes into another body; the firm man does not grieve about it.[5]

Just as a man casts off worn-out clothes and puts on new ones, so also the embodied Self casts off worn-out bodies and enters others which are new. Weapons cut It not, fire burns It not, water wets It not, wind dries It not. This Self cannot be cut, burnt, wetted, nor dried up. It is eternal, all-pervading, stable, immovable and ancient.[6]

The Lord explains that the objects of the physical world are all subject to change, that our existence on Earth is impermanent, that everyone is destined to die. The only true reality, the one that never alters, is the all-pervading Supreme Self.

Most of us, like Arjuna, have formed emotional attachments to our loved ones and would need to have Krishna explain more convincingly how the above philosophy of life could possibly have any relevance for us. Any one of us might ask the same questions that Arjuna poses throughout *The Gita.* When Krishna sees that Arjuna doesn't respond to the philosophical explanation, he tries to persuade Arjuna by telling him he must set an example by enacting his purpose in life as a warrior. He must act for the sake of dharma and serve as an example to others. But Arjuna is still stuck in his great difficulty: He has to go out and kill people. How on earth can this be a good action? Arjuna says, "If You think that knowledge is superior to action, O Krishna, why then do You ask me to engage in this terrible action? . . . Tell me that one way for certain by which I may attain bliss."[7]

In full warrior's regalia, the great hero sits in his chariot at Krishna's feet, not willing to move until he is satisfied with the answers. Arjuna is like a child asking repeated questions to the Mother of the Universe. Krishna, with the patience of a mother, replies, "Freedom from activity is never achieved by abstaining from action. Nobody can become perfect by merely ceasing to act. In fact, nobody can rest from activity even for a moment . . . therefore you must perform every action sacramentally, and be free from all attachment to results. . . . Do your duty always, but without attachment. That is how a man reaches the ultimate truth; by working without anxiety about results."[8]

With this teaching Krishna takes us below our superficial judgments about war. It is not the kind of action that matters, but the spirit in which the action is performed. Krishna explains that Arjuna must enact his role as a warrior without concern for the outcome.

Still, it would be easy for many to misunderstand the above philosophy. Some might take it as a license to kill or to harm others. However, Krishna clearly warns us that we must avoid the pitfalls that could arise when we confuse nonattachment with not caring.

This brings Arjuna to the next question. He wants to know why people are driven to do the opposite of good, why they are compelled to commit sins. Still in exterior definitions of "goodness," he thinks he should become a wandering renunciate instead of remaining a warrior.

Krishna describes an evil act as one motivated by the desire for power. When we attempt to take control over matters that are not in our hands, when we give up our spiritual values for the sake of personal aggrandizement, we become like the wicked cousin in *The Gita*—the blind king's arrogant son was compelled to dominate at all costs.

The practical advice Krishna offers for avoiding the destructive outcome of greed and vanity is to cultivate an attitude of nondoership. Rather than claiming that we are great and powerful because we have accomplished this or that, Krishna counsels us to remember that it is divine energy that acts through us. In reality, we don't *do* anything; we are simply instruments for the doing. Krishna says, "In all cases, all actions are done by the qualities of Nature only. He whose mind is deluded by egoism thinks, 'I am the doer.' "[9]

For example, if we could envision that our bodies are filled with the permeating force of Mother Nature, and that it is she who is the fundamental cause of all our actions, we would enter into a state of inner peace while performing our actions. We would know that it is never we who cause anything to happen. We would simply experience ourselves as manifestations of the never-ending flow of detached divine love. We would be in a state of surrender.

To explain the concept of nondoership, Krishna tells Arjuna that it is important to do what we are born to do or suited to do. We each have particular gifts that function as part of the greater whole. We are not just seemingly separate waves taking our journey to the shore—there are many similar but unique swells. The divine charioteer warns Arjuna of the difficulties he would encounter by abandoning his special gifts and his job in life: "Better is one's own duty, though devoid of merit, than the duty of another well discharged. Better is death in one's own duty; the duty of another is fraught with fear or productive of danger."[10]

To further clarify the concept of keeping to our unique life tasks, it can be helpful to observe the innocent behavior of wild animals. Beasts don't wonder about what to do, they simply act spontaneously. Each divinely designed creature serves a special and original function that is perfectly balanced in relationship to all the other creatures. Mountain lions kill deer for sustenance. This seemingly destructive act thins the deer populations so they don't eat up all the plants. The big cats kill off only weak animals so that the deer generate strong and healthy genes. Vultures and jackals eat dead, leftover prey and keep the woods and prairies clean.

It would be silly even to try to imagine a deer attempting to be like a lion, a bee struggling to be like a flower, or a bird splashing its wings to be like a fish. It would be even stranger to envision a deer taking pride of responsibility for being a deer; it simply is filled with the divine energy of deerness and takes no thought in expressing that gift to its fullest. When we express our own unique gifts with attitudes of detachment, without envy or greed, there is a sense of love and dedication in our work that gives deep meaning and purpose. There is no plant, no animal, no human on earth that can take the job of another living thing and be happy or successful.

Krishna tells all of us through Arjuna that the way to attain peace is not by giving up our actions, but by abandoning our inner torments and endless yearnings. Lord Krishna attempts to convince Arjuna that, as a warrior, he is simply a vessel through which divine activity takes place. Krishna advises that by adopting a detached and compassionate mental attitude, all pain and suffering is destroyed.

The Gita suggests that if at any point we become distraught because we seem to have ended up in the wrong job, or we've come to a point where we don't think anything we do in life is worthwhile, or we are disappointed in our fellow humans in the workplace and at home, we need only to remember to seek counsel, to take refuge in the divine navigator. Once we are clear, the truth can be revealed.

Just as Arjuna takes an eternal moment in time to suspend the imminent battle, it may be that we must take retreats in solitude, in religious settings, or in nature where we can quietly communicate with the supreme charioteer within. There are many ways to enter that eternal moment in time in order to commune with the Mother or Krishna before continuing the sacred battle of life—including meditation, contemplation, and prayer.

One of *The Gita*'s messages shows us that states of mental confusion and emotional distress like Arjuna's can be critical launching pads for spiritual awakening. At the same time, it warns us not to run away from life's lessons by avoiding our daily tasks. It is not necessary or even recommended for all of us to become monks or nuns as an expression of our spiritual quest. Like Arjuna, we may feel as though we would like to give up our life as we know it rather than continue in our present state of despair. But Krishna advises that our release from suffering does not come through escaping our purpose in life, or by taking on a false sense of goodness. It comes through experiencing our divine nature within the context of our daily lives.

Arjuna's mind continues to harbor doubts. He becomes anxious. He doesn't understand how his present difficulty can be overcome, nor does he think he can ever enjoy inner peace. He finds that his mind is too restless and "as difficult to control as the wind." Arjuna asks Krishna what would happen if he becomes deluded or fails in his effort to be detached from the fruits of his labor. He's afraid he will "perish like a rent cloud, supportless, deluded on the path of Brahman [God]."[11]

Krishna reassures Arjuna that even a little practice, even the mere desire to know the truth, will bring great benefits. "O Arjuna, neither in this world, nor in the next world, is there destruction for him; none who does good, O My son, ever comes to grief."[12]

Meanwhile, on the battlefield in ancient India, armies of mighty warriors watch, poised with weapons in hand. Yet Arjuna is oblivious to everything around him except Krishna. He is intent upon understanding why he has to fight. He does not stop pursuing Lord Krishna with his inquiries until he is satisfied with the answers. Krishna never loses patience with Arjuna's tenacious quest. The great hero poses questions, listens attentively, understands partially, asks more questions, and continues to harbor doubts. With each thought-provoking issue, with each explanation from Lord Krishna, Arjuna's heart softens in a progressive and gradual process.

Eventually Arjuna exhausts his more practical queries. At this point in the story, Krishna's words have purified Arjuna's mind, making Arjuna eager to hear about the essence of Krishna himself. Now he tells Arjuna not about the individual person of Krishna, but about the imperishable Supreme Self with which Krishna is identified. In a voice filled with divine honey, the blessed lord says,

> I am the father of this world, the mother, the dispenser of the fruits of actions and the grandfather.[13] ... I am the goal, the supporter, the Lord, the witness, the abode, the shelter, the friend, the origin, the dissolution, the foundation, the treasure-house, and the seed which is imperishable.[14]

Even after hearing such an elaborate portrayal, Arjuna is not content. He wants to know more: "Tell me again in detail, O Krishna, of Your Yogic power and glory; for I am not satisfied with what I have heard of Your life-giving and nectar-like speech."[15]

Arjuna's divine charioteer peels away Arjuna's mental and emotional layers, creates a tender cushioning inside the fibers of his being, and goes on describing his divine powers:

> I am the source of all; from Me everything evolves.[16]
>
> I am the Self seated in the hearts of all beings; I am the beginning, the middle and also the end of all things.[17]
>
> Among weapons I am the thunderbolt; among cows I am the wish-fulfilling cow called Kamadhenu; I am the progenitor, the god of love.[18]

Among the purifiers I am the wind . . . among the fishes I am the shark.[19]

And I am all-devouring Death, and the prosperity of those who are to be prosperous; among the feminine qualities I am fame, prosperity, speech, memory, intelligence, firmness and forgiveness.[20]

Among the seasons I am the flowery season.[21]

I am the splendor of the splendid.[22]

Among secrets I am silence; knowledge among knowers I am.[23]

At the end of the list of qualities, Krishna tantalizes Arjuna with this one statement: "But, of what use is the knowledge of all these details, O Arjuna? I exist, supporting this whole world by one part of Myself."[24]

Arjuna's curiosity is piqued. In the noble manner expected of his times, Arjuna pauses to express gratefulness for hearing about the secret of the Self. But he hungers for more. He yearns to know Krishna's true identity. Arjuna says, "O Supreme Person, I wish to see your cosmic form. If You think it possible for me to see it, O Lord of the Yogins, then show me Your imperishable Self."[25]

Reminiscent of Chandra Pillai's vision of Mother as Devi, Arjuna witnesses Krishna expand and shine with the brilliance of a million suns. The great warrior quivers and shakes at the sight. The hair on his body stands on end as he speaks these words:

Having seen Your immeasurable form with many mouths and eyes, O mighty-armed, with many arms, thighs and feet, with many stomachs and fearful with many teeth—the worlds are terrified and so am I. . . . On seeing Your Cosmic Form touching the sky, shining in many colors, with mouths

wide open, with large fiery eyes, I am terrified at heart and
find neither courage nor peace. . . .[26]

In the midst of his experience Arjuna manages to describe to Krishna a scene from his vision in which all the
warriors, all his uncles, friends, and grandfathers, meet their
demise:

> Verily, just as many torrents of rivers flow towards the ocean,
> even so these heroes in the world of men enter Your flaming
> mouths. As moths hurriedly rush into a blazing fire for their
> own destruction, so also these creatures hurriedly rush into
> Your mouths for their own destruction.[27]

Arjuna falls to his knees, places his palms together in
prayer position, begs for mercy, and asks Krishna to explain
the terrible sight.

Lord Krishna says,

> I am the full-grown world-destroying Time, now engaged in
> destroying the worlds. Even without you, none of the war-
> riors arrayed in the hostile armies shall live. . . . Verily by Me
> have they been already slain; therefore, be a mere instrument,
> O Arjuna.[28]

Filled with tears of joy and exhilaration, Arjuna can barely
speak. He realizes that the person he had dealt with casually
as a friend is one and the same as the divine form that blazes
radiantly in front of him. Even though he always had known
Krishna was an incarnation of God, he had not grasped the
notion fully. Pleading with Krishna to return to his more
easily recognizable human form, Arjuna bows down to him,
prostrates at his feet, and praises him again and again. With
choked voice he says,

I am delighted, having seen what has never been seen before; and yet my mind is distressed with fear. Show me your previous form only, O God; have mercy, O God of gods, O Abode of the universe.[29]

Arjuna calms down when Krishna resumes his more familiar self, wearing golden silk garments and a peacock feather in his long black hair. Like Arjuna, many of us may *want* to see the cosmic form, but the reality of fully unveiled divinity could present us with both an ecstatic and terrifying vision. In Chandra Pillai's case, he would have preferred to remain forever in the vision of Devi.

Krishna reminds Arjuna that what he has seen is rare and that there is only one way to see what he has just witnessed: through surrender, through pure devotion in action. "He who does all actions for Me, who looks upon Me as the Supreme, who is devoted to Me, who is free from attachment, who bears enmity towards no creature, he comes to Me, O Arjuna."[30]

Without any trace of doubt, Arjuna's vision of Krishna's cosmic form, which is no less than the rising and burning of Mother Kundalini, shows him that he is only a vehicle for the divine, that he is not the doer. He has seen that all the warriors who oppose him in battle are like moths flying into a flame, into all-devouring time, to their own destruction. Death is inevitable.

Arjuna now understands that he must fight to fulfill his life purpose; he must enter the battle as a sacramental offering.

However, even though Arjuna recognizes that the key to inner peace is to engage in this particular war with an attitude of compassion and detachment, he wants to know how. How can he continue to perform his duty in life and at the same time be freed from the wheel of karma, the cycle of birth and death? How can he practice divine surrender on a daily basis?

Krishna says,

> He who is the same in pleasure and pain, who dwells in the Self, to whom a clod of earth, stone and gold are alike, who is the same to the dear and the unfriendly, who is firm, and to whom censure and praise are as one, who is the same in honor and dishonor, the same to friend and foe. . . .[31]

Krishna says that rather than being bound by a "hundred ties of hope," we can liberate ourselves forever by nurturing qualities such as straightforwardness, harmlessness, charity, gentleness, modesty, and purity of heart.[32] Throughout the entire *Gita*, Krishna describes many attitudes to adopt for helping to close the gates of endless suffering.

The Bhagavad Gita ends with these words from the blind king's seer:

> Thus I have heard this wonderful dialogue between Krishna and the high-souled Arjuna, which causes the hair to stand on end. . . . Wherever is Krishna, the Lord of Yoga; wherever is Arjuna, the wielder of the bow, there are prosperity, victory, happiness and firm policy; such is my conviction.[33]

≈

Love in Daily Routines or, Work as Worship

Wherever your work be—in the kitchen, the cowshed or the toilet— let that be your temple.[34] . . . If one puts his [her] heart and soul into an activity, it will be transformed into a tremendous source of inspiration.[35]
                                                            —Ammachi

As mentioned in Part IV, at my ashram in Pennsylvania we used to read aloud one chapter from *The Bhagavad Gita* twice a day after meditation. The more I heard it, the more it penetrated into my psyche. I would remember parts of it while cooking, cleaning, or working in the garden. I would attempt to apply its principles to any work at hand. It helped me approach my daily tasks in a sacred way.

When I took my first retreat in the Pennsylvania ashram, we were taught how to use *The Bhagavad Gita* as a guide in one of the first tasks we were asked to do: cleaning the bathrooms with a toothbrush, and keeping silence while we worked. We were to imagine that our hands and the toothbrush were instruments of the divine and that the tiles, grout, and porcelain toilet bowl were manifestations of the supreme. We were to focus on the task only, not the outcome.

Most of us thought this to be an absurd notion in the beginning, until we had done it a few times. After a few days of this activity—it took over an hour to clean one very small bathroom—I was surprised to find a sense of peace and timelessness come over me. My negative attitude toward the cleaning job gradually shifted into one of love.

Children, you should develop an attitude of bowing down to anything and everything. Keep the plate of food in front of you and bow down to the food before eating and bow down to the plate after eating. An attitude to prostrate to anything at any time should come. In this way, an awareness, "for what am I doing this," will arise. . . . Prostrate to the cloth you will wear. Bow down to the water with which you will take a shower. During these occasions of bowing down, you will have a pure resolve to see the same consciousness in everything whether with form or without.

—Ammachi

Two years later, long after my many bathroom cleaning exercises were over, my negative attitude reappeared. My guru had put me in a position of leadership, organizing the office, developing programs, and assuming some of the responsibility for keeping the ashram's daily schedule. Eventually, I became quite proud, and I failed at being kind and compassionate in my role. In response, my guru at the time asked me to remain silent, to eat meals in my room in the bungalow, and to spend the day cleaning all six bathrooms (not with only a toothbrush!), including the two outhouses, and when I was done with that, to pick weeds.

Obviously my guru felt I needed to do some inner reflecting. Actually, I was delighted to be in silence and by myself, but I was incensed about having to scrub bathrooms. I thought I had already had that lesson. In protest, I didn't clean perfectly. To further challenge my pride, a fellow devotee reprimanded me for my negligence—I had missed some dust on ledges and in corners. Picking weeds gave me a chance to be outdoors where no one bothered me, but even in that I didn't attempt to do my best.

> *The mind is nothing but thoughts. Thoughts, when intense,*
> *become actions. Actions, when repeated, become habits. Habits*
> *form character. Therefore, to get rid of the mind, first we should*
> *change the quality of our thoughts.*[36]   —Ammachi

I couldn't stop my negative thinking. I kept hoping my guru wouldn't notice and would let me quit latrine and weed duty. After a couple of weeks of this *tapas* I realized that by refusing to change my attitude and by resisting, not surrendering, I was the cause of my own suffering. When I accepted my failure in the leadership position and gave in to the task at hand, I began to feel inner peace and joy.

From that moment on, I began to sing devotional songs while scrubbing and to concentrate on cleaning with feelings of love. Outside during weed picking, another change took place. I discovered that the unwanted plants had a particular sound if I pulled them out just so. This delicate crunching noise meant I had gotten all the root. Just to be able to hear that perfect separation between root and earth, I would use my bare hands so that I could hold the weed exactly where it came up from the ground, squeeze it gently, and pull. After a few weeks of singing in the bathroom and listening to weeds, I began to feel an inexplicable love that ran through me nearly every day for the remainder of my four months of this activity.

While these joyous feelings did not remain with me always, this training set the foundation for me to be able to bring love into any task when I remember to do so.

> *Do not talk while working. . . . Replace talking with the singing of*
> *the Divine Name. In this way you will be able to stop the inner*
> *babbling. Glorifying or praising the Lord is, in fact, the process of*
> *awakening your own inner Self.*[37]   —Ammachi

Bringing love into any job is still another way to practice surrender. One secret is to try to live in the moment, releasing the attempt to control the past and future. Ammachi explains: "The past and future are movements of the mind. . . . The mind attains a state of stillness when it rests in the present moment. . . . That is what is known as remembrance of God."[38]

However, trying to live moment by moment may seem impractical in day-to-day living, especially when we have a family and a job. Ammachi gives some very sound advice. She says that for an ordinary person who has worldly responsibilities to completely forget the past and the future isn't possible. And we don't have to do that. Yet when there is pressure for perfection on the job, for meeting deadlines, or for getting household tasks done, it is best not to have interference from the past and the future. Such worries will prevent us from carrying out our duties properly.

Ammachi reminds us that an action always takes place in the present moment. To be able to carry it out well, using all our talents and capabilities, we have to concentrate 100 percent on the work at hand in the moment. Brooding or dreaming about something else will interfere with our concentration. Ammachi suggests that before we begin any task, we should consider relevant past mistakes or failures, make all calculations and planning, prepare the mind beforehand for the job we are about to do. Once the work has begun, all our attention should be on what we are doing at that time. Ammachi says that if we are in the middle of a task and we remember something related to the job, "pause, go to the repository of the past, and find what you need to know. Then come out of there and continue with what you were doing, putting all your heart and soul into it."[39]

In the Love in Daily Routines practice, use the above stories and suggestions, including the teachings from *The Bhagavad Gita*. Try changing your mental attitude toward work for a few hours each day. Whatever your job—professional or domestic—make the effort to approach it as a sacramental offering. Ammachi explains further:

> The product of an action performed with love will have a discernible presence of life and light in it. That reality of life and love will fill peoples' minds with immense attraction.
>
> Life is a precious gift. The human body is a rare gift. Work with love while you are still healthy.... Do your work and

perform your duties with all your heart. Try to work self-lessly with love. Pour yourself into whatever you do. Then you will feel and experience beauty and love in every field of work. Love and beauty are within you. Try to express them through your actions and you will definitely touch the very source of bliss.[40]

≈

Love Can Blossom
Even Out of the
Darkest Shadow

There is love and Love. You love your
family. . . . But you do not love your
neighbor. . . . You love your son or daughter,
but you do not love all children. You love
your father and mother, but you do not love
everyone. . . . Hence, this is not Love; it is
only love. Transformation of this love to Love
is the goal of spirituality. In the fullness of
Love blossoms the beautiful, fragrant flower
of compassion.   —Ammachi

When the unbreakable bond with the beloved has been
established, surrender spontaneously occurs. In this way,
love can grow in the most unusual or even the most impossible of situations. It is a well-known fact that the lotus
blossom—a flower used in Hindu symbolism to represent
Lakshmi or Kamala, the goddess of love, abundance, and
beauty—grows out of slime and muck. The following
story illustrates the unfathomable way in which love trans-
forms. In her diaries, *An Interrupted Life,*[1] Etty Hillesum, a
sophisticated Jewess from Holland during the Nazi era,
describes her relationship with her analyst, Julius Spier,
whom she refers to as "S." Out of one of the blackest shad-

ows of our century blossomed a love beyond most human understanding.

Etty Hillesum describes herself before she met the man who was to transform her life and initiate the opening of her heart: "Deep down something like a tightly-wound ball of twine binds me relentlessly and at times I am nothing more or less than a miserable, frightened creature. . . ."[2] Recognizing that something inside her was "locked away," she sought the help of Spier, who worked with clients in an unusual way. He wrestled with them, not a normally recommended form of therapy. After the physical rolling around, he would discuss issues that came up and proceed from this base. According to many clients, he was endowed with an unusual ability to offer a detached but profound love, resulting in emotional and physical transformation beyond the scope of most psychological settings.

In the beginning Etty's feelings about him were mixed. Sometimes she felt disgusted with him. At other times she was arrogant and didn't think his work could benefit her. Occasionally she "fell under the spell of the inner freedom that seemed to emanate from him, of the suppleness, ease, and singular grace of his heavy body."[3] Yet she admitted that within one week "he worked wonders with me, almost in spite of myself. Gymnastics, breathing exercises, and illuminating, liberating words about my depression, my attitude to others and the like. Suddenly I was living differently, more freely, more flowingly. . . ."[4]

Within the first few sessions, Etty Hillesum established herself as different from his other clients when one day she threw him on the floor during one of their wrestling matches, something that no one else had ever done. And, over time, she did it again and again. She explains why she was impressed in these potentially embarrassing moments:

He was so "free," so guileless, so open, so unaffected in his movements, even as we tumbled about together on the ground. And even when I, held tightly in his arms and finally tamed, lay under him, he remained "objective," pure, while I surrendered to the physical spell he emanated. It all seemed so innocent, this wrestling, new and unexpected, and so liberating. It was not until later that it took hold of my fantasies.[5]

Most of Spier's female clients were infatuated with him, but it was with Etty that he invited intimacy beyond the client-professional relationship. In the beginning, in part because he was thirty years older, in part because he was her therapist, she didn't notice how much she loved him. Gradually, haltingly, she opened to her love for him, recognized that her feelings for him didn't fall into the category of her expectations of romantic love. They both grappled with classic inner battles between spirit and matter—she sometimes would comment that physical lovemaking with him rarely equaled the immensity of the love she felt.

In the beginning, Etty was often torn with jealousy, wanted to own him, have him all to herself. The budding stages of intimacy were fraught with the usual doubts, the well-known feelings of despair that can come up with any couple at different junctures throughout their relationship. Even though they each had separate lovers—Etty, the man she lived with, and Spier, a woman in England to whom he was betrothed—the love they had for each other became so all-consuming, so full of dignity and respect, that something unusual happened. In a slow, hesitating fashion, they moved beyond the normal boundaries of temporal love and sank down inside themselves to divine love.

During her psychological, philosophical, and spiritual training with Spier, Etty became relentless with herself, always turning difficulty into an opportunity to examine her own inner workings. When World War II broke out and many complained with great bitterness, Etty wrote in her diary, "I believe that I will never be able to hate any human being for his so-called 'wickedness,' that I shall only hate the evil that is within me, though hate is perhaps putting it too strongly even then."[6]

Etty and Spier's relationship blossomed during the insidious infiltration of Holland by the Nazi regime. As Jews, they were made to follow restrictions that were not too offensive in the beginning, but that grew more and more intolerable and menacing as time passed. At first it was simply a matter of wearing Stars of David to mark them as Jews, then they were made to take their daily strolls on back streets, then they were not allowed to ride bicycles or public buses or be seen in public parks. When Etty's feet were covered with blisters from having to walk long distances, she blamed no one and mustered up a humorous, often philosophical mental attitude.

While Jews were being banned from grocery stores, prohibited from playing pianos, and sent to concentration camps, Etty noticed that Spier, also a Jew, focused not on the harassment of the times, but on his patients. She wrote, "[He] sees six patients a day and gives all he has to each one. He breaks them open and draws out the poison and delves down to the sources where God hides Himself away."[7]

The Nazi invasion caused Etty to suffer both physically and emotionally, but the attitude she developed toward the gradual infusion of the German occupation was out of the ordinary, as is evident from these words in her diary:

We must learn to shoulder our common fate; everyone who seeks to save himself must surely realize that if he does not go another must take his place. As if it really mattered which of us goes. Ours is now a common destiny and that is something we must not forget.[8] . . . Most of us in the West don't understand the art of suffering and experience a thousand fears instead. We cease to be alive, being full of fear, bitterness, hatred and despair. God knows, it's only too easy to understand why. But when we are deprived of our lives, are we really deprived of very much?[9]

Westerbork concentration camp was established in Holland as a holding place for Jews who eventually would be sent to such sites as Auschwitz. Etty had connections and was able to locate a job that would keep her from being forced to go. However, she did not want to be treated differently; if her people were going to suffer, she wanted to be with them, so she entered herself into the camp.

Her own words best describe how her love for another human being had grown into an all-encompassing love. Etty had been released from the Jews' stark barracks because of illness when she wrote:

Those two months behind barbed wire have been the two richest and most intense months of my life, in which my highest values were so deeply confirmed. I have learned to love Westerbork.[10] How is it that this stretch of heath land surrounded by barbed wire, through which so much human misery has flooded, nevertheless remains inscribed in my memory as something almost lovely? How is it that my spirit, far from being oppressed, seemed to grow lighter and brighter there? . . . There among the barracks, full of hunted and persecuted people, I found confirmation of my love of life.[11]

During her convalescence, Spier, who had not yet been required to enter a concentration camp, died a natural death. During her mourning, Etty recalled having written:

> My heart will always fly to you like a bird, from any place on earth, and it will surely find you. . . . You had become so much a part of the Heaven that stretches above me that I had only to raise up my eyes to be by your side. And even if they flung me into a dungeon, that piece of Heaven would still spread out within me and my heart would fly up to it like a bird. . . .[12]
>
> We used to feel so certain that we would help each other bear the sorrows of our age. Now he lies a wasted corpse under a stone . . . yet . . . I was able to commit myself unreservedly to another, to bind myself to him and to share his sorrow. And did he not lead me to God, after first paving the way with his imperfect human hand?[13]

Etty was warned that she probably would not be allowed out of the camp again if she were to go back, that the barbed wire and the SS guards had been increased. However, she would not be stopped from joining the fate of her people. In the few days she had before returning to Westerbork, she wrote:

> God, grant me the great and mighty calm that pervades all nature. If it is Your wish to let me suffer, then let it be one great, all-consuming suffering, not the thousand petty anxieties that can break a human being. Give me peace and confidence. . . . All those worries about food, about clothing, about the cold, about our health—are they not so many denials of You, my God?[14]

In Westerbork, she spent most of her time consoling and helping others. When there was time, she would find some corner where she would write letters to friends on bits of paper.

> You know, if you don't have the inner strength while you're here to understand that all outer appearances are a passing show, as nothing beside the great splendor (I can't think of a better word right now) inside us—then things can look very black here indeed. Completely wretched, in fact, as they must look to those pathetic people who have lost their last towel, who struggle ... with moldy bread ... who are miserable when other people shout at them or are unkind, but who shout at others themselves without a thought; or to those poor abandoned children whose parents have been sent on transport, and who are ignored by the other mothers. ... You should see these poor mothers sitting beside the cots of their wailing young in blank and brute despair.[15]

In the few weeks before she was to be transported to a more final destination, Etty worried about her parents—she did not want to watch them suffer. As she watched many cargo trains being loaded with Jews, she would have moments of struggle with prejudice and terror upon seeing "oafish, jeering faces [of the guards], in which one seeks in vain for even the slightest trace of human warmth."[16] Yet in the midst of watching unimaginable cruelty and agony, she wrote:

> You have made me so rich, oh God, please let me share out Your beauty with open hands. My life has become an uninterrupted dialogue with You, oh God, one great dialogue. Sometimes when I stand in some corner of the camp, my feet planted on Your earth, my eyes raised towards Your Heaven, tears sometimes run down my face, tears of deep emotion

and gratitude. At night, too, when I lie in my bed and rest in You, oh God, tears of gratitude run down my face, and that is my prayer ... [that] all my creative powers are translated into inner dialogues with You; the beat of my heart has grown deeper, more active and yet more peaceful, and it is as if I were all the time storing up inner riches.[17]

Etty's last diary entries were in Westerbork, September 1943. She died in Auschwitz in November 1943, at the age of twenty-nine. Those she had left behind in the Nazi concentration camp in Holland spoke of her sparkling humor and of the love and kindness she had given them.

> *The more you love a person, the more you surrender to him. This is what happens even in a normal love affair between a man and a woman. The lover and the beloved surrender to each other's wishes and wills, as the love between them grows into fullness. His likes become hers and vice versa. Surrender is nothing but giving up one's individuality, giving up one's likes and dislikes for a higher goal. Even in ordinary love both the lover and the beloved give up their likes and dislikes, which constitute their individuality, for the sake of their love. In spirituality, the seeker renounces all that he has to the Supreme Principle, God.[18]* —Ammachi

The example of Etty Hillesum's story, her uncompromising surrender to the conditions in the concentration camp, her compassion to others, her acceptance of the inhumanity of the Nazi guards, is testimony to the absolute peace that pure love brings. Etty's ability to view the blatant tragedy of her outer world was colored by the mirror of her inner character. Etty's life story, her relatively commonplace beginnings, her transfiguration through love, and her confrontation with one of history's worst travesties against humanity, offers hope for our own spiritual transformation.

For some of us, to greet all circumstances in life with divine love might take years of rehearsal, as shown in my own stories throughout this book. I began my spiritual practices in 1970 and, for whatever reason, still do not feel love under all circumstances. What is it that propels me forward? It is the memory of unconditional love and the absolute peace of it; it is in hearing stories such as Etty Hillesum's; it is reveling in the celebration of life in nature: birds singing, rain moistening a lush forest, deer grazing in a meadow, streams gurgling over rocks, flowers carpeting an alpine meadow.

Still, many of us might wonder about the necessity for travail in life. When asked why there is sorrow in the world, Ammachi had said that without sadness we would not grow spiritually. Ammachi's own childhood is yet another example of the benefit of approaching difficulties with an attitude of unconditional love. No matter how much Ammachi's parents chastised and beat her, no matter how much housework she did in a day, Ammachi became more and more firm in her resolve to hold her beloved Krishna in her heart every second of every day. Her love of Krishna alone brought happiness.

Ammachi tells us that one way to approach surrender is to remember the possibility of death. Arjuna, when facing the demise of his dear ones, finally succumbed to his weakness, leaving his heart open to listen to Krishna. Etty Hillesum's confrontation with death propelled her into a constant communion with God. Personally, I have difficulty trying to remember about death all the time, but when I do my life is richer because I act out of today, not tomorrow. My brushes with death through skin cancer and asthma have taught me about the value of powerlessness and failure, and that divine love is the only refuge. Ammachi suggests that in the presence of death our sense of helplessness contributes to learning humility. She explains that "humility is surrender; surrender is bowing low to all existence. Then there can be no ego. Once you become egoless, there is no more death."

Part VI

Contentment and Yearning

When you see life, and all that life brings you, as a precious gift, you will be able to say yes to everything.

—Ammachi

Saying Yes
to Everything

*Contentment comes only when you are
surrendered, only when you have the attitude
of complete acceptance. . . . A contented
person will have enthusiasm and vigor . . .
[and the attitude] that life and everything
that happens in life is a gift.*   —Ammachi

My relationship to Mother intensified my long-time desire
to swim with dolphins, close relatives to the whale, one of
my original symbols for the great Mother. I believed being
with dolphins in the wild was the only major experience I
still seriously wanted before giving up my life as I knew it.

A couple of years ago in India I decided to go on my first
bus trip with Ammachi. I'd heard about these trips—the
crowded conditions, the long hours, the absence of bathroom stops. Until now I had avoided these journeys because
I was too sick and a little afraid of more *tapas.* Many devotees had reported that the most difficult of all these trips
with Amma was the one to Calicut, a thirteen-hour ride to
northern Kerala. This year I was well and in a mood to go.
My mind was relishing saying yes to everything.

Feeling like a child about to venture out on its first picnic,
I climbed onto one of the three buses and settled into my as-
signed seat. Just before the coaches were ready to roll away,
about fifteen Indian ashram resident women scrambled on

board, filling the aisles. I thought, "My God! Are they going to travel standing up? Or was there some mistake?" When the drivers started the engines and revved the motors, I realized it was no error; quickly I offered to hold some of their parcels in my lap. At first they hesitated, but when I insisted they handed me a couple of their satchels. I noticed only two or three other Western women following suit.

After an hour and a half or so, the buses pulled off onto the side of the road. Oh great! A chance to pee! I thought. But soon was surprised to notice that only the men got off. At my age, sometimes there is a sense of urgency about the need to urinate. I got a little worried. I expressed my concern to one outspoken woman who then turned to the one in charge and said in a loud voice, "Savitri has to go to the toilet!" I was a little embarrassed and also relieved. Following after me, all the women got down from the bus and used the primitive facilities of some kind person who lived in the house near where we had stopped. Then Ammachi's white car seemed to appear out of nowhere. I was thrilled and started to run to her, but noticed everyone standing at a respectful distance, so I did, too. After I returned to the bus, a veteran of touring with Amma snapped, "There's something you need to know about traveling with Amma: only the men get off, no peeing, and it doesn't mean anything when Mother drives up."

I responded, "But it did mean something."

She raised her eyebrows disdainfully. "What?" she said.

"It was fun," I answered.

About an hour later we stopped again, this time for a picnic. All the food, cooked in the morning before departure and stored on top of the coaches, was served to us by Ammachi. Everyone was in a meditative mood and ate in silence while birds chirped and crows chattered, waiting in the coconut palms, ready to swoop down to grab a stray morsel.

Amma advised us to hurry; otherwise we wouldn't make it to the river before dark. Amma loves to swim. Since we all were looking forward to a dip in the water with her, we scurried back to our seats and the buses roared away. After some time, I got up to offer my place to one of the Indian women, and so did three or four other Westerners. It was a heartwarming way to share. At one point my seatmate was standing and I was sitting, chatting with one of the Indian women who spoke nearly perfect English; she was very curious about my background. After some time, she said, "I'd better get up now or Mother will scold me for being lazy." Her remark helped me understand why they had been so reluctant in the beginning to hand over their parcels—this bus tour was a form of *tapas* for them, as it was for all of us. It was not meant to be a pleasure trip; we were to chant our mantras, not waste energy talking to our neighbors, and, if possible, hold our urine.

Nevertheless, my mood of contentment made everything about the trip a source of immense inner joy for me—the crowded conditions, the small seats, the bumpy roads, even the irritable moods of some. As I stood, swaying with the curves, giving with my knees to the bumps, I saw a river and got very excited. "Surely we will stop soon, before it gets dark," I thought. But no; we sped along next to the river for an hour, then away into villages and clusters of thatched huts. The swim with Mother, one of the aspects of the trip I was especially looking forward to, seemed to be slipping into dusk.

Now, long after I'd sat down and night had fallen, I was more or less resigned that we wouldn't go swimming. All at

once we pulled over. "Why are we stopping?" I said, knowing it was too early for us to have arrived at Calicut.

"The river is here," said one of the Indian women.

Still quite comfortable with whatever would happen, yet
still yearning to swim with Mother, I asked, "Should we take
our suits?" We were to have kept either a swim dress or Punjabi outfit in a plastic bag for swimming.

One Western ashram resident said, "No. It's too dark."

More than one Indian girl said, "Bring your suit."

Some of us agreed that the Indians would know best
about the chances for swimming, so I brought my Punjabi
set. Outside it was black. No moon. My eyesight is not that
great at night. One of the Indian girls held my hand down
the dirt road to the wide, sandy banks of the river. We rested
at the river's edge, clustered around Mother, who sat in a
folding chair giving *darshan* to villagers who happened to be
on the beach or had gotten wind of her presence. I lay down,
happy to be on my back, yet wishing we could swim. Finally,
I asked Ammachi's personal attendant if Mother was going
to swim later. She frowned and said curtly, "How can we in
the dark?"

I didn't know the answer, but I also knew that with
Mother, anything is possible. After about an hour of hugging
villagers, Amma looked around at all of us, then said in English, "Swimming? Disappointed?"

Some said yes under their breaths, but most, including
myself, kept very quiet, glancing at one another like children
not sure of the rules of the game. Suddenly Mother got up,
wandered away from the group to sit in the sand; someone
lit a candle and propped it up next to her. I happened to be
resting right there and felt pleasure in my good fortune as
others crowded in. All at once Amma changed places again.
Most everyone rustled after her but I remained by the can-

dle, somehow hoping she would return. I could tell by the silent shuffling of the group that she had shifted again, and then again—a game of hide-and-seek in the night.

Time lost all meaning. I had no idea how long we'd been on the beach when suddenly a police car drove down the dirt road and two policemen got out of a jeep carrying Coleman lanterns. Lights, I thought as I peered here and there trying to see where Ammachi was. Then I happened to spot her in her red swim dress heading for the river. I scurried after her, ripped off my clothes, got into my "suit," and was one of the first of the hundred or so to splash into the knee-deep water's edge. Amma was pushing some devotees in. I longed for her to do the same to me. With a big smile on my face, I shuffled very slowly toward her, inviting her with my mind to dunk me. In what seemed like an eternal second, her hand snapped out, fast as a karate chop, grazing me in the chest with such force that I flopped onto my back, fully submerged.

A deep yearning to swim alongside Amma rose into my heart; I imagined myself paddling next to her. She swims like a dolphin, I'd heard, literally wiggles her body and doesn't use her arms. I am a good swimmer and was confident I'd be able to keep up. However, my desire seemed fruitless as I stood in the chest-deep water at the outer edge of the dense circle of devotees crowded around her. Suddenly she disappeared under the water and emerged right next to me, undulating down the river. I thrashed after her in my best speed-racing mode, rubbing slightly against her body. Then, without realizing it, I was floating downstream, alone, after she had abruptly stopped. Again she was surrounded by devotees, and once more I looked on longingly, thinking surely it had been an accident that she slipped through the crowd and appeared where I just happened to be standing. All at once she sank underwater. Everyone was looking here and there to see where she'd gone. Then, after slithering through the devotees, she broke the water where I stood and led me swimming downstream next to her.

I was in bliss. No longer needing to be near her, knowing there was no mistake that she had singled me out, I floated in the warm river water gazing at the expanse of stars in the heaven above. I didn't even notice when Mother left the river. By the time I'd gone to shore and changed my clothes, Ammachi was sitting next to a fire, still in her swim dress with a white towel wrapped around her shoulders, stirring a huge pot of chai, a milky spiced tea. We sang devotional songs while we waited for our hot drink.

The next morning during the chanting of the thousand names of the Mother of the Universe, my mind drifted to my river experience, to Ammachi and the billions of stars overhead. In a flash I realized that she was my dolphin and I the baby, wiggling my tail as fast as I could to keep up with my mother.

The above story reveals aspects of stage six along the Path of the Mother, in which feelings of contentment and yearning enter in, playing back and forth. In this stage we are more serene, more balanced. Sadness, anger, despair, happiness, and joy are experienced as enriching sensations, flowing through us as naturally as waves lapping onto the shore. Our lives are more harmonious, not necessarily the occurrences themselves, but rather the way in which we perceive them. Our minds are not so bothered by the past or the future, or by what someone said or did, or at least we let uncomfortable feelings come and go more easily than we used to. Since we don't tend to cling to past events or worry about the future, a quiet space is created inside of us in which we yearn for Mother to be with us in everything we do and say.

In this stage we begin to realize that everything we do is guided by Mother. Her consistent patience with all our concerns—health, finances, relationships—has opened our hearts so that we now trust almost every aspect of her motherhood. Her dedicated concern for our every desire has brought us to a point where we feel a comfortable faith in her counsel.

It is said that Mother will give us everything we want until the day we want what she wants to give us: merging as one with the absolute. In stage six, no matter what our life task is—householder, professional, or renunciate—our desire for objects of the material world begins to fade. We become content with very little because we recognize that our wealth lies in Mother's love.

In ancient Hinduism, during the third stage of life,[1] after the children are raised, elderly couples used to retire to the forest to an ashram or special meditation hut. The husband and wife would leave the cares of the world behind and begin focusing on the supreme. In the present-day world, this loss of interest in accumulating wealth and temporal pleasure is a very gradual process that can happen at any time. While it can enrich our lives to experience this stage in our early years, it is bound to happen as we approach old age and death.

No matter how old we are, in the later spiraling of stage six, Mother becomes our only goal in life. The more empty our minds become, the more we might cry out like small children asking Mother to come closer. At this point, a fire kindles within, and we develop an intense longing to be identified with her, with the universal self.

*   *

Cathi Schmidt, a small cheerful woman with wide-open hazel eyes, and the wife of Steve Schmidt, is an example of a person for whom the objects of the physical world hold little interest, and for whom contentment and yearning prevail. However, before she experienced this sixth stage along the path, she endured many years of despair. Even though Cathi seemed to have everything anyone could ever want—healthy children, a good husband, financial security, a beautiful home on thirty-five acres, and a sound body—she yearned for something beyond all of this, but she didn't know what was missing.

Before meeting Steve, Cathi had moved to Santa Fe after having lost her mother, a couple of friends, and some pets. She was in a deep depression until finally she couldn't stand to be alive. One day she said, "Okay, God, you just do something, or get me out of here, right now! This is the very, very end of my rope. I'm finished." After that, Cathi said,

> Something happened—the whole air around me, everything changed. From that instant onward I had this feeling of impending greatness, with the thought that something really incredible was about to happen. It was the most wonderful thing in my whole life to have been down as far as I could get, and suddenly to have this hand reach down and seem to say, "All right, I'll rescue you. It's going to be all right, just wait a few more weeks."

Three weeks later Cathi received a phone call from a friend inviting her to a party. She and her friends drove out of Santa Fe into the hills along a long dirt road, and finally arrived at a little stone house among piñons and ponderosa pines. When Cathi walked into the house, she saw a fellow sitting on the floor, introduced herself to him, and found out he'd moved to Santa Fe only two days before. She secretly harbored feelings of superiority that she'd been in Santa Fe for two whole months. As they sat talking, Cathi thought Steve was a nice guy but not exactly her type. However, it turned out he was looking for someone to build a fence to enclose a yard for his dog, and Cathi had been studying carpentry. Steve hired her to put the fence together, and after that they started going out.

Cathi described what happened:

There was more to the meeting with Steve than a cute guy with a dog: he was studying yoga and had a guru. All my life I'd had these philosophical beliefs about the oneness of everything, and that there could be only one God for all religions. But I'd never read anything about it and didn't know there were millions of people in India following a similar philosophy. So when I met Steve and saw pictures of his guru, I got curious. When Steve started telling me about his guru's teachings, right then and there I saw a soul mate in Steve. He was the first person I ever knew who believed exactly the same way I did. Meeting with this wonderful man marked the end of my big depression. Not only did he become my best friend, but also the one who opened the way to my spiritual life. I now knew what the feeling of impending greatness had been.

Eventually Steve and Cathi got married and had two children. Since 1974 they'd been attending *satsang* with a group that had the same guru in common. Later they held the devotional singing in their home every Friday night. Then, their guru of that time died, and their association with that spiritual group ceased. After the calamity of the death of their guru, Steve and Cathi maintained a Friday-night *sat-sang* in their home. Cathi describes her dilemma with regard to that group:

> The music was always the same and I was so bored with it, so desirous of some other way. I even thought of joining a jazz band or a rock group, because musically there was nothing appealing to me about our *satsang* chanting.
>
> Soon another incredible thing happened. Steve and I had been living on five acres of land. The neighbors there were upset because we had horses. Since we didn't want to bother our neighbors, we tried to find another plot. After looking for a long time without results, we decided to move to another town. That exact day we found land advertised in the paper—the very land where we'd met in the little stone house. It was amazing. We'd never dreamed in our wildest imagination we could buy this land. It was too sacred to us, too special. The exhilaration after having purchased this land was so great it took away my boredom with the music and with not having a guru in the body.
>
> After we built our adobe home, it was very clear that I had everything anyone could ever have wanted. However, I was happy for a short time only. Even though I wasn't struggling in any way, something was wrong. Life felt hollow. I had to force myself to deal with life; I had to force myself to be happy and not morose. I would walk around every day wondering what was the matter, wondering why I felt that some huge piece was missing out of my life. It was as though a fire had gone out, and everything inside me was all charcoal and ashes. I was very depressed and didn't know what to do. I felt guilty looking at all the people who weren't married and wanted to be, who didn't have kids and wanted children, who didn't have money, or food, or a house, and wanted all of these. I felt ashamed for feeling so low all the time.
>
> Right in the middle of my dark mood, out of the blue,

came Earl. He'd joined our meditation group and was talking about a woman guru called Ammachi. I thought, That's nice. A woman guru. Interesting. The next week Earl brought a videotape of Ammachi hugging everyone. Seeing this, I had no doubt that she was a saint. Then Earl said, Oh, by the way, she's coming to America and to New Mexico.

At the time I didn't think a person should have a second guru, but I didn't mind helping this woman saint out if she needed it, and actually thought it would be an honor to do so. Earl asked us if we would host her in our house, which we were happy to do. In the process, I never considered I would have anything to do with her beyond that.

Meanwhile Steve was having experiences: he'd start crying when he'd think about Ammachi or when he'd play one of her old *bhajan* tapes. I thought that was interesting and great that this was happening to him, but was certain nothing like that was going to take place for me. Nevertheless, I was excited she was coming, and got on the phone to tell as many people as I could about it. I didn't want to be embarrassed that she would come all this way and there'd be no one here for her programs.

Then Ammachi came and we got caught up in a whirlwind of exciting peace. It was the most peaceful yet chaotic experience I could ever have imagined. We always had the house clean, neat, and tidy. We were too old for the days when everyone used to come and crash in our living room. We had a guest room for that purpose. Our house, which we normally were pretty uptight about, was a mess within minutes after Ammachi arrived. As soon as Mother came, everyone went into the kitchen and started cooking; the whole place was in shambles—all the cleaning I'd done for four months—clothes all over the laundry room, mustard seeds in oil, and spices all over the kitchen, including weird bags of unknown substances, and plates of food that someone was trying to hide in every cabinet, and sleeping bags all over. It was just amazing. But I just loved it because all the people traveling with Mother were all so adorable, so humble and unpretentious.

I remember thinking before they came that this was going to be a test case, because if I experienced them as uptight, I wasn't ever going to ever do this again. I'd no more interest in being involved with tense and inflexible people like the ones surrounding my previous guru. After the first half hour I clearly saw that was not going to be the case. This group of young Indian men and one Australian woman, Mother's personal attendant, were so humble about everything. They were constantly apologizing and expressing how sad they were that they'd made a mess in the kitchen or that they didn't know to put the shower curtain inside the bathtub, causing the bathrooms to flood. They never made me feel as though they were saying to themselves, "We're the holy people in your house, and you should be so honored that we're here." It wasn't like that at all. They were always making us feel like we were the special ones and they were the ones that were causing all the trouble. I fell in love with them all.

Just to give an idea of how chaotic it was, many of the people who came to meet Mother for the first time never left; they were sleeping all over the living room, the dining room. We'd be walking over bodies when we got up in the morning. We'd go in to use the bathroom and find a stranger in the shower. It was like this for a couple of weeks. We were in such a cloud of sweet euphoria, we didn't really mind at all.

Meanwhile the whole entourage, including those Americans who had met Mother for the first time, came and went from Taos a couple of times. I stayed behind to clean the house, scrubbing the bathrooms, the kitchen, and cleaning the carpets. On one of those occasions Mother came back from Taos while I was vacuuming. I wasn't expecting her when she walked through the front door and disappeared down the hall into her room. I'd put a soft, white towel in the bathroom and she was wearing it like a shawl. It was so adorable. Now I'll never part with that towel. A week later, the day she was leaving Santa Fe for good, she said to me, "Mother feels so sad, Mother feels so sorry that she didn't stop and talk to you when you were cleaning the carpets, but Mother had been up all night and she was so tired."

I was so touched by her concern. Yet her kindness was just one example of many experiences I'd had with Ammachi: I'd sometimes be feeling so full of love for her, then something like that would happen in which she would show me what infinite love was. It was the same with humility: I'd be feeling so humble in her presence, then I'd look at her concern with every detail of someone's life, and say to myself, "Oh, but that's infinite humility."

I was drawn in. After about the first three days, I remember crying a little bit and thinking, If I really let myself love Mother and I accept her as my guru, that's going to mean I have to completely bury the first one; I'll have to admit he's dead and gone and that's it. And that's what I did; then and there I accepted that Mother was really going to be it now.

If somebody had told me, You're going to meet a beautiful woman who will be your mother for you, your divine deity, your inspirational guru, and, in addition, the greatest musician alive who will teach you and bring you a gift of the most beautiful music you've ever heard, I would think, Get a life! That's not going to happen. But that's exactly what did happen. I would have been afraid to have conceived of someone so extraordinary. I didn't want to admit my deepest desires, because I didn't think I deserved to have them come true.

While Mother was in our home, I'd cry incessantly. Partly I was crying out of relief that someone like Mother existed, and simultaneously out of the pain that she would not be standing there in the hall for the rest of my life. In these times of despair, she'd look at me and say, "Smile." In the beginning, I couldn't understand why she gave me this simple directive.

Even though Mother had told us she would come back to Santa Fe, I was extremely sad when she left. Her departure was the beginning of the big thing that would happen every year for about the first five or six years. After we got over the shock and the wonderfulness of it, we knew it would be many months before we would see her again. We had to settle back into life, and I didn't want to. I wanted to get back to having Mother here and fifteen people asleep on the floor. Once having experienced that, I didn't want to let it go. I hadn't felt that good in my whole life. I didn't want to go back to not feeling good.

Meanwhile, the euphoria of the visit tapered off, and I started sinking down into depression again. At the same time, I was never completely the same: something inside had changed. Where it had been totally dark, there now was this little light. Mother'd started to turn on the light inside and so the black tunnel had a little light at the end. But it was a long tunnel to get through every year from July to June. I'd think: Oh, God, I'll never be able to do it. How can I possibly wait until next June?

Here I was with two kids in public schools, a husband who went to work every day, and a *satsang* group that met only once a week. From Friday night at ten P.M. to the next Friday at seven-thirty P.M. it was regular householder life. Luckily everyone in the family had fallen in love with Mother. Steve felt every bit as strongly as I did, and the children, too. But the children were children, Sanjay, six, and Devi, nine; while they got to know her in their own unique individual ways, it was life as normal for them.

I'd be thinking there was something wrong with me, that I could be so morose as a mother of our two children. I had to fake enthusiasm about events like Halloween, the next school project, the soccer game, the basketball game, and the cheer-leading tryouts. I felt so guilty because my first duty was to my children. Of course, I was insanely in love with my children, just as possessing and doting as any mother, but there was a part of me that wanted to run off and be with Mother.

I wanted to go to India to help break the long gap between visits. It was a wrenching pain to wait; it was all I could do to bear it. When I was faced with the notion of leaving for a while, I didn't think the family could handle things without me. One year I did have a ticket to go, but that was the year of the Gulf War, and Steve's parents were beside themselves with worry and fear, so I canceled the trip.

Cathi looked off into the distance as she continued to speak:

I was not at all integrated for the first few years. It was very hard. It wasn't like Mother had come and therefore suddenly everything was wonderful, or that I now had this great spiritual life that enhanced my worldly life. It wasn't like that. In the beginning, everything was a complete split. Everything about Mother was a total delight, and everything about normal life was dull.

That first year, the time between Mother's first visit and her next one seemed like an eternity. However, over the next few years, gradually the *satsang* group expanded, we had a little bookstore in our dining room, and the summer program had gotten so big I had to start preparations in April. Right after Mother's first visit, I stopped singing the boring songs we used to chant every Friday and started learning and leading Mother's songs, both the Sanskrit and the Malayalam ones. Increasing all of these activities helped make the time between her visits easier.

Slowly Mother's work in Santa Fe expanded, as my duties

as a mother began to shrink. When you give your kids the car keys, forget it, it's "Bye, Mom." Then we built the temple and had some retreats given by a couple of the swamis during the fall months; we also hosted other activities, such as Mother's birthday celebration. These events occupied my time, so that I was happier. Now I was doing more of what I wanted to. Anything having to do with Mother had a delectable sweetness to it. While I knew that I needed to find that sweetness in my entire life, including with my family, that way wasn't yet my experience. So it remained very hard for me for quite a long time.

One of the elements that helped me eventually understand the sacredness of householder life was my association with Mother's renunciates. They'd be in our home with Mother every summer, and a couple of them would stay with us during the year conducting retreats or classes, first in our house, then later in the temple and ashram. I'd grown up with the idea that I had to get spiritual in order to receive divine grace, that the less human I could become, the more spiritual I'd be. Surprisingly, what I learned from Mother's swamis was exactly the opposite. I'd watch their sometimes childlike behavior; I'd observe them admitting that they were hungry or tired, that they liked or disliked this or that kind of food, or that they were sad to be separated from Ammachi. Seeing their vulnerability helped me learn to admit I was human; to do so was part of becoming more humble, more innocent, more happy.

In addition, these same swamis would show concern for the worldly details of our lives—the welfare of our children, our health, Steve's problems at work, and on and on. It was very interesting to me that these renunciates, who'd given up everything to live with and serve Mother, paid attention to our normal life. What it did was to validate my householder existence. Gradually, I realized that our family life was also sacred. Before, I'd thought the only worthwhile spiritual path was that of a renunciate. I began to get it: my worldly life wasn't something to get through until I was a little older and could do some spiritual practices. My family life *was* my spiritual practice; I didn't have to go to India for it, or wait until I got older; and I didn't have to cut myself off from it. Family life, as well as monastic life, was imbued with every possibility of bringing to it my devotion for the divine.

One year I watched Steve getting *darshan*. I was sitting on the stage at an odd angle from Mother, behind her and a little far back. Even though she was always glancing at certain individuals, she'd have to turn too far around to look at me. When I saw Steve in her lap, I thought, Now that's true love. She's giving him what he really needs—perfect, unconditional love. Just as that thought was passing through me, Mother whipped her head around at a peculiar angle and shot a glance at me. I was stunned and thought, Okay, Mother. I get it—he's yours and I've got to be *really* nice to him. In that moment, I understood Mother was showing me that I was to strive for that same unconditional love—that was to be my goal.

Still, in the first few years I felt I could never have the kind of infinite love Mother showed us. Our kids were great reminders; early on they started calling Steve and me on our behaviors. They'd say, "You aren't following Mother's teachings. You're supposed to have patience." Or they'd point out after the first couple of years when we'd been going on parts of Mother's tour, "You go following Ammachi all over, but you don't listen to anything she says." And they were right. After listening to countless talks Mother would give about loving our family members, and after watching her give *darshan* to entire families over and over again, I realized Mother was showing us to love each other in the same way. For example, one year I told myself, "If I keep arguing with Steve, one of these days Mother's going to say something to me and I may argue with her, since I've got this pattern going." Since that was the last thing in the world I wanted to do, I thought I'd better start right now with the people in my family and not fight back, hoping that if one day Mother would start scolding me, I wouldn't start fighting back out of habit.

Gradually I began to see that because our family had Mother in common, no matter what it looked like on the outside, everything was so much better for us. We'd be in Mother's web of sweetness, in the feeling that's so hard to describe, that special womb of love; we were all getting that massage of the heart. We'd each remember different things Mother had done with us, and we'd share these moments together. Bit by bit, Mother's teaching began to seep into all of us on a very deep level. Then, somehow, I began carrying this love with me all year long.

At the same time, our kids were having American teenage experiences in public high schools the same as most kids— their music, style of dress, and social life. On obvious levels Sanjay and Devi rebelled the same way other kids did, and I acted just as obnoxiously as any normal parent. However, none of these things bothered me as much as they had years ago, during the time when my heart had been newly captured by Mother. I no longer felt the split even while attending the children's high school programs or picking Sanjay up from parties at two in the morning in the days before he had his own car. As a full-time mom—cooking, cleaning, doing their errands, doing all manner of things that were part of my householder job—I never could have been so busy with the Amma Center as I am now. Now Devi's graduated from college and has been accepted to law school, and Sanjay is in college.

I asked Cathi if she had anything else to add, any more teachings from Mother that helped her become so content and full of joy. She remembered something important:

Back when all my struggles were still going on, one day I was bemoaning the fact that over the years Mother hadn't given me very many spiritual instructions as she had to other devotees. Suddenly it occurred to me that I hadn't paid attention to the one thing Mother used to tell me over and over again, which was to smile. I realized that when Mother would tell me to smile, she meant it for a very serious reason. She was saying it because I had a strong need to do that in order to improve myself. It was easy for me to smile at *satsang* and around Mother and the swamis, but in the first few years after I'd met Mother, I'd not been smiling very much around my family. Instead, with Steve and the kids I was often moody and sullen. I concluded that if I didn't start smiling I wasn't going to make much progress.

From then on I decided to force myself to smile. In the beginning smiling felt fake; I couldn't understand how forcing such an act would achieve anything. I told myself to just try it for a while. After a half a day of smiling at everyone, I suddenly started feeling better, even though the smiling didn't feel real. Then I began to notice that everywhere I went, when I smiled at people, they smiled back. Soon I started getting addicted to getting all these smiles back, and imagined that it must have been nice for others to have somebody smiling at them. Smiling seemed like a good practice.

Noting that nowadays Cathi was prone not only to generous smiling but also to frequent giggling and laughing, I asked if her constant smiling was an indication that she felt an inner peace and joy most of the time. She answered, "I'm definitely a different person now."

Cathi's tale is an example of the nonlinear aspect of the stages, showing how they can come in any order and any

style. With Cathi, stages one and two were happening simultaneously from the moment she met Ammachi. Cathi's
shadow experience came in the beginning, as seen in her
depressions before meeting Steve, again before meeting
Ammachi, and still again after meeting Mother. Cathi's profound agony around raising her two children is typical of the
shadow: she couldn't see the pure love that lay beneath her
anguish. Much like a child herself, a newborn spiritual baby,
she wanted only to be with Mother. Ammachi's words describe Cathi's state:

> Just as crying is the only manner of expression a child uses to
> let its wishes be known—be it hunger, thirst or pain—in the
> beginning stages of spirituality you have only one way of ex-
> pressing your heart, and that is through shedding tears of in-
> tense longing. The Master will bind you with his [her] love
> and he [she] will become the absolute center of your life.[2]

Mother offered hope and a promise of love even as Cathi
waded through her split around family life and spiritual life.
Even though Cathi *knew* she was to find Mother's love in
her children and husband, it took burning with Mother's
love to bring Cathi to stage five, the point of surrender. Only
then could she remember the one critical discipline Mother
had given her, the directive to smile. And since Cathi was
an emotional person, prone to deep feelings and sensitivi-
ties, she also received subtle disciplines through observing
Mother and the swamis; these spiritual lessons seeped in,
helping Cathi to realize the truth of family life as a vital
spiritual setting.

The yearning Cathi felt in the beginning, both before she
met Ammachi and during the several years after, can be
viewed as a foreshadowing of the kind of divine longing that

accompanies feelings of contentment and inner peace. The painful and unpleasant aspect of yearning that often precedes stage six belongs to any of the stages, and particularly to stage four, the shadow part of the journey.

These characteristic feelings of gnawing despair could be likened to our craving to meet our soul mate. The shadow is evidenced because, like Cathi, we might have a sense of hopelessness or unworthiness to have something so wonderful happen to us. Then, when we finally meet the long-awaited partner, we might fall into despair again when he leaves town. Even though we might know he will return in a few months or in a year, getting through the day can become an agonizing struggle. The shadow in this case may have to do with lifetimes of suffering over loss of parent or partner or child. Because we are still in the shadow, the separation from the loved one leaves us with a sense of futility.

Over the years, when we experience our lover returning from the long absences time and time again, we begin to feel more confidence in the purity and constancy of the love we have for one another. Our never-ending focus on the lover can be seen as a kind of *tapas*. As the forest dweller's one-pointed search for his master's lion-god cleansed his mind, we eventually become purified by our love. Our mind and heart become unclouded. Now when our beloved is away, our yearning for her feels uplifting, and we often sense her residing within us. Along with feelings of contentment during these periods of separation, we yearn to be in her arms; we suffer an inexplicable joy in our hunger to be joined once again.

Mother is like the beloved. Gradually our love for her burns away our interest in anything other than being in her love. In the process we begin to experience everyone as her and everything we do as service to her—our job, our family, even our recreation. Cathi Schmidt gradually became able to experience more contentment than ever before. At the same time, she freely admits to falling into moments of feeling unworthy and inadequate, even to the point of shedding tears of sadness and crying in solitude to Mother about jealousies and frustrations.

Another of Cathi's secrets to her contentment lay in her musical expression. Even before she'd met Ammachi, she had used song to cheer her soul. During the several years after her own mother died, Cathi wrote many folk tunes to express her grief; it was the only way she knew how to deal with her mother's death. During the early years after Cathi had met Ammachi, song lent solace during Ammachi's long absences; in more recent years, composing tunes and writing lyrics provided an outlet for Cathi's divine longing.

≈

Singing

When you sing bhajan *[devotional songs] imagine that your Beloved Deity is standing right before you. Imagine that your Beloved is dancing to the rhythm of the song and that you are blissfully dancing hand in hand with Him or Her.*

—Ammachi

It is no secret that song opens the heart. Any tune sung with love is a form of devotion.

Religions and spiritual traditions all over the world use chanting, rhythm, and tune as integral aspects of their practices. At Ammachi's ashram in India and on all her world tours, she sings *bhajans* every evening. There are more than forty-five volumes of cassette tapes of the devotional songs that she and her devotees have written, some even in English.

Cathi Schmidt's story of music as a spiritual practice might help us get a sense of how to approach singing. In the first days of meeting Ammachi, Cathi was snobbish about choosing only Sanskrit and Malayalam songs for the *satsang* group. She preferred those languages to less musical and common-sounding English songs. In addition, English was not a holy language like Sanskrit, Latin, Hebrew, or Greek, each of which carried with its ancient messages a vibration of spirituality.

One day Rita, a devotee from Taos, asked Cathi to write English words for one of Ammachi's Malayalam songs. While Cathi was well aware of the difficulty of Ammachi's language for most Westerners, she was afraid such an act might be considered blasphemous. Nevertheless, she created the popular English version of one of the Malayalam *bhajans*, "There Is No Need to Speak in Words to the Divine Mother,"[3] and everyone loved it, including Ammachi and the swamis.

The overwhelming success of her first effort made her reconsider the language problem; she had to admit the power of singing together while understanding the words. As a result, Cathi has created English lyrics for many Malayalam songs, and has been composing words and tunes resulting in a collection of English *bhajans*.[4]

Personally, listening to these songs has brought tears to my eyes many times, and I've watched the same happen in a hall full of devotees. I asked Cathi how she felt when she sang. Did her musical experiences bring tears to her eyes? She answered:

Yes. Absolutely. What would happen was this: just before I'd come up with a line to a song, something would build up. I'd get a fiery knotted place in me, and I'd want to say something to Mother so badly and I didn't know how. Then, when a really beautiful line would come and express itself in words, I'd get a feeling as if suddenly the rain had sprinkled down and washed everything, and I'd feel soothed. The knot inside me had come undone, the flame subsided, and there'd be a sweet feeling inside of me that almost re-created the experience of yearning to be in Ammachi's lap, then at last finding myself in her arms.

Unlocking divine feelings by singing in the English language is a very powerful experience; it's something everyone can relate to, that they're actually expressing thoughts, not just making nice sounds.

Looking out the window, Cathi seemed transported to the moment of yearning when she wrote her first English *bhajan*, "Teach Me the Language of Your Heart." She described the experience:

I was standing at my kitchen sink one day. I really wanted to tell Mother something, but what was it, and how could I possibly do it? How could I possibly tell Mother how I felt? I didn't even know. And I didn't speak Malayalam. I felt hopeless. What did I want to tell her and what did I want her to do? I wanted her to do something; I wanted her to teach me something. I wanted her to . . . then it just came to me like a flash. Boom: "Teach me the language of your heart." Then, I thought, Oh, that's cool. Then my mind went, Mother does so much with her eyes: "Teach me the language of your eyes." Again I said to myself, Look at how she touches us! I could say, "Teach me the language of your touch." And so words to the song came to me: boom, boom, boom, all at once.

> *Teach me the language of your heart*
> *Only your love will bring peace inside me*

Teach me the language of your smile
Looking at you all my sorrows vanish

Teach me the language of your voice
Help me to speak only words of kindness

Teach me the language of your eyes
Deep in your gaze is the truth I long for

Teach me the language of your light
Feeling your strength I will fear no darkness

Teach me the language of your touch
Please let me stay in your arms forever

Teach me the language of your heart
Only your love will bring peace inside me
Promise me that you will always guide me
I need to know you are right beside me

Teach me the language of your heart.[5]

Then I played around and wrote a little tune for it. But I thought no one would ever want to listen to it. For three months I kept it a secret. One day I went over to Dawn and Mark's house to do a little *bhajan* practice. I said to them, "I'm going to sing this song I wrote, and if you really can't stand it, you can tell me and I'll never sing it again." When I sang it, they started crying, and when it was over they told me it was beautiful. I couldn't believe them. "Really?" I said. "You like it?"

Cathi reflected on her state of consciousness as she composes: "When I look inside my mind, there was no way that those beautiful words were a formation of my own creation—they came from another place, that's clear. The inspiration was way beyond this form of mine." Cathi's experience with song can be compared to Arjuna in his position as a warrior. Krishna had advised Arjuna to fight without a sense of "I" or "mine," without the feeling that "I am doing it," recognizing that "it is being done through me."

If Cathi Schmidt had to break through barriers to sing her compositions in front of others, imagine my difficulty getting through mine with the simplest of songs. When I was a child, I carried a tune quite well. When I was a teenager, I sang in the church choir. In my early twenties, I played guitar to accompany my folk singing. Later, something happened, and it became difficult for me to stay on key; maybe it's because I'd stopped singing, or maybe someone told me I was off key. Even today, after years of singing with Ammachi, I tend to be a little flat, and sometimes wander away from the tune. However, I love to sing, and that's what matters. Additionally, I have noticed after singing with Ammachi as much as I do—at home, in my car, in the woods—my ability to carry a tune has improved, and my joy while singing has increased immeasurably.

Most of my singing is done alone or in group, not as a leader. You will need to discover what setting is best for you. In singing practice, flood your heart with song—sing while you work, while you plant the garden, clean house, tend to your children, cook, hike, drive your car, sit at your altar. Let song express your longing for divine love; let it comfort you when you feel depressed; let it express feelings of joy. If you have the inclination, write down your own songs, or put your own words to known tunes as Cathi Schmidt did.

Singing any familiar melody you love will do. Some examples to get you started: "Let It Be" (Lennon/McCartney), "Michael, Row Your Boat Ashore" (spiritual), "We Are Climbing Jacob's Ladder" (spiritual), "You'll Never Walk Alone" (from *Carousel*), "Somewhere Over the Rainbow" (from *Wizard of Oz*), "The Hills Are Alive with the Sound of Music" (from *The Sound of Music*), "Oh, Danny Boy" (Irish ballad), and "Down Yonder Green Valleys" (camp song). Begin now recalling songs that express feelings of longing or joy, and create a notebook full of them to help you remember to sing.

Sing along with CDs or cassette tapes.

≈

The Bittersweet
of Yearning

*Our longing to see God should be like the
intense desire that we would have to escape if
someone were coming to kill us. Our painful
longing to see God should be like the pain we
should have while dying in the midst of a
blazing fire. If you are unable to call God the
whole day, try at least until noon.*

—Ammachi

As we saw with Cathi Schmidt, this yearning for God or
Mother can bring its share of morose suffering before we
open to the indescribable pleasure unique to divine longing.
With Etty Hillesum we witnessed how love can transport us
beyond our normal understanding of suffering into a sweet
bitterness that is difficult to explain. While in the concentration camp, Etty Hillesum wrote how suffering can be turned
into something beautiful, even desirable:

> The *idea* of suffering (which is not the reality, for real suffer-
> ing is always fruitful and can turn life into a precious thing)
> must be destroyed. And if you destroy the ideas behind
> which life lies imprisoned as behind bars, then you liberate
> your true life, its real mainsprings, and then you will also
> have the strength to bear real suffering, your own and the
> world's.[1]

The Sufi poet Rumi writes:

> *The way of love is not*
> *a subtle argument.*
>
> *The door there*
> *is devastation.*
>
> *Birds make great sky-circles*
> *of their freedom.*
> *How do they learn it?*
>
> *They fall, and falling*
> *they're given wings.*[2]

In Western culture, many Catholic mystics have provided us with records of the glorious anguish that can accompany a relationship with the divine beloved. Their story of pain may repel us at first. Most of us do not want to suffer any more than we already have. The voice of St. Therese of Lisieux offers us a very human glimpse into the gentle beauty of surrendering into divine love's trials.

The "little flower," as St. Therese of Lisieux called herself, was the youngest of nine children. Born in 1873, her family feared she would meet the same fate as four of her little brothers and sisters, each of whom died before she was born. Her mother was too ill to breast-feed her sickly baby, so a midwife, Therese's first adoptive mother, nursed her to good health.

Before they were married, Therese's mother and father had harbored the desire to be monastic. The love that kindled their religious sentiment was reflected naturally in the raising of their five girls. The sisters often would play at being nuns and practiced their beliefs fervently. Therese, who was too young to go to mass, would wait at home impatiently for her sister, Celine, three years older, to bring her a slice of the holy bread. One time Celine forgot. Little Therese insisted Celine make her some. So Celine took a loaf of bread from the kitchen cupboard, recited a Hail Mary, made the sign of the cross, and gave a slice to Therese. She ate it and said it tasted just as good as the blessed bread from church.

Therese was spoiled by her sisters and her parents, never had to make her bed or clean house, and was called "my little queen" by her father. Her sisters loved her, too, and rejoiced in her position as Daddy's favorite. Therese's mother wrote about her in a letter:

> Celine seems naturally good. . . . But I can't be too sure how the little minx [Therese] will turn out, for she's a little madcap. She is more intelligent than Celine, but nothing like as gentle and she is stubborn beyond words. It's quite impossible to budge her when she says no. . . . Yet she has a heart of gold and is very affectionate and without a trace of slyness. It's amusing to see her coming running to me to confess her faults: "Mummy, I've given Celine a push and I've thumped her, but I won't do it again." She says that every time she has done anything wrong.[3]

As she grew older, her self-honesty served her inner quest, and her stubbornness transformed into an unbending will to love God with every fiber of her being.

Therese divides her life into three periods, with the first running until age four. Her profoundly passionate nature and her inclination to love deeply were evident from the beginning. She remembers in great detail family outings among the flowers and trees. In her autobiography, *Saint Therese of Lisieux: The Story of a Soul,* she wrote:

I can still feel the deep emotion I felt when I saw the fields of wheat starred with poppies, cornflowers, and daisies. I was already in love with far distances, with open spaces, and with great trees. . . . Truly, the whole world smiled on me. My path was strewn with flowers, and my own happy temperament also made life pleasant.[4]

Her mother's death catapulted her into the second period of her life, a time marked by loss and despair. She became timid, quiet, and easily provoked to tears. She describes her state:

I was never cheerful except within the family circle, and there the greatest love and kindness surrounded me. Daddy's affection seemed enriched by a real motherly love, and I felt that both you [her second to the eldest sister] and Marie [her eldest sister] were the most tender and self-sacrificing of mothers. God's little flower would never have survived if He had not poured His warmth and light on her. She was still too frail to stand up to rain and storm. She needed warmth, the gently dropping dew and the soft airs of spring. She was never without them, for Jesus gave them to her, even amidst the bleak winter of her suffering.[5]

Pauline, her sister and second mother, had coached Therese for her first confession so well that Therese believed that when she spoke to the priest she spoke to God Himself. Later she came to believe that there was no such thing as an intermediary between her and God, but rather that He dealt with her directly.

Another painful loss came when Pauline entered the convent of Carmel. Therese had understood that Pauline would wait for her as she had promised. Pauline had told her that they would go together to be hermits in a far-off desert. Therese wrote:

> How can I express the agony I suffered. In a flash I understood what life was. Until then I had not seen it as too sad a business, but now I saw it as it really was—a thing of suffering and continual partings. I cried bitterly, for I knew nothing then of the joy of sacrifice. . . .
>
>   I shall never forget how tenderly you [Pauline] comforted me. You explained what life in Carmel was like and it seemed wonderful. . . . I felt that Carmel was the desert where God wanted me to hide myself too. . . . I was certain it was a call from God. I longed to enter Carmel, not because of you, but solely because of Jesus. Many thoughts came to me that I can't put into words, but they filled my heart with peace.[6]

Soon after her sister's departure, Therese fell ill. She called it a "strange illness," because she was often delirious and said things that were unrelated or didn't make sense. Her third adoptive mother, her sister Marie, sat beside her, and, like any good mother, knew what was best for her more than the doctors did. One day, after many months of despair as to the likelihood of her recovery, all her sisters gathered around her bed to pray to a statue of the Mother Mary. Therese also turned toward the heavenly Mother and asked her to take pity on her. "Suddenly the Blessed Virgin glowed with a beauty beyond anything I had ever seen. Her face was alive with kindness and an infinite tenderness, but it was her enchanting smile which really moved me to the depths."[7] Therese's pain vanished and tears of joy filled her eyes.

Marie prepared Therese for her first communion. In the chapel, while kneeling at the altar, she felt the "first kiss of Jesus." She declared: "I love You and I give myself to You forever!" She and Jesus gazed at each other until "Therese had disappeared like a drop of water lost in the depth of the ocean. Only Jesus remained—as Master and King."[8] She wept with joy.

On Christmas Eve, at age thirteen, she entered the third period of her life. At home after Mass before the opening of surprise packages out of the magic shoes, Therese overheard her father say, "Thank goodness it's the last time we shall have this kind of thing!" And, indeed, Therese was too old to participate in the childhood celebration, but they had continued the practice because she was still the baby of the family. Celine also had overheard her father's irritated comment and cautioned Therese not to go downstairs, told her she was sure to burst into tears of shame and make her father very unhappy. But in that moment something happened inside of Therese that caused a permanent change in her. She was not mortified as she would have been in the past. She went downstairs and opened the presents with gaiety and joy, to the delight of her father and her sisters. Celine watched in amazement. Therese never again was subject to bouts of self-pitying shyness and self-consciousness, something she had toiled for ten years to overcome. She saw the experience as a conversion, a grace bestowed by her Lord Jesus. "Love filled my heart, I forgot myself and henceforth I was happy." Therese described the implications:

One Sunday when I was looking at a picture of Our Lord on the Cross, I saw the Blood coming from one of His hands, and I felt terribly sad to think that It was falling to the earth and that no one was rushing forward to catch It. I determined to stay continually at the foot of the Cross and receive It. I knew that I should then have to spread It among other souls. The

cry of Jesus on the Cross—"I am thirsty"—rang continually
in my heart and set me burning with a new, intense longing. I
wanted to quench the thirst of my Well-Beloved. . . .[9]

At age fourteen, Therese longed to enter Carmel to join
her sisters Marie and Pauline. Her sister Celine also intended to become a Carmelite nun. She chose the day of
the Feast of the Pentecost to tell her father her wish. In the
garden Therese sat and then strolled with her father. Their
tears mingled as he willingly gave permission to his little
queen. However, many obstacles arose before the day of her
glory would come. Church officials, including an influential
bishop, did not agree to let her enter at so young an age.

Celine and Therese went with their father on a group tour
to Rome, a religious pilgrimage. In an unprecedented moment, during an audience with the Pope, when Therese's
turn in line came to kneel before the Holy Father, she went
against all protocol and asked to speak to him. With obvious
interest, he leaned forward to listen to her request. He told
her that if it was God's will, she would enter Carmel at
age fifteen. But that was not enough for the strong-willed
Therese. She wanted him to say yes, folded her hands on his
knee, and begged. Church officials had to pull her away.

After numerous delays, permission was granted for her to
enter Carmel at the young age of fifteen. There she was to go
through many periods of darkness, which included sleeping
through prayers and communion thanksgiving chants. She
figured Jesus, like any good parent, would love her even
while she slept. She describes her experiences of the dry
darkness with which she was often overcome:

When I sing of the bliss of heaven and the eternal possession
of God, I get no joy from it, for I am singing only of *what I*

want to believe. Sometimes, I admit, a tiny ray of sunshine pierces the darkness and then, for a second, my suffering stops. Instead of comforting me, the memory of this makes the darkness blacker.[10]

In the monastery she learned to love suffering for her Lord through hard work, inadequate nourishment, cold sleeping arrangements, blame for things she didn't do, harsh reprimands from the Mother Superior, and difficulties with other Carmelite sisters. She saw everything as an opportunity to learn charity, to test her ability to love God under all conditions. In the midst of her trials, she was peaceful, happy, and filled with gratitude. But she found it difficult to communicate her imperfections and her inner experiences to her superiors. An older nun understood what she was going through and summed up the nature of Therese's dilemma and the nature of her saintliness. As Therese told it:

> At recreation one day she [the old nun] said: "It strikes me, my child, that you cannot have much to say to your superiors."
> "Why do you think that, Mother?"
> "Because your soul is very simple, but when you are perfect, you will be more simple still. The nearer one gets to God, the simpler one becomes."[11]

Soon after her final vows, she became ill with tuberculosis. When the first cough of warm blood came out of her mouth in the night, she was exhilarated that soon she would go to heaven to join with her Beloved forever. In the last months before her death, at age twenty-three, she wrote:

> Ah, since that day [of my vows] I have been soaked and engulfed in love. There is not a second when this merciful love

does not renew and cleanse me, sweeping every trace of sin from my heart. It's impossible for me to fear purgatory. I know I do not deserve even to enter that place of expiation, but I know also that the fire of love cleanses more than the flames of purgatory. I know too that Jesus does not want us to suffer uselessly, and that He would not inspire me with such desires unless He meant to fulfill them.[12]

It is impossible for me to grow bigger, so I put up with myself as I am, with all my countless faults. But I will look for some means of going to heaven by a little way which is very short and very straight, a little way that is quite new. We live in an age of inventions. We need no longer climb laboriously up flights of stairs. . . . I was determined to find a lift to carry me to Jesus. . . . It is Your arms, Jesus, which are the lift to carry me to heaven. And so there is no need for me to grow up. In fact, just the opposite: I must stay little and become less and less.[13]

I no longer want anything except to love until I die of love. I am free and fear nothing.[14]

It was months after the last rites had been made over her that she was to die. She never ceased being a delight to the community. She joked and amused the other nuns until her end. The bell to announce her impending death rang twice over a couple of months. But she did not die, only suffered beyond human understanding.

In her final hours she said to Pauline, "Mother, isn't this the agony yet? Am I not going to die yet?"

"Yes, child, it is the agony—but perhaps God wishes it to go on for a few hours still."

"Very well," Therese said. "So be it—oh, I don't want to suffer less." She turned to the crucifix, looked at it long. In her last whisper she said, "Oh, I love him—my God—I—love—you."[15]

≈

Cultivating Contentment and Yearning

Inner peace always follows in the wake of pain. To reach the state of joy, you first have to experience pain. Pain in the beginning and lasting happiness at the end is far superior to happiness in the beginning and long-lasting pain at the end. —Ammachi

Before beginning contentment and yearning as a practice, it is important to continue addressing this seemingly undesirable common thread that links all the stories throughout the Path of the Mother: that of suffering.

Who wants heartache? And why? As with Adam and Eve, our existence during the difficult time of the *Kali Yuga* holds the inevitability of suffering. So how can we sublimate sorrow into joy?

Within the confines of the barbed-wire fence, Etty Hillesum managed to see beauty and feel rapture. We know that her love of God and of her beloved Spier was her inspiration, but with regard to the *Kali Yuga*, what are the additional implications of her experience? "Looked at from one standpoint," according to Ammachi, "all four yugas, *Krita*, *Treta*, *Dwapara*, and *Kali*, exist in us at the same time. The yugas are dependent on one's [inner] nature."[16] If the strife inherent in the *Kali Yuga* is a creation of our own minds, then, as with Etty Hillesum, it is possible for all of us to make a shift in our perception of the world around us.

How can we experience the river of love rushing through us? Since love's expression does not always pour out from a spontaneous uprising, what else can we do in a very practical way to help us to become unhesitating lovers of the divine? The answer has to do with passionate prayer and with a subtle modification in the attitude with which we approach our spiritual practices.

A hint lies in the story of Therese of Lisieux when she writes about her persistence to love even through the darkest and driest periods of her quest. Her efforts gave her a sense of peace and gratefulness. Her yearning to experience Jesus in everything led her to practice changing her mental perspective in the simplest of ways:

> Formerly one of our nuns managed to irritate me whatever she did or said. . . . I did not remain content with praying a lot for this nun who caused me so much disturbance. I tried to do as many things for her as I could, and whenever I was tempted to speak unpleasantly to her, I made myself give her a pleasant smile and tried to change the subject. . . . When I was violently tempted by the devil and if I could slip away without her seeing my inner struggle, I would flee like a soldier deserting the battlefield. And after all this she asked me one day with a beaming face: "Sister Therese, will you please tell me what attracts you so much to me? You give me such a charming smile whenever we meet." Ah, it was Jesus hidden in the depth of her soul who attracted me, Jesus who makes the bitterest things sweet![17]

As St. Therese's efforts to smile and speak kindly might seem not genuine, your own efforts to practice the following suggestions may feel forced initially. With a lot of patience, you just have to make yourself do them and rest in between. Cathi Schmidt's smile felt fake in the beginning and soon brought feelings of inner peace and joy. Over time, as the slate of our minds becomes more and more blank, with fewer negative tendencies and fewer negative reactions to life's situations, our yearning and contentment become more natural, more childlike in nature, more sweet like nectar.

From the Sufi mystic, Rumi:

> *When you are with everyone but me,*
> > *you're with no one.*
> *When you are with no one but me,*
> > *you're with everyone.*
> *Instead of being so bound up with everyone,*
> > *be everyone.*
> *When you become that many, you're nothing,*
> > *empty.*[18]

There are three parts to the practice of cultivating contentment and yearning: 1. Developing humility, 2. Seeing everything as Mother, or Accepting everything, and 3. Praying, or Crying for Mother.

1. Developing humility:

Only the feeling of nothingness and humility will help us reach the state of perfect fullness, the experience that "I am everything."

—Ammachi

Humility is a word often used in spirituality and religion. Cathi Schmidt described it in her experience with Ammachi and the swamis. The forest dweller, by his very position in life and through his honest ignorance, demonstrated humility. Ammachi was quoted in the Introduction, in the story about the mahatma pouring tea for the scholarly seeker, advising us to become innocent beginners, to bow down before all creation in humility.

In actuality, humility is another word for contentment.

Most of us associate humility with self-deprecation, with giving up our innate gifts and talents. Or we might associate it with a false presentation of who we really are. In fact, real humility is quite the opposite. It is a state of unpretentiousness in which we are satisfied with who we are and have no fear in admitting our weaknesses or human qualities. In addition, rather than trying to be in control, we've learned to credit all our actions and accomplishments to the divine. We are surrendered and open to love. We are innocent like children. Because we are not laden with expectation, everything we do seems to "work," and our lives are filled with divine energy and abundance. Jesus was referring to humility in his Sermon on the Mount when he said, "Blessed are the meek: for they shall inherit the earth."

Rumi wrote:

> Sometimes a lover of God may faint
> in the presence. Then the beloved bends
> and whispers in his ear, "Beggar, spread out
> your robe. I'll fill it with gold."[19]

Ammachi tells us that there are two ways to realize the absolute. One is to become bigger and bigger until we are aware that everything is in us, and we are in everything. The only problem here is that we are liable to let our egos become big, do too much thinking in the process, and forget about the divine being big inside. As with the forest meditator, it is difficult for love to come in if we are puffed up. The easiest way is to become very small, then the beloved can enter into us, causing us to feel very big with love.

Ammachi's advice is similar to Therese of Lisieux's, who wrote about staying small like a child so Jesus could carry her. Jillellamudi Mother said, "To make one who hops like a frog (in pride) move like an earthworm (in humility) is my way."[20] Perhaps the snake in the Garden of Eden was showing us the way of humility when she accepted God's commandment: "Upon your belly you shall go, and dust you shall eat all the days of your life."[21]

Krishna taught Arjuna that humility has to do with letting the divine move through him. The same is true for all of us. Putting all our heart and soul into life is part of humility. Rumi wrote:

> Life freezes if it doesn't get a taste
> of this almond cake [love].
>   The stars come up spinning
> every night, bewildered in love.
>   They'd grow tired
> with that revolving, if they weren't.
>   They'd say,
> "How long do we have to do this!"
>
> God picks up the reed-flute world and blows.
> Each note is a need coming through one of us,
> a passion, a longing-pain.
>   Remember the lips
> where the wind-breath originated,
> and let your note be clear.
> Don't try to end it.
> Be *your* note.
> I'll show you how it's enough.[22]

2. Seeing everything as Mother, or accepting everything:

When you are full of love and compassion, you cannot say no to anything, you can only say yes.   —Ammachi

To accept everything doesn't mean sitting back and doing nothing. It doesn't mean we refuse to help someone in need, or that we think it's okay for our neighbors to mistreat their children. It has more to do with cultivating dispassion and with developing the witnessing consciousness, the *sakshi bhava* mentioned in Part I under Witnessing Meditation.

Ammachi says there are three ways most of us approach problems or difficulties—we want to change the person or situation, we tend to blame others, or we try to run away. Ammachi suggests there is a fourth way, which is the spiritual approach. It has to do with reperceiving or changing our mental attitude. It has to do with accepting everything as a blessing. This practice is reminiscent of those of Selfless Service and Work as Worship. The difference is in the fine-tuning of our inner musical instrument.

To begin, try acknowledging anything and everything that comes your way as a divine gift, including the seemingly negative events such as illness, mental distractions, professional setbacks, loss of financial security. At first, try assuming this mental attitude with simple disturbances such as the car that pulled out in front of you without stopping at the intersection, the bus that made you late to work, the friend who complained during lunch.

As Therese of Lisieux tried to be kind to difficult nuns, as Cathi Schmidt forced herself to smile, try to reperceive people and events that you normally and previously had experienced as bad or negative. The benefits of such mental changes may come only in glimpses at first, as shown in the Work as Worship practice, in my story of picking weeds and cleaning bathrooms in my Pennsylvania ashram.

Another way to approach this practice is to envision everything that comes your way as Mother's holy food—in India it is referred to as Mother's *prasad*, a sweet preparation offered to the deity during rituals, as visualized in Meditating on the Beloved Deity practice. When someone gets angry at you, or is rude to you, or ignores you, or does something you think is insufferable, imagine it as Mother handing you some exotic, delicious pudding, and slipping it into your mouth with her fingers.

Still another suggestion is to acknowledge what comes to you as a balancing act, a tipping of the scales of life, the law of cause and effect, or karma. If you are not familiar with karma, an illustration of its meaning can be seen when you hit a baseball. The law of cause and effect dictates that the ball will go some distance before gravity takes over and the ball falls to the ground. It is the same with our actions. If we've done something in the past, either good or bad, we will reap the effect of it. For instance, if you drink several cups of coffee, and you're not a regular coffee drinker, chances are you'll get quite jittery and talkative. Sometimes this happens even if you are a coffee drinker. Another example could be speeding in your car one too many times. Eventually you are likely to get a ticket. Another example of karma might have happened in grade school when you helped a new kid in class. Then a few years later a new classmate took you under her wing when you moved to another town.

With karma, as with the laws of physics, we don't always know what caused the result. For instance, before we knew about meteors, we wouldn't have known what created their craters. Before we had world communication, we might not have known that an earthquake somewhere else in the world shook the ocean swells into tidal waves. So it is with karma. We don't always know what we might have done to reap either the positive or the negative results. We don't know why bad things happen to good people or good things happen to bad people. It could be that we receive a result today from an action of lifetimes ago.

To bring the rounds of karma to a halt, it is beneficial to acknowledge both the difficult and the easy things in life as a completion of our individual soul's balancing act. One way to do this is to adopt a grateful attitude no matter what comes our way—to say "thank you" no matter what, to hold love and kindness, no matter what.

Bit by bit, after trying over and over again, and failing over and over again, we will get glimpses of seeing every seemingly negative and positive event or person that comes our way as a heavenly gift. Ammachi suggests we envision all difficult things that come our way as the Divine Mother's will and all wonderful things as Mother's grace.

All the stories in this book reveal the feeling of inner peace in the moment of welcoming difficult experiences. The forest dweller was more than willing to search for his master's lion, traveling long distances, over hills, under bramble bushes, going without food and water. Indra, albeit out of pride, accepted his plight concerning the mystery of the Great Light, chanted while waiting for it in the dark. Chandra Pillai, with the analytical probing of a scientist, sometimes fearing that he might get drawn into a cult, eagerly questioned Ammachi about everything, ultimately developing a strong desire to know who Ammachi really was. Cathi Schmidt was overcome by the darkness of her own mind, struggled through her split world of family and spirituality, strongly resisting in the beginning and ultimately giving in to the practice of smiling, and of accepting family as her path.

If you always say no to life, to all the experiences that life brings you, you will be miserable and you will get bored. . . . To accept is

to say yes to everything. Everything may go wrong in your life,
but still you find yourself saying, "yes, I accept." The river says
yes to everyone. All of Nature says yes, except human beings. A
human being can say both yes and no. . . . When you see life, and
all that life brings you, as a precious gift, you will be able to say yes
to everything.[23] —Ammachi

3. Praying, or crying for Mother:

Children, crying has the power to make the mind completely one-
pointed. . . . When we cry we can forget everything effortlessly. . . .
The agony caused by the longing to see God is not sorrow; it is
bliss. . . . Some people would say the crying for God is a mental
weakness . . . the happiness experienced from God and the thought
of Him is everlasting. That "weakness" is sufficient for us.

—Ammachi

What happens when we are face-to-face with the divine—a sunset, a holy person, the beloved? Sometimes we cry. These tears of joy and remembering represent the inexplicable rapture brought on by the grief and sorrow experienced while yearning for the divine beloved.

Some spiritual seekers, rather than striving for final liberation, actually long to hold that unbearably ecstatic separation between themselves and God so that they will forever feel the yearning. To convince us of the intoxicating effects of the wine of divine suffering, we have the testimonies of Catholic mystics such as Teresa of Avila and St. Francis of Assisi, Hindu mystics such as Ammachi and the sixteenth-century princess Mirabhai, and Muslim mystics such as Rumi. All the accounts in this book demonstrate this unique longing, including the bitter craving in Irina Tweedie's account and the ecstatic yearning in Etty Hillesum's story.

Ammachi assures us that when we cry for Mother she will

come. She cannot refuse us. If forcing a smile feels false, trying to bring on tears for Mother may seem like an impossible task. For me this divine sadness can be stimulated by writing about my experiences with Ammachi, or by creating fictional accounts of my visions of her. Without fail, when I write or read these stories to myself or others, I cry. It is a delightful form of purification that brings peace and joy to my heart.

For Cathi Schmidt, crying for Mother transpired while singing or composing. For others, the tears of divine yearning are brought on during a guided visualization of Mother. One devotee I know had a knack of being able to sit down at his altar and somehow bring on tears of devotion. He had heard Ammachi say that ten minutes of crying was worth an hour of meditation. Powerful experiences with our loved one can cause tears. Affection for a horse or cat or dog arouses this same divine love.

Once we no longer care to experience conflict and struggle, we can call on the Mother of the Universe, upon whose breast rests the promise of the milk of love and the return to paradise.

In India, during my meditation experience on the roof when I searched inside myself and shed tears of longing, I finally understood why Ammachi tells us we should cry while thinking of our beloved deity. When Ammachi walked past me during the rooftop meditation and left me lamenting, I wanted to be blessed with the same delicious feeling of crying for Mother every day for the rest of my life. My palpable experience of an inexplicable joy let me know the truth of Ammachi's words:

> Just call out, but let the call come from your heart. Just as a child cries out for food or to be . . . cuddled by [her] his mother, call out to [Her] Him with the same intensity and in-

nocence. . . . Children . . . no other sadhana will give you the bliss of divine love as effectively as sincere prayer.[24]

Ammachi explains that we don't have to undergo any academic training to love the supreme being. When we cry and pray to Mother, she must reveal herself. She cannot sit silent and unmoved when we call her like that.

Etty Hillesum, at the end of her time in Westerbork, with tears of emotion, asked God to let all her creative energy become inner dialogues with the divine; Ammachi suggests that we pray for love's own sake. To pray for nothing more than to love Mother, no matter what happens in life, is the only real happiness.[25]

> *Children . . . try to pray until your heart melts and flows down as tears. It is said that the water of the Ganges purifies whoever takes a dip in it. The tears which fill the eyes while one is remembering God have tremendous power to purify one's mind. These tears are more powerful than meditation. Such tears are verily the Ganges.*[26] —Ammachi

Many people, including myself and Ammachi's mother, Damayanti Amma, were used to the concept of prayer that involved asking to have desires met. "Dear Lord, this is my desire. Please fulfill it," or "I don't want that to occur. Don't make it happen." When we pray like this, essentially we are giving instructions to the supreme being to satisfy our own wishes. We are assuming we know more than Mother or God.

I still sometimes find myself unwittingly praying for what I want, not simply turning my life over to Mother, or remembering to pray for others. Things come up—my car battery goes dead, my computer crashes, I lose solar power because of too many cloudy days. Without thinking, I ask for help with these things that, at the moment, seem critical in my life. I forget to be grateful for everything that comes my way.

Any prayer, no matter how it is expressed, is better than none. In prayers of supplication, at least we are making some contact with Mother and have the understanding that everything is due to her. In addition to prayers for ourselves, Ammachi recommends that we pray for the welfare of others and for the peace of the world. On her world tour she leads every gathering in the following prayer, an English translation of the Sanskrit chant:

> *May all the beings in this world and in all other worlds be peaceful and
>   happy*
> *May all the beings in this world and in all other worlds be peaceful and
>   happy*
> *May all the beings in this world and in all other worlds be peaceful and
>   happy*
> *Om, peace, peace, peace*

As St. Therese on her deathbed said she didn't want anything except to die of love, as Etty Hillesum communed with God in the concentration camp, Ammachi says to pray until we ourselves become the offering, until we are consumed by the flames of divine love.

> Prayer is an offering, an offering of one's own life. . . . Once
> you become the offering, once your whole being is in a state
> of constant prayer . . . what is left is Love. Prayer can perform
> this miracle. Crying can accomplish this feat. What is the pur-
> pose of meditation? It is to become love. It is to attain One-
> ness. Thus there is no better meditation technique than
> praying and crying to the Lord.[27]

As Ammachi on the beach during her liberation experi-ence pleaded with the Mother to come, Ammachi advises us to pour our hearts out to Mother.

Mother, please come to me. I am your helpless child wandering around in the darkness. I have no power without you. I thought I had, but now I understand that I am helpless and cannot see. I am nothing without you. Guide me, lead me, help me. Don't ever leave me. Take me into your arms and hold me there forever.[28]

—Ammachi

≈

Epilogue

All of life moves in cycles; the whole universe is cyclic. Just as the earth moves around the sun in a regular cycle, all of Nature moves in a cyclic pattern. The seasons move in a circle: spring, summer, autumn, winter, then spring again, and so forth. From the seed comes the tree, the tree again provides seeds, and the seeds grow into trees. It is a circle. Likewise, birth, childhood, youth, old age, death, and again birth. It is a continuous circle. Time moves in a circle, not in a straight line. Karma and its results must inevitably be experienced by every living being until the mind is stilled and one is content in one's own Self. . . .

Reactions are the results of actions performed in the past. It goes on and on. Death is not the end; it is the beginning of another life. As the circle of life turns around, the actions of the past bear fruit. We cannot say when the fruit will come, what the fruit will be or how it will come. It is a mystery known only to the Creator. If you have faith, you believe; otherwise, you deny it. Whether you believe or not, the fruits come, the law of karma operates. But do not try to analyze how or why, because the cycle of karma is as mysterious as God. Karma, too, is beginningless, but it ends when one drops the ego, when one attains the state of Realization.

Try to forget about the cycle of karma. There is no meaning in thinking about the past. It is a closed chapter. Whatever is done is done. Prepare yourself to confront the present.

The power of karma veils our real nature, while at the same time it creates the urge to realize the Truth. It helps us to go back to our real existence. The circle of karma is a great transformer, if you have the eyes to see it. It lets us know the great message: "This life of yours is the effect of the past. Therefore beware, your actions in the present determine your future. If you do good [follow your dharma] you will be rewarded accordingly, but if you commit mistakes or perform evil actions [acts of ignorance that are against dharma], such actions will return to you with equal strength."
And to the true spiritual seeker, the great message says, "It is better if you can stop the circle completely. Close the account and be free forever."[1]
                                                            —Ammachi

Appendix I: For Further Reading

Amritaswarupananda, Swami. *Ammachi: A Biography of Mata Amritanandamayi*. San Ramon, Calif.: Mata Amritanandamayi Center, 1994. For books, cassettes, videotapes, and photos of Ammachi, go to www.mothersbooks.org or call the Mata Amritanandamayi Center at 888-524-2662.

Amritaswarupananda, Swami. *Awaken, Children! Dialogues with Sri Sri Mata Amritanandamayi*, vols. II–IX. San Ramon, Calif.: Mata Amritanandamayi Center, 1990, 1991, 1992, 1993, 1994, 1995, 1996, 1998. Highly recommended. These books are Ammachi's scripture.

Awaken, Children!: Dialogues with Sri Sri Mata Amritanandamayi, vol. I. Adapted and translated by Swami Amritaswarupananda. Vallickavu, Kerala, India: Mata Amritanandamayi Mission Trust, 1989. An excellent account of Mother's discipline in a Hindu monastic setting. Along with the other *Awaken, Children!* books, this too is Ammachi's scripture, but perhaps more appealing to the Indian than the Western mind.

Brunton, Paul. *A Search in Secret India*. Bombay: BI Publications, 1980. The story of a man's spiritual journey and ultimate meeting with the Indian saint, Ramana Maharshi, Brunton's guru.

Conway, Timothy. *Women of Power and Grace: Nine Astonishing, Inspiring Luminaries of Our Time.* Santa Barbara, Calif.: The Wake Up Press, 1994. Stories of twentieth-century women saints from various traditions.

The Essential Rumi. Translated by Coleman Barks with John Mayne. San Francisco: Harper San Francisco, 1995.

Eternal Wisdom: Upadeshamritam, vols. I and II. Translated into English by Dr. M. N. Namboodiri from materials compiled by Swami Jnanamritananda Puri. San Ramon, Calif.: Mata Amritanandamayi Center, 1997 and 1999. More dialogues with Ammachi.

Fischer, Louis. *The Essential Gandhi: His Life, Work, and Ideas; An Anthology.* New York: Vintage Books, 1962. Gandhi used *The Bhagavad Gita* as a guide in his nonviolent movement toward an independent India. He is a supreme example of nondoership, the philosophy of karma yoga or love in action.

Ganguli, Anil. *Anandamayi Ma: The Mother Bliss-Incarnate.* Calcutta: Shree Shree Anandamayee Charitable Society, 1983. A twentieth-century Indian saint.

The Gospel of Sri Ramakrishna. Translated by Swami Nikhilananda. Originally recorded in Bengali by M., a disciple of the Master. New York: Ramakrishna-Vivekananda Center, 1942. A detailed account of Ramakrishna, including dialogues.

Godman, David, ed. *Be as You Are: The Teachings of Sri Ramana Maharshi.* New York: Penguin Books, 1992. Dialogues with this twentieth-century saint put forth the concept of self-inquiry. Ramana Maharshi attained enlightenment at age seventeen, and was drawn to the sacred hill of Arunachala in Tiruvanamalai, South India. His ashram sits at the base of the famous Shiva hill.

Gottlieb, Lynn. *She Who Dwells Within: A Feminist Vision of a Renewed Judaism.* San Francisco: Harper San Francisco, 1995. A powerful model for ways to bring Mother back into Western religions, in this case Judaism.

Hallstrom, Lisa Lassell. *Anandamayi Ma (1896–1982)*. New York: Oxford University Press, 1999. The newest version of the story of the Indian saint Anandamayi Ma.

Hillesum, Etty. *An Interrupted Life: The Diaries of Etty Hillesum, 1941–1943*. Translated by Jonathan Cape Ltd., London. New York: Pantheon Books, 1983.

Isherwood, Christopher. *Ramakrishna and His Disciples*. Hollywood: Vedanta Press, 1965. Paramahamsa Ramakrishna was known as the God-intoxicated sage. He was an avatar, husband of Mother Sarada Devi, devotee of Kali, and guru to Swami Vivekananda (who brought Indian spirituality to the West at the turn of the twentieth century).

Le Joly, Edward. *Mother Teresa of Calcutta, A Biography*. San Francisco: Harper & Row, 1977, 1983. An excellent example of a tireless nun's selfless service to the poorest of the poor all over the world.

Osborne, Arthur. *Ramana Maharshi and the Path of Self-Knowledge*. New York: Samuel Weiser, 1973. The story of Ramana Maharshi.

Roberts, Bernadette. *The Experience of No-Self: A Contemplative Journey*. Albany, N.Y.: State University of New York Press, 1993. A personal account of a former Catholic nun's spiritual awakening.

Roberts, Bernadette. *The Path to No-Self: Life at the Center*. Albany, N.Y.: State University of New York Press, 1991. Recommended only after reading her personal account, *The Experience of No-Self*.

Saint Teresa of Avila. *The Life of Saint Teresa of Avila*. Translated by J. M. Cohen. New York: Penguin Books, 1957. The story of a sixteenth-century saint, a Catholic Divine Mother.

Saint Teresa of Avila. *The Interior Castle*. Translated by Kieran Kavanaugh, O.C.D., and Otilio Rodriguez, O.C.D. New York: Paulist Press, 1979. A remarkable personal account of spiritual unfolding.

Saint Therese of Lisieux. *The Autobiography of Saint Therese of Lisieux: The Story of a Soul*. Translated by John Beevers. New York: Image Books, Doubleday, 1989 (new edition). An enchanting account of the short life of a twentieth-century Catholic saint.

Schiffman, Richard. *Mother of All: A Revelation of the Motherhood of God in the Life and Teachings of the Jillellamudi Mother.* Andhra Pradesh, India: Matrusri Printers, 1983. American version soon to be released by Blue Dove Press.

Tweedie, Irina. *Daughter of Fire: A Diary of a Spiritual Training with a Sufi Master.* Nevada City, Calif.: Blue Dolphin Publishing, 1986.

Venkataraman, T. N. *Maharishi's Gospel.* Tiruvannamalai, India: Sri Ramanasramam, 1979. Dialogues with Sri Ramana Maharshi.

Appendix II:
Centers and
Tours

Ammachi Centers All Over the World

There are two main centers that can provide the most updated information about Ammachi's ashrams and *satsang* groups scattered all over the United States, Europe, Australia, India, Japan, and other parts of the world.

U.S.A.

Mata Amritanandamayi Center or M.A. Center
P.O. Box 613
San Ramon, CA 94583-0613
Ph: 510-537-9417
Fax: 510-889-8585
E-mail: macenter@ammachi.org
Website: http://www.ammachi.org

If you are interested in locating a *satsang* group (a gathering together to sing devotional songs, chant, and meditate) in your area, go to Ammachi's website at www.ammachi.org.

India

Mata Amritandamayi Math (Ammachi's main ashram)
Amritapuri P. O., Kollam—690 525
Kerala, India
Ph: 011-91-475-896178
E-mail: mata.quilon@sm1.sprintrpg.ems.vsnl.net.in

The growing number of small ashrams in India include Calicut, Trivandrum, Madras, Pune, Bombay, and Delhi.

For information on Ammachi's charitable organizations all over India (major hospital, schools, technical schools, hospices, orphanages, schools for deaf, homes for the homeless, etc.), write or call M.A. Center in California, M.A. Math in India.

Ammachi's World Tour Itinerary

The exact nature of the tour schedule changes every year. As of this writing, Ammachi usually travels for six months out of the year. Call the M.A. Center in San Ramon or check their World Wide Web site, http://www.ammachi.org, for updated information. If in India, the M.A. Math.

In the United States from June to mid-July, Ammachi travels to places such as Seattle, Wash.; San Ramon, Calif. (Bay Area); Los Angeles, Calif.; Santa Fe, N.M.; Dallas, Tex.; Chicago, Ill.; Washington, D.C.; New York, N.Y.; Boston, Mass. Places vary slightly from year to year.

In Europe in October, Ammachi travels to various countries such as France, Switzerland, Sweden, Germany, England, Italy, and Spain.

In November 1996, Ammachi began including a short visit to the United States.

Japan has been included on her tour schedule in late May. There is an M.A. Center in Tokyo.

In April, Ammachi sometimes includes Australia and Singapore in her tour to Reunion Island and Mauritius.

Ammachi usually travels to North India in February and March.

Appendix III:
Endnotes

Introduction

1. Story and message about innocent beginners is from a dialogue with Ammachi in Swami Amritaswarupananda, *Awaken, Children! Dialogues with Sri Sri Mata Amritanandamayi*, vol. VII (San Ramon, Calif.: Mata Amritanandamayi Center, 1995), 69–71. The last sentences spoken by the mahatma are from p. 71.
2. Ibid., 69.
3. Ammachi in Swami Amritaswarupananda, *Awaken, Children!*, vol. VII, 75.

Ammachi

1. Ammachi's story is taken from Swami Amritaswarupananda, *Ammachi: A Biography of Mata Amritanandamayi*. (San Ramon, Calif.: Mata Amritanandamayi Center, 1994).
2. Swami Amritaswarupananda, *Awaken, Children! Dialogues with Sri Sri Mata Amritanandamayi*, vol. IV (San Ramon, Calif.: Mata Amritanandamayi Center, 1992), 144–46.

3. Swami Amritaswarupananda, *Ammachi: A Biography of Mata Amritanandamayi*, 50.

4. "Mother's Message," *Amritanandam: A Quarterly Journal Dedicated to Mata Amritanandamayi*, vol. XII, no. 2 (San Ramon, Calif.: Mata Amritanandamayi Center, 1997), 4.

5. Ammachi in *Eternal Wisdom: Upadeshamritam*, vol. I, translated into English by Dr. M. N. Namboodiri from materials compiled by Swami Jnanamritananda Puri (San Ramon, Calif.: Mata Amritanandamayi Center, 1997), 169.

6. Swami Amritaswarupananda, *Ammachi: A Biography of Mata Amritanandamayi*, 110.

7. Ibid., 140–41, 145.

8. Ibid., 142–43.

9. Ibid., 152.

10. AIMS, Amrita Institute of Medical Sciences & Research Center, is an eight-hundred-bed hospital in Cochin, Kerala, India. The purpose of the institute is to provide outstanding research, education, and complex diagnostic and patient care services in a nonprofit, charitable setting. Specialties include open-heart and neurosurgical services and kidney transplantation.

Hinduism and the Mother

1. Story and hymn adapted from *Devi Mahatmayam (Glory of the Divine Mother)*, trans. Swami Jagadiswarananda (Madras: Sri Ramakrishna Math, 1953).

2. Elaine Pagels, *The Gnostic Gospels* (New York: Vintage Books, 1979), 48. "While Catholics revere Mary as the mother of Jesus, they never identify her as divine in her own right: if she is 'mother of God,' she is not 'God the Mother' on an equal footing with God the Father!"

3. Ibid., 57.

4. Ibid. The Gospel of Mary has been omitted from the New Testament. In it, in answering a question about an argument she had with Peter, Jesus tells Magdalena that whoever the Spirit in-

spires is divinely ordained to speak, whether man or woman (p. 65). In the Gnostic gospel, *Dialogue of the Savior*, Mary Magdalena is included as one of the three disciples chosen to receive special teachings ". . . she spoke as a woman who knew the All" (p. 64).

See also Mary R. Thompson, SSMN, *Mary of Magdala: Apostle and Leader* (New York and Mahwah, N.J.: Paulist Press, 1995).

5. Ajit Mookerjee, *Kali the Feminine Force* (New York: Destiny Books, 1988), 12.

6. Ibid.

7. Ibid., 23.

8. Refers to the unbroken lineage of Shankaracharya Jagadgurus since the time of Shankara. The personal story in the text was experienced while Sri Abhinava Vidyathirtha, 35th Jagaguru, presided. Shankara was an incarnation of Lord Shiva. An exponent of the philosophy of nondualism, he helped eliminate exclusivity among certain Hindu religious sects.

9. Sarada is the presiding goddess in the Temple at Sringeri. She is considered to be both Shakti and Shaktiman (Shiva) and is the representation of God as she.

10. *The Greatness of Sringeri* (Bombay, India: Tattavaloka, 1991), 15.

11. Ibid., 16.

12. Ammachi in Swami Amritaswarupananda, *Awaken, Children! Dialogues with Sri Sri Mata Amritanandamayi*, vol. II (San Ramon, Calif.: Mata Amritanandamayi Center), 103.

13. Ibid., 55.

14. Ammachi in Swami Amritaswarupananda, *Awaken, Children!*, vol. VII, 34.

15. Ammachi in Swami Amritaswarupananda, *Awaken, Children!*, vol. VI, 180.

16. Martin Palmer and Jay Ramsay with Man-Ho Kwok, *Kuan Yin: Myths and Prophecies of the Chinese Goddess of Compassion* (San Francisco: HarperCollins Publishers, 1995), xi. All the material on Kuan Yin in this passage is taken from Palmer's book.

17. Ibid., 135. Poem is entitled "Into the Green."

18. Some of this information is liberally adapted from Harish Johari, *Tools for Tantra* (Rochester, Vt.: Destiny Books, 1986).
19. Ibid.
20. Ammachi in Swami Amritaswarupananda, *Awaken, Children!*, vol. VI, 95.
21. Ammachi in Swami Amritaswarupananda, *Awaken, Children!*, vol. III, 75.

Kundalini Shakti

1. For further information about Kundalini awakening as part of the spiritual journey, see the stories of Irina Tweedie and Bernadette Roberts in The Personal Shadow in Part IV of this book.

For in-depth accounts of Kundalini awakening, see Swami Amritaswarupananda, *Ammachi: The Life of the Holy Mother Amritanandamayi* (San Ramon, Calif.: Mata Amritanandamayi Center, 1994); Irina Tweedie, *Daughter of Fire: A Diary of a Spiritual Training with a Sufi Master* (Nevada City, Calif.: Blue Dolphin Publishing, 1986); Bernadette Roberts, *The Experience of No-Self: A Contemplative Journey* (Albany, N.Y.: State University of New York Press, 1993); and Teresa of Avila, *The Interior Castle*, trans. Kieran Kavanaugh, O.C.D., and Otilio Rodriguez, O.C.D. (New York: Paulist Press, 1979).

For information on a transpersonal psychologist's view of Kundalini awakening, see Stan Grof and Christina Grof, *Spiritual Emergency* (New York: J. P. Tarcher, 1989) and Bonnie Greenwell, *Energies of Transformation: A Guide to the Kundalini Process* (Saratoga, Calif.: Shakti River Press, 1995).

For a story on the difficulties of Kundalini awakening when there is no expert spiritual guidance, see Gopi Krishna, *Living with Kundalini: The Autobiography of Gopi Krishna* (Boston, Mass.: Shambhala, 1993).

For technical information on the chakras, see Ajit Mookerjee, *Kundalini: The Arousal of the Inner Energy* (Rochester, Vt.:

Destiny, 1982) and Harish Johari, *Tools for Tantra* (Rochester, Vt.: Destiny, 1986).

Ramana Maharshi, an Indian saint of the twentieth century, says the following regarding the sometimes frightening difficulties around Kundalini awakening and resultant exalted states: "The fear and the quaking of one's body while one is entering samadhi [intense absorption on the object of meditation, resulting in consciousness of Self] is due to the slight ego-consciousness still remaining. But when this dies completely, without leaving even a trace, one abides as the vast space of mere consciousness where bliss alone prevails, and the quaking stops." From David Godman, ed., *Be as You Are: The Teachings of Sri Ramana Maharshi* (New York: Penguin Books, 1992), 154. Relevant to fear and terrifying notions about *nirvikalpa samadhi* (meditative experience of the bliss of Self) related to Kundalini awakening, Ramana Maharshi says, "If those who have all the Upanishads and Vedantic [Hindu scriptures] tradition at their disposal have fantastic notions about nirvikalpa, who can blame a westerner for similar notions? . . . All this is due to their viewing it intellectually." (*Be as You Are*, 153.) "Nirvikalpa is chit—effortless, formless consciousness. Where does the terror come in, and where is the mystery in being oneself? To some people whose minds have become ripe from a long practice in the past, nirvikalpa comes suddenly as a flood, but to others it comes in the course of their spiritual practice, a practice which slowly wears down the obstructing thoughts and reveals the screen of pure awareness 'I'—'I.' Further practice renders the screen permanently exposed." (*Be as You Are*, 154.)

2. *The Srimad Devi Bhagavatam*, 4th ed. (Allahabad, India: Munshiram Manoharlal Publishers, 1992), 1167.

3. Ibid., 1168. Quote has been altered and adapted.

4. Ammachi in Swami Amritaswarupananda, *Awaken, Children! Dialogues with Sri Sri Mata Amritanandamayi*, vol. III (San Ramon, Calif.: Mata Amritanandamayi Center, 1991), 102.

5. Ammachi in Swami Amritaswarupananda, *Awaken, Children!*, vol. V, 19.
6. Ammachi in Swami Amritaswarupananda, *Awaken, Children!*, vol. II, 103–04.
7. Ibid., 103.
8. Ammachi in Swami Amritaswarupananda, *Awaken, Children!*, vol. VII, 21.
9. Ammachi in Swami Amritaswarupananda, *Awaken, Children!*, vol. II, 101.
10. Ammachi in Swami Amritaswarupananda, *Awaken, Children!*, vol. V, 66.
11. Ammachi in Swami Amritaswarupananda, *Awaken, Children!*, vol. II, 108.
12. Ibid., 109.
13. Ammachi in Swami Amritaswarupananda, *Awaken, Children!*, vol. II, 111–12.

Jillellamudi Mother

1. Richard Schiffman, *Mother of All: A Revelation of the Motherhood of God in the Life and Teachings of the Jillellamudi Mother* (Bapatla, India: Matrusri Printers, 1983).
2. Ibid., 87.
3. Ibid., 90.
4. Ibid., 116.
5. Ibid., 118.
6. Ibid., 119.
7. Ibid., 154.
8. Ibid., 165.
9. Ibid., 167.
10. Ibid., 171.
11. Ibid., 346.
12. Rodney Alexander Arms, ed. *Talks with Amma* (Bapatla, India: Matrusri Printers, 1980), 63.
13. Ibid., 86–87.

14. Ibid., 59.
15. Ibid., 89.
16. Richard Schiffman, *Mother of All*, 279.
17. Ibid., 314.
18. Ibid., 316–17.
19. Ibid., 319–20.
20. Ibid., 345.
21. Ibid., 354.
22. Ibid., 356.
23. Ibid., 358.
24. Ibid., 354.
25. Ibid., 347.
26. Ibid.
27. Ibid., 354.
28. Ibid., 357.
29. Ammachi in Swami Amritaswarupananda, *Awaken, Children!*, vol. VII, 31.
30. Ibid., 29.
31. Ibid., 22.

The Lure of Divine Love

1. Kali Yuga, the age of the decline of righteousness, is the last of Hinduism's four ages. The topic is discussed at length in Part IV of this book.
2. Ammachi in Swami Amritaswarupananda, *Awaken, Children!*, vol. IV, 222.
3. Ammachi in Swami Amritaswarupananda, *Awaken, Children!*, vol. II, 109–10.
4. Marie Watts wrote many books and recorded her teachings on tape after moving to Vista, California. Among them, *The Ultimate* (San Gabriel, Calif.: Willing Publishing Co., 1957).
5. Ammachi in Swami Amritaswarupananda, *Awaken, Children!* vol. VI, 110.

The Lover and the Beloved

1. Adapted from one of the Hindu scriptures of ancient legends, *The Shiva Purana,* vol. I (Delhi, India: Motilal Banarsidass, 1970).
2. Ammachi in Swami Amritaswarupananda, *Awaken, Children!* vol. II, 64.
3. A bodhisattva in Buddhism is similar to the Hindu avatar. It is a God-realized soul who comes back to help people who wish to attain the same goal.

Penetrating Deep into the Mind

1. Ammachi in Swami Amritaswarupananda, *Awaken, Children! Dialogues with Sri Sri Mata Amritanandamayi,* vol. VII (San Ramon, Calif.: Mata Amritanandamayi Center, 1995), 221–25.

Who Is the Guru?

1. Ammachi in Swami Amritaswarupananda, *Awaken, Children! Dialogues with Sri Sri Mata Amritanandamayi,* vol. IV (San Ramon, Calif.: Mata Amritanandamayi Center, 1992), 65.
2. Ibid.
3. Mata Amritanandamayi, *Amritanandam* (fourth quarter 1993), back cover.
4. Ammachi in Swami Amritaswarupananda, *Awaken, Children!,* vol. V, 57–58.
5. Ammachi in Swami Amritaswarupananda, *Awaken, Children!,* vol. IV, 153–54.
6. Ammachi in Swami Amritaswarupananda, *Awaken, Children!,* vol. VI, 224.
7. Ibid., 225.
8. Ammachi in Swami Amritaswarupananda, *Awaken, Children!,* vol. III, 6.
9. Ammachi in Swami Amritaswarupananda, *Awaken, Children!,* vol. VI, 179–80.
10. Ibid.

11. Ammachi in Swami Amritaswarupananda, *Awaken, Children!*, vol. VII, 44.

12. Ammachi in Swami Amritaswarupananda, *Awaken, Children!*, vol. VI, 225.

13. Ammachi in Swami Amritaswarupananda, *Awaken, Children!*, vol. VII, 54.

14. Ammachi in Swami Amritaswarupananda, *Awaken, Children!*, vol. VI, 225.

15. Ammachi in Swami Amritaswarupananda, *Awaken, Children!*, vol. VII, 44.

16. Ammachi in Swami Amritaswarupananda, *Awaken, Children!*, vol. VI, 225.

17. Ibid., 224.

Tapas

1. Based on a story told by the Holy Mother Ammachi. Swami Amritaswarupananda, *Awaken, Children! Dialogues with Sri Sri Mata Amritanandamayi*, vol. V (San Ramon, Calif.: Mata Amritanandamayi Center, 1993).

2. Ibid., 25.

3. Ammachi in Swami Amritaswarupananda, *Awaken, Children!*, vol. VII, 65.

4. Ammachi in Swami Amritaswarupananda, *Awaken, Children!*, vol. V, 122.

5. Quotation from Anandamayi Ma in Timothy Conway, *Women of Power and Grace* (Santa Barbara, Calif.: The Wake Up Press, 1994), 160.

6. Ammachi in Swami Amritaswarupananda, *Awaken, Children!*, vol. VI, 187.

7. Mary Craig, *Mother Teresa* (London: Evans Brothers Limited, 1983), 23.

8. Ibid., 29.

9. Ammachi in Swami Amritaswarupananda, *Awaken, Children!*, vol. VI, 186.

10. Sri Sri Mata Amritanandamayi Devi (Ammachi), *May Your Hearts Blossom: An Address at the Parliament of World's Religions* (given in Chicago in 1993), trans. Swami Amritasarupananda (Amritapuri, Kerala, India: Mata Amritanandamayi Mission Trust, 1994), 28–29.

Kali

1. "Kali," with a long "a," literally means, "the black" and refers to Goddess Kali. The word *Kali*, with a short "a," refers to Kali Yuga or the Age of Materialism and has to do with dissension and strife.
2. M., a disciple of the Master, *The Gospel of Sri Ramakrishna*, trans. Swami Nikhilananda (New York: Ramakrishna-Vivekananda Center, 1992).
3. Ramya and Jyoti, "Kali: The Divine Force Behind the Universe," *Amritanandam*, vol. XII, no. 1 (San Ramon: Mata Amritanandamayi Center, 1997), 36.
4. Description based on Elisabeth U. Harding, *Kali: The Black Goddess of Dakshineswar* (York Beach: Nicolas-Hays, Inc., 1993) and Ramya and Jyoti, "Kali: The Divine Force Behind the Universe."
5. Ramya and Jyoti, *Amritanandam*, 28.

Demons Within and Without

1. *Webster's New World Dictionary of the American Language* (Cleveland and New York: The World Publishing, 1953).
2. Creation story based on Wendy Doniger O'Flaherty, *Hindu Myths: A Sourcebook Translated from the Sanskrit* (New York: Penguin Books, 1978).
3. Elaine Pagels, *The Origin of Satan* (New York: Random House, 1995).
4. Ibid., 49.
5. Ibid., xvi.

6. Ammachi in Swami Amritaswarupananda, *Awaken, Children!*, vol. III, 165.
7. Ammachi in Swami Amritaswarupananda, *Awaken, Children!*, vol. VII, 66–67.
8. Ibid., 186.

The Religious Shadow

1. Please note: In an attempt to clarify the religious shadow, none of the interpretations in the following paragraphs are meant as a criticism of the Judeo-Christian traditions in their purest essence. They are meant to illuminate possible distractions that might have led us away from the core of spirituality inherent in all religions.
2. Swami Amritaswarupananda, *Awaken, Children! Dialogues with Sri Sri Mata Amritanandamayi*, vol. VII (San Ramon, Calif.: Mata Amritanandamayi Center, 1995), 86.
3. Ibid., 90–91.
4. Arthur Avalon, *The Tantra of the Great Liberation (Mahanirvana Tantra)* (New York: Dover Publications, 1972), cxlii.
5. Ammachi in Swami Amritaswarupananda, *Awaken, Children!*, vol. III, 17.
6. Ammachi in Swami Amritaswarupananda, *Awaken, Children!*, vol. II, 103.
7. Ammachi in Swami Amritaswarupananda, *Awaken, Children!*, vol. III, 17–18.
8. Genesis 3:6 Revised Standard Version.
9. Some qualities to be expected during Kali Yuga are described by Arthur Avalon in *The Tantra of the Great Liberation*, 9–10: "[Kali Yuga is an age] full of evil customs and deceit. . . . Men will become . . . maddened with pride . . . heartless, harsh of speech, short-lived, poverty-stricken . . . addicted to mean habits. . . . They will be heretics, impostors, and think themselves wise. . . . They will be without faith or devotion, and will do japa [repetition of God's name] and puja [worship] with

no other end than to dupe the people.... The only sign that they are Brahmanas [priests] will be the thread [sacred cloth] they wear."

10. Riane Eisler, *The Chalice and the Blade: Our History, Our Future* (San Francisco: HarperSanFrancisco, 1987).

11. Genesis 3:20 Revised Standard Version.

12. "Asherah, another form of the Canaanite Goddess, continued to be worshipped alongside Yahweh in the Solomonic temple for two-thirds of its existence." From Rosemary Radford Ruether, *Sexism and God-Talk: Toward a Feminist Theology* (Boston: Beacon Press, 1983), 36. Ruether provides an evolutionary view of how the god/goddess relationship shifted to a male orientation and subsequent subjugation of the female.

According to Susannah Herschel in her book, *On Being a Jewish Feminist: A Reader* (New York: Shocken Books, 1983), the Jewish Sabbath celebration is an acknowledgment of the connubial embrace of God and his Shekinah, or bride, anticipating the ultimate union of male and female as one.

See also Lynn Gottlieb, *She Who Dwells Within: A Feminist Vision of a Renewed Judaism* (San Francisco: HarperSanFrancisco, 1995). Gottlieb discusses Shekinah at length. She also writes about the Kabbala, the tree of life, including the role of the feminine in it.

13. Genesis 3:13 Revised Standard Version.

14. Genesis 3:24 Revised Standard Version.

The Family Shadow

1. For a discourse on the ideal life of the goddess cultures of Old Europe, see Riane Eisler, *The Chalice and the Blade: Our History, Our Future* (San Francisco: HarperSanFrancisco, 1987).

2. Patricia Garfield describes one such group, the Senoi Indians of Malaysia, in her book *Creative Dreaming* (New York: Ballantine Books, 1976). In the inland jungles, amid sounds of chattering birds and sporting monkeys, a typical Senoi family joins to-

gether around the breakfast table to share and discuss their dreams. The entire community life of these hill-dwelling islanders exists around the events of the dream world. From the time they are small children, they learn to control their dreams as a way to understand their interconnectedness to all things visible and invisible. At the morning meal, grandparents, brothers, sisters, aunts, uncles, parents, teenagers, and small children share their dreams. Children are congratulated for having dreams, and are encouraged to defeat the lions and tigers of their dream world, and to turn dream enemies into friends or allies.

Subduing aggressors, conquering danger, and changing difficult situations into positive ones are among the essential principles of dream activity for the Senoi. They value positive dream outcomes like being reborn if they have died or turning a frightening falling incident into a pleasant flying experience. It is considered powerful to receive gifts from dream enemies. Everyone is encouraged to seek pleasure and exciting adventures in dreams. Adults consider it auspicious to enjoy sex until orgasm is reached.

The contents of the dreams are carried into worldly activities. Children, often with the help of an older sister or brother, are assisted while they express dream images through play or crafts. Adult villagers spend hours discussing how they can implement dream information into community living. Almost all major and minor decisions are determined on the basis of dreams. These family- and community-oriented people whose lives intimately revolve around their unique spirituality are known to be cooperative, peace loving, and psychologically well adjusted.

3. Ammachi in Swami Amritaswarupananda, *Awaken, Children! Dialogues with Sri Sri Mata Amritanandamayi,* vol. IV (San Ramon, Calif.: Mata Amritanandamayi Center, 1992), 148–49.

4. Gertrude J. Williams and John Money, eds., *Traumatic Abuse and Neglect of Children at Home* (Baltimore: The Johns Hopkins University Press, 1982).

5. Karen Jo Torjesen, *When Women Were Priests* (San Francisco: HarperSanFrancisco, 1995).

6. Gertrude Williams and John Money, *Traumatic Abuse and Neglect of Children at Home*, 15.

7. Ibid., 17.

8. Adapted from Swami Amritaswarupananda, *Ammachi: A Biography of Mata Amritanandamayi.* (San Ramon, Calif.: Mata Amritanandamayi Center, 1994).

9. Ibid., 28.

10. Ammachi in Swami Amritaswarupananda, *Awaken, Children!*, vol. IV, 145–50.

11. Ammachi in Swami Amritaswarupananda, *Awaken, Children!*, vol. III, 165.

The Personal Shadow

1. Ammachi in Swami Amritaswarupananda, *Awaken, Children! Dialogues with Sri Sri Mata Amritanandamayi*, vol. IV (San Ramon, Calif.: Mata Amritanandamayi Center, 1992), 247.

2. Irina Tweedie, *Daughter of Fire: A Diary of a Spiritual Training with a Sufi Master* (Nevada City, Calif.: Blue Dolphin Press, Inc., 1989).

3. Ibid., 104.

4. Ibid., 105.

5. Ibid.

6. Ibid.

7. Ibid.

8. Ibid., 108–09.

9. Ibid., 110–11.

10. Ibid., 111.

11. Ibid., 820.

12. Ibid., 604.

13. Ibid., 810.

14. Bernadette Roberts, *The Experience of No-Self* (Albany: State University of New York Press, 1993).

15. Story taken from Bernadette Roberts, *The Experience of No-Self.*
16. At the time of her search in the libraries, she was not familiar with the writings of Meister Eckhart. Much later, she found some aspects of his accounts to parallel her experience.
17. Bernadette Roberts, *The Experience of No-Self*, 53–55.
18. Ibid., 66.
19. Ibid., 67–68.
20. Ibid., 72.
21. In David Godman, ed., *Be as You Are: The Teachings of Sri Ramana Maharshi* (New York: Penguin Books, 1992), 148, Ramana Maharshi defines *sahaja nirvikalpa samadhi*, often referred to as sahaja samadhi. "This is the state of the jnani [wise one] who has finally and irrevocably eliminated his ego. Sahaja means 'natural' and nirvikalpa means 'no differences.' A jnani in this state is able to function naturally in the world, just as any ordinary person does. Knowing that he is the Self, the sahaja jnani sees no difference between himself and others and no difference between himself and the world. For such a person, everything is a manifestation of the indivisible Self."
22. I referred to her state as "a level of realization" because it is possible to have attained to the irreversible feelings of oneness and still not be fully enlightened. Even at this stage, there can be *vasanas* or tendencies in very subtle ways. Only a fully enlightened teacher can know the extent of Bernadette's or anyone's realization. People who have attained levels of realization and not full realization will talk about still discovering more about the universe. For fully realized souls, like Ammachi or Ramana Maharshi, there is nothing more to be revealed.
23. For a concise and detailed definition of the unitive state as distinguished from the state of no-self (same as *sahaja nirvikalpa samadhi*), see Bernadette Roberts, *The Path to No-Self: Life at the Center* (Albany, N.Y.: State University of New York Press, 1991). For a personal account of the unitive state, see Teresa of Avila, *The Interior Castle*, trans. Kieran Kavanaugh, O.C.D., and Otilio Rodriguez, O.C.D. (New York: Paulist Press, 1979).

In David Godman's *Be as You Are*, p. 154, Ramana Maharshi also defines the difference. "In samadhi itself there is only perfect peace. Ecstasy comes when the mind revives at the end of samadhi, with the remembrance of the peace of samadhi. In devotion the ecstasy comes first. It is manifested by tears of joy, hair standing on end and vocal stumbling. When the ego finally dies and then sahaja is won, these symptoms and the ecstasies cease."

In Swami Amritaswarupananda, *Awaken, Children!*, vol. II, p. 274, Ammachi explains why we see moods in realized souls even though they live in the constant bliss of realization: "Even though they [realized souls] all experience samadhi, one can see different moods in them corresponding to the spiritual practices which they have been following. The moods that were seen in Sri Ramakrishna were not the same as in Ramana Maharshi. The same is true of other Realized Souls as well. Therefore, even though they were all great souls, their Realization manifested differently. This depends on the path through which they attained the goal."

24. See Elaine Pagels, *The Gnostic Gospels* (New York: Vintage Books, 1979). Gnostic Christian mystics were considered heretical when the Roman church ruled, starting around 100 C.E.

25. Ibid., 128. From the Gospel of Thomas: ". . . Rather, the Kingdom is inside of you and it is outside of you. When you come to know yourselves, then you will be known, and you will realize that you are the sons of the living Father. But if you will not know yourselves, then you dwell in poverty, and it is you who are that poverty."

26. Bernadette Roberts, *The Experience of No-Self,* 209, footnote 9.

27. Ammachi in Swami Amritaswarupananda, *Awaken, Children!*, vol. VII, 221–24.

28. Ibid. The material in this paragraph is adapted from Ammachi's own words.

29. Ammachi in Swami Amritaswarupananda, *Awaken, Children!*, vol. II, 181.

Releasing Gradually

1. Ammachi in Swami Amritaswarupananda, *Awaken, Children! Dialogues with Sri Sri Mata Amritanandamayi,* vol. II (San Ramon, Calif.: Mata Amritanandamayi Center), 102.
2. Ammachi in *Awaken, Children!,* vol. V, 206.
3. Ammachi in *Awaken, Children!,* vol. IV, 151–54.
4. Ammachi in *Awaken, Children!,* vol. IX, 72.
5. Ammachi in *Awaken, Children!,* vol. VI, 135.

The Song of God: The Bhagavad Gita

1. Except where indicated, all the quotes are from Sri Swami Sivananda, trans., *The Bhagavad Gita* (U.P., India: The Divine Life Society, 1969). I have taken the liberty of changing "thee" and "thou" to "you," and of making a few more changes to put the text into more modern language.
2. Ibid., 3:5.
3. Ibid., 2:9.
4. Ammachi in Swami Amritaswarupananda, *Awaken, Children! Dialogues with Sri Sri Mata Amritanandamayi,* vol. IX (San Ramon, Calif.: Mata Amritanandamayi Center, 1998), 69–70.
5. Sri Swami Sivananda, *The Bhagavad Gita,* 2:12–13.
6. Ibid., 2:23–24.
7. Ibid., 3:1–2.
8. Swami Prabhanananda and Christopher Isherwood, trans., *The Song of God (The Bhagavad Gita)* (New York: Penguin, 1941), 45–47 (third discourse).
9. Sri Swami Sivananda, *The Bhagavad Gita,* 3:27.
10. Ibid., 3:35.
11. Ibid., 6:38.
12. Ibid., 6:40.
13. Ibid., 9:17.
14. Ibid., 9:18.
15. Ibid., 10:18.

16. Ibid., 10:8.
17. Ibid., 10:20.
18. Ibid., 10:28.
19. Ibid., 10:31.
20. Ibid., 10:34.
21. Ibid., 10:35.
22. Ibid., 10:36.
23. Ibid., 10:38.
24. Ibid., 10:42.
25. Ibid., 11:3–4.
26. Ibid., 11:23–24.
27. Ibid., 11:28–29.
28. Ibid., 11:32–33.
29. Ibid., 11:45.
30. Ibid., 11:55.
31. Ibid., 14:24.
32. Ibid. Taken from the sixteenth discourse.
33. Ibid., 18:74 and 78.
34. Ammachi in Swami Amritaswarupananda, *Awaken, Children! Dialogues with Sri Sri Mata Amritanandamayi,* vol. V (San Ramon, Calif.: Mata Amritanandamayi Center, 1993), 211.
35. Ibid., 125.
36. Ammachi in Swami Amritaswarupananda, *Awaken, Children!,* vol. II, p. 106.
37. Ammachi in Swami Amritaswarupananda, *Awaken, Children!,* vol. IV, 246.
38. Ammachi in Swami Amritaswarupananda, *Awaken, Children!,* vol. IX, 173.
39. Ibid., 171.
40. Ammachi in Swami Amritaswarupananda, *Awaken, Children!,* vol. V, 125–27.

Love Can Blossom Even Out of the Darkest Shadow

1. Etty Hillesum, *An Interrupted Life: The Diaries of Etty Hillesum* (New York: Pantheon Books, 1983).

2. Ibid., 1.

3. Ibid., 3.

4. Ibid., 4.

5. Ibid.

6. Ibid., 80.

7. Ibid., 119.

8. Ibid., 146.

9. Ibid., 128–29.

10. Ibid., 174.

11. Ibid., 177.

12. Ibid., 169.

13. Ibid., 189.

14. Ibid., 190.

15. Ibid., 203.

16. Ibid., 215.

17. Ibid., 205.

18. Ammachi in Swami Amritaswarupananda, *Awaken, Children! Dialogues with Sri Sri Mata Amritanandamayi*, vol. IV (San Ramon, Calif.: Mata Amritanandamayi Center, 1992), 62–63.

Saying Yes to Everything

1. The four stages of life in Hinduism are: 1. *Brahmacharya*, a time for keeping celibacy and studying scriptures and other spiritual practices. 2. *Grihastha*, a time for marriage, profession, and raising a family. 3. *Vanaprastha*, a time for retiring to the forest. 4. *Sannyasa*, a time to renounce all aspects of the world.

2. Ammachi in Swami Amritaswarupananda, *Awaken, Children! Dialogues with Sri Sri Mata Amritanandamayi*, vol. VII (San Ramon, Calif.: Mata Amritanandamayi Center, 1995), 216.

3. English Bhajans, vol. I, *Satsang* members, Amma Center of New Mexico (CD and cassette tape).

4. English Bhajans, vols. I–IV.

5. English Bhajans, vol. I.

The Bittersweet of Yearning

1. Etty Hillesum, *An Interrupted Life: The Diaries of Etty Hillesum* (New York: Pantheon Books, 1983), 187.

2. Coleman Barks, trans., *The Essential Rumi*, (Edison, N.J.: Castle Books, 1997), 243.

3. John Beevers, trans., *The Autobiography of Saint Therese of Lisieux: The Story of a Soul*, (1957; reprint, New York: Doubleday, 1989), p. 24.

4. Ibid., 27.

5. Ibid., 30.

6. Ibid., 41.

7. Ibid., 47.

8. Ibid., 52.

9. Ibid., 63.

10. Ibid., 119.

11. Ibid., 92.

12. Ibid., 111.

13. Ibid., 114.

14. Ibid., 119.

15. John Clarke, O.C.D., trans., *Saint Therese of Lisieux: Her Last Conversations* (Washington, D.C.: Institute of Carmelite Studies, 1977), 206.

16. Swami Amritaswarupananda, *Awaken, Children! Dialogues with Sri Sri Mata Amritanandamayi*, vol. III (San Ramon, Calif.: Mata Amritanandamayi Center, 1991), 17.

17. Beevers, *The Autobiography of Saint Therese of Lisieux*, 126–27.

18. From "Emptiness," in Coleman Barks, *The Essential Rumi*, 28.

19. From "Birdsong from Inside the Egg," in Coleman Barks, *The Essential Rumi*, 274.

20. Ibid., 356.

21. Genesis 3:13 Revised Standard Version.

22. From "Each Note," in Coleman Barks, *The Essential Rumi,* 103.

23. Ammachi in Swami Amritaswarupananda, *Awaken, Children!,* vol. VII, 127.

24. Ammachi in Swami Amritaswarupananda, *Awaken, Children!,* vol. V, 19–20.

25. Ammachi in Swami Amritaswarupananda, *Awaken, Children!,* vol. III, 106–07.

26. Ibid., 25.

27. Ammachi in Swami Amritaswarupananda, *Awaken, Children!,* vol. V, 30.

28. Adapted from Ibid., 30–32.

Epilogue

1. Ammachi in Swami Amritaswarupananda, *Awaken, Children! Dialogues with Sri Sri Mata Amritanandamayi,* vol. III (San Ramon, Calif.: Mata Amritanandamayi Center, 1992), 61–65.

Index

ABOUT THE AUTHOR

Savitri L. Bess is a transpersonal therapist, workshop facilitator, and fiber artist who has been awarded both a Fulbright and an NEA grant. She has been on the Path of the Mother for more than twenty-seven years.

While living as a monastic at the Holy Shankaracharya Order in Stroudsburg, Pennsylvania, Savitri studied Hindu philosophy and religion. Later she became a therapist and founded and directed the Center for Creative Consciousness in Tucson, Arizona, where she taught yoga and meditation and conducted workshops. After immersing herself in visual, emotional, and spiritual expression of the dark, Savitri met Mata Amritanandamayi, a Holy woman believed by many to be the Black Mother Kali incarnate. Savitri traveled to India to live with this Holy Mother, also known as Ammachi, on and off for several years. Savitri now resides at the Amma Center of New Mexico ashram in Santa Fe, New Mexico, where she completed this book.